POCKETS

ANIMALS
OF THE
WORLD

P9-DJL-093

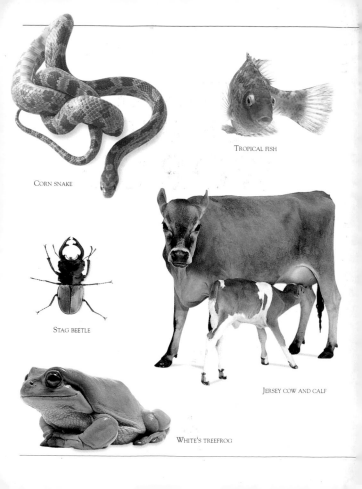

CORN SNAKE

TROPICAL FISH

STAG BEETLE

JERSEY COW AND CALF

WHITE'S TREEFROG

P O C K E T S

ANIMALS
OF THE
WORLD

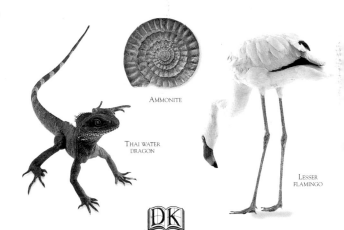

AMMONITE

THAI WATER
DRAGON

LESSER
FLAMINGO

DK

DK PUBLISHING

LONDON, NEW YORK,
MELBOURNE, MUNICH, and DELHI

Writers and consultants: David Alderton, Steve Brooks, Dr. Barry Clarke,
John Farndon, Mark Lambert, Laurence Mound, Scarlett O'Hara, Barbara Taylor,
Steve Parker, Joyce Pope, David Taylor

Produced for Dorling Kindersley by
PAGE*One*, Cairn House, Elgiva Lane, Chesham, Buckinghamshire HP5 2JD

REVISED EDITION
Project editor Steve Setford
Designer Sarah Crouch
Managing editor Linda Esposito
Managing art editor Jane Thomas
DTP designer Siu Yin Ho
Consultants David Alderton, Jonathan Elphick,
George C. McGavin, Mark O'Shea, Richard Walker
Production Erica Rosen
US editors Margaret Parrish, Christine Heilman

Second American Edition, 2003
Published in the United States by
DK Publishing, Inc., 375 Hudson Street,
New York, New York 10014

07 08 10 9 8 7 6 5 4

The material in this book originally appeared in the following
DK Pocket titles: *Birds, Cats, Dogs, Encyclopedia, Horses, Insects,
Mammals, Nature Facts, Reptiles, Sharks.*

Copyright © 2003 Dorling Kindersley Limited

All rights reserved under International and Pan-American Copyright Conventions.
No part of this publication may be reproduced, stored in a retrieval system, or
transmitted in any form or by any means, electronic, mechanical, photocopying,
recording or otherwise, without the prior written permission of the copyright owner.
Published in Great Britain by Dorling Kindersley Limited.

A Cataloging-in-Publication record for the First American Edition of this book
is available from the Library of Congress.

ISBN 13: 978-0-7894-9603-4

Color reproduction by Colourscan, Singapore
Printed in China

See our complete product line at
www.dk.com

CONTENTS

BIRDWING
BUTTERFLY

GREEN MANTELLA

ARMADILLO

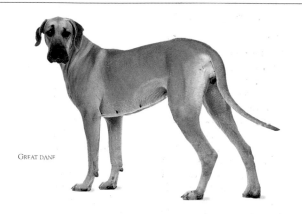

GREAT DANE

HOW TO USE THIS BOOK

These pages show you how to use the *DK Pockets Animals of the World*. The book is divided into seven sections about the animal kingdom. There is also an introductory section about the origins of animal life, and how animals are classified. At the back of the book, there is a comprehensive index.

HEADING AND INTRODUCTION
Every spread has a subject heading. This is followed by the introduction, which outlines the subject and gives a clear idea of what these pages are about.

Label

Heading

Introduction

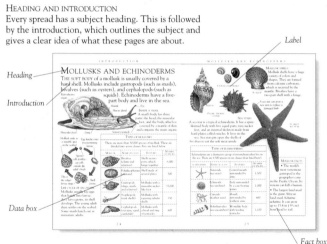

Data box

Fact box

DATA BOX
Some pages have data boxes, which contain detailed numerical information. This box gives data about types of mollusk.

FACT BOXES
Many pages have fact boxes. The information in these is related to the main topic on the page.

LABELS
For clarity, some pictures have labels. These give extra information about the picture, or provide clearer identification.

SIZE INDICATORS
In some sections of this book, you will find clear symbols next to photography. These indicate the average size of an animal.

Size indicator

RUNNING HEADS
Across the top of the pages there are running heads. The lefthand page gives the section, the righthand the subject.

Running head

REAR-FANGED SNAKES
SNAKES WITH FANGS in the back of their mouth are found in both the Old and New Worlds, and, as with other groups of snakes, they vary greatly in color, size, and habitat. They are not as efficient as front-fanged snakes at injecting venom, and so most species are harmless to humans. Large rear-fanged snakes, however, can be dangerous.

IN THE TREETOPS
HIGH UP IN THE RAINFOREST CANOPY it is light and warm and there is plenty of food: especially fruits, seeds, and insect life. Bird life includes large bird predators such as eagles which patrol the treetops looking for prey. Canopy birds, such as parrots and toucans, climb well and have strong feet for grasping branches.

Caption

Annotation

ANNOTATION
Pictures often have extra information around them, which picks out features. This text appears in *italics*, and uses leader lines to point to details.

CAPTIONS
Each illustration in the book is accompanied by a detailed, explanatory caption.

INDEX
There is an index at the back of the book that alphabetically lists every subject. By referring to the index, information on particular topics can be found quickly.

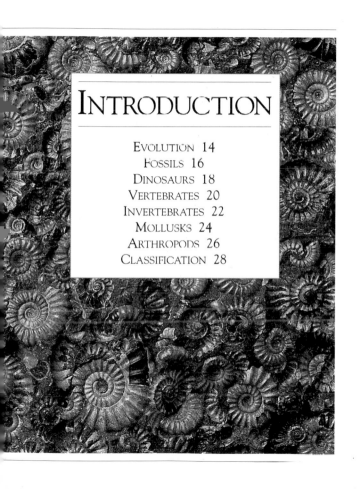

INTRODUCTION

EVOLUTION

SINCE LIFE appeared 3.8 billion years ago, millions of different creatures have come and gone. As habitats altered, some life forms survived by adapting to change, while others died out. This gradual change over time is known as evolution.

PORPOISE'S FRONT FLIPPER

"Finger" bones form a powerful flipper for swimming

Two sets of short "arm" bones

Two sets of long bones make up the arm

Five sets of finger bones make up the hand

ADAPTATION
Evidence for evolution comes from the adaptation of the forearm in humans and porpoises – two related species that live in very different habitats, land and water.

HUMAN ARM

LIFE FORMS THROUGH THE AGES
By working out when certain rocks formed, and then studying the fossils found in them, paleontologists – who study the life forms of the past – have built up a remarkable picture of the way species have changed since the dawn of the Cambrian period 545 million years ago. Little is known of Precambrian life forms because very few fossils remain.

PRECAMBRIAN	PALEOZOIC	
	Cambrian	Ordovician

4,600–545 mya
Single-celled life forms, such as bacteria and algae, appear, then soft multi-celled life forms, such as worms and jellyfish.

545–495 mya
No life on land. Invertebrates flourish in the seas. First mollusks and trilobites.

495–443 mya
First crustaceans and early jawless fish appear. Coral reefs form. Sahara glaciated.

HOW EVOLUTION WORKS

According to Darwin's theory of evolution, only the best-adapted members of species survive to breed, leading to a gradual change in living organisms over millions of years. His theory challenged the accepted 19th-century view that life forms did not change after being created by a deity (god).

CHARLES DARWIN (1809–1882)

The theory of evolution was developed by English naturalist Charles Darwin after studying animals and plants during a world voyage. He published his findings in 1859 in his book *On the Origin of Species*.

EVOLUTION OF THE HORSE

Hyracotherium
This animal of 50 million years ago had four toes on its front feet.

Mesohippus
Mesohippus, which lived 30 million years ago, had three toes on its front feet.

Merychippus
One of Merychippus's three toes formed a large hoof. Merychippus existed 20 million years ago.

Equus (modern horse)
Modern horses, which have a single toe or hoof on each foot, evolved about 2 million years ago.

Silurian	Devonian	Carboniferous	Permian

443–417 mya
First jawed fish. Huge sea scorpions hunt in the sea. Small land plants colonize the shore.

417–354 mya
Age of sharks and fish. Insects and amphibians appear on land. Giant ferns form forests.

354–290 mya
Warm swampy forests leave remains that will turn to coal. First reptiles.

290–248 mya
Reptiles diversify, conifers replace tree ferns. Mass extinction as Earth turns cold

FOSSILS

THE REMAINS of living things preserved naturally, often for many millions of years, are called fossils. Most fossils are formed in rocks; however, remains can also be preserved in ice, tar, peat, and amber. Fossils tell us nearly all we know about the history of life on Earth.

Spider trapped inside resin

SPIDER IN AMBER
Amber is fossilized tree resin that may also preserve trapped insects.

AMMONITES BECAME EXTINCT 65 MYA

KINDS OF FOSSILS
Many fossils form on the seabed, so shells and sea creatures are very common. Fossils of land animals and plants are rarer. Footprints, burrows, or droppings may also be preserved.

Fossilized shell

MESOZOIC			CENOZOIC		
Triassic	Jurassic	Cretaceous	Tertiary		
				Palaeocene	Eocene

248–206 mya Mammals and dinosaurs appear. The climate warms and seed-bearing plants dominate.	206–142 mya The age of the dinosaurs. The first known bird, Archaeopteryx, appears.	142–65 mya First flowering plants. Period ends with a mass extinction that wipes out dinosaurs.	65–55 mya Warm, humid climate. Mammals, insects, and flowering plants flourish.	55–34 mya Mammals grow larger and diversify. Primates evolve.	

1. ANIMAL DIES
The body of a dead animal lies decaying on the surface of the land.

2. REMAINS SINK
Gradually, the body becomes covered with sand or mud.

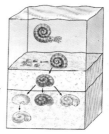

FOSSILIZATION AT SEA
Dead organisms sink to the seabed and are buried. As the sediment turns to rock, their remains are either chemically altered or dissolve to leave a cavity, which may fill with minerals to form a cast.

3. BONES ALTER
Over time, the bones are altered, and the sand and mud turn to rock.

4. FOSSIL IS EXPOSED
Eventually, weather and erosion expose the fossil at the surface.

Oligocene	Miocene	Pliocene	Quaternary	
			Pleistocene	Holocene

34–24 mya *First humanlike creatures appear. Hunting birds thrive. Some mammals die out.*	*24–5 mya* *Climate cools, and forests shrink. Deerlike hoofed mammals flourish. First hominids.*	*5–2 mya* *Cold and dry. Mammals reach maximum diversity. Many modern mammals appear.*	*2 mya–10,000 ya* *Ice Ages. Homo sapiens evolves. Mammoths and saber-toothed tigers die out.*	*10,000 ya to present Humans develop agriculture and technology. Human activity threatens many species.*

DINOSAURS

FOR 160 MILLION YEARS the Earth was dominated by giant reptiles called dinosaurs, including *Seismosaurus*, the longest creature ever to walk on land. Then, 65 million years ago, all the dinosaurs mysteriously died out.

Light bones for flying

Wings of skin

Furry body

PTEROSAUR
While dinosaurs ruled the land, giant reptiles, like Pterosaur, flew in the air.

DINOSAUR GROUPS
Scientists divide dinosaurs into two orders according to the arrangement of their hipbones. Saurischians have lizardlike hips and include both plant and meateaters. Ornithischians have bird-like hips and are all plant eaters. The two orders are divided into five subgroups.

Muscular tail balanced the front of the body

Long neck for browsing in treetops

Ruff

Horn

SALTASAURUS

STYRACOSAURUS

Sauropods (Saurischians) were huge, long-necked four-legged planteaters.

Marginocephalians (Ornithischians) had a bony ruff and horns for self-defense.

TYRANNOSAURUS

STEGOSAURUS

CORYTHOSAURUS

Thyreophorans (Ornithischians) were spiny-backed planteaters.

Theropods (Saurischians) were two-legged meateaters.

Ornithopods (Ornithischians) had a horny beak and birdlike feet.

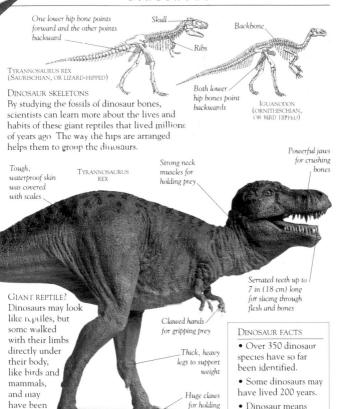

One lower hip bone points forward and the other points backward

Skull

Backbone

Ribs

TYRANNOSAURUS REX
(SAURISCHIAN, OR LIZARD-HIPPED)

DINOSAUR SKELETONS

By studying the fossils of dinosaur bones, scientists can learn more about the lives and habits of these giant reptiles that lived millions of years ago. The way the hips are arranged helps them to group the dinosaurs.

Both lower hip bones point backwards

IGUANODON
(ORNITHISCHIAN, OR BIRD-HIPPED)

Tough, waterproof skin was covered with scales

TYRANNOSAURUS REX

Strong neck muscles for holding prey

Powerful jaws for crushing bones

Serrated teeth up to 7 in (18 cm) long for slicing through flesh and bones

GIANT REPTILE?

Dinosaurs may look like reptiles, but some walked with their limbs directly under their body, like birds and mammals, and may have been warm-blooded.

Clawed hands for gripping prey

Thick, heavy legs to support weight

Huge claws for holding prey on the ground

DINOSAUR FACTS

• Over 350 dinosaur species have so far been identified.

• Some dinosaurs may have lived 200 years.

• Dinosaur means "terrible lizard."

VERTEBRATES

ONLY ABOUT five percent of all animals have backbones, and these are called vertebrates. There are more than 50,000 different species of vertebrate, divided into classes of mammals, birds, fish, reptiles, and amphibians. Their sense organs and nervous systems are well developed, and they have adapted to almost every habitat.

GORILLA SKELETON

BACKBONE
Vertebrates have a skeleton of bone, with a backbone, two pairs of limbs, and a skull that protects the brain. Inside are the heart, lungs, and other organs.

REPTILES
Lizards, snakes, crocodiles, and geckos are reptiles. They all have a tough, scaly skin. Young reptiles hatch from eggs, and look like tiny versions of their parents. This chameleon is a type of lizard.

Spines along backbone give protection from attack

Scaly skin

MADAGASCAN CHAMELEON

Female frog lays eggs, called frogspawn

Male fertilizes spawn

ANIMAL REPRODUCTION
In vertebrates, offspring are created when males and females come together and the male's sperm join the female's eggs. This is called sexual reproduction, and usually involves mating. A few animals are neither male nor female, and they reproduce asexually.

Prehensile tail for holding onto branches

SENSES

Mammals and other vertebrate animals have senses to help them find their way, locate food, and avoid enemies. For land animals, such as this caracal, sight, hearing, and smell are the most important senses. Sea creatures rely more on smell and taste to escape danger and find food.

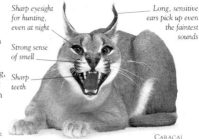

Sharp eyesight for hunting, even at night

Long, sensitive ears pick up even the faintest sounds

Strong sense of smell

Sharp teeth

CARACAL

FISH

With streamlined bodies covered in slippery scales, these vertebrates are perfectly suited to life in the water.

TWINSPOT WRASSE

Scales covered in slimy mucus

BIRDS

The only animals that have feathers are birds, and most of them are powerful fliers. Birds have a beak, or bill, instead of teeth, and all reproduce by laying eggs.

COUNT RAGGI'S BIRD OF PARADISE

RED-EYED TREE FROG

Large eyes spot prey

AMPHIBIANS

Frogs, toads, newts, and salamanders are amphibians. These vertebrates spend part of their lives in water and part on land. They all reproduce by laying eggs.

Long legs for jumping

PORCUPINE

Spiny quills protect body

Fur helps keep body warm

MAMMAL

A mammal is usually covered by fur or hair. It gives birth to live young, which it feeds with milk.

INVERTEBRATES

NINETY-FIVE PERCENT of all animals are invertebrates, which means they have no backbone. They include jellyfish, sponges, starfish, coral, worms, crabs, spiders, and insects.

Intestine

Body shape maintained by fluid

Dorsal blood vessel

Gizzard (part of stomach)

Ovary

Spermatheca (reproductive organ)

Ventral nerve cord

Mouth

EARTHWORM CROSS-SECTION

Hard shell to protect soft body

Soft body

Eyes on stalks

MOLLUSKS

These soft-bodied invertebrates are often protected by a hard shell. Most mollusks, such as squid and octopuses, clams, mussels, and scallops, live in water, but some, like snails and slugs, live on land.

WORMS

A worm is an animal with a long soft body and no legs. There are many different kinds, including flatworms, tapeworms, earthworms, roundworms, and leeches.

Echinoderms have a five-part body plan.

Ossicles are hard plates just under the skin that keep the body rigid

Arm

STARFISH AND URCHINS

Starfish, sea urchins, and sea cucumbers are all of echinoderms. All are predators, and most have sucker-tipped "tube feet" through which they pump water to move along and feed. The five broad arms of a starfish can wrench open a shellfish to suck out the contents.

Underside of arm is covered with fluid-filled tube feet for moving and feeding

Arm

LIFE CYCLE
Each invertebrate has its own life cycle, but most species lay eggs. Some go through several larval stages; others hatch as miniature adults.

Buds break away as free-swimming adults

Jellyfish

Fertilized larva

Polyp divides into eight-part buds

Larva grows into a polyp

SPIDER

ARTHROPODS
Insects, spiders, and lobsters are all arthropods. They have jointed limbs and a tough external skeleton.

CROSS SECTION OF A JELLYFISH

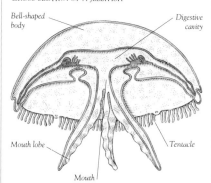

Bell-shaped body

Digestive cavity

Mouth lobe

Tentacle

Mouth

Jellyfish, anemones, and coral are all kinds of cnidarians – sea creatures with a mouth surrounded by tentacles. These tentacles usually carry a sting to stun or kill prey. Some cnidarians, called polyps, always attach to solid objects, such as a rock; others, called medusas, move by contracting their bell-shaped bodies.

SPONGES
These primitive sea creatures feed by drawing water into the holes in their soft bodies and filtering out any food.

INVERTEBRATE FACTS
• Up to 500 million hookworms may be found in a single human.

• Roundworms are probably the most numerous animals on Earth.

MOLLUSKS AND ECHINODERMS

THE SOFT BODY of a mollusk is usually covered by a hard shell. Mollusks include gastropods (such as snails), bivalves (such as oysters), and cephalopods (such as squids). Echinoderms have a five-part body and live in the sea.

Reproductive organ

Mantle

Eye

Mucus gland

Muscular foot

Lung

Sensory tentacle

INSIDE A SNAIL
A snail's body has three parts: the head, the muscular foot, and the body, which is covered by a mantle of skin and contains the main organs.

Mollusk sinks to a suitable spot on the seabed

Egg hatches into freeswimming larvae

Sperm cells fertilize egg cells outside the adult's body

This is the veliger larvae stage

Shell forms

LIFE CYCLE OF AN OYSTER
Mollusks usually lay eggs that hatch into larvae. As a larva grows, its shell develops. The young adult then settles on the seabed. Some snails hatch out as miniature adults.

TYPES OF MOLLUSKS			
There are more than 50,000 species of mollusk. These are divided into seven classes. Five are listed below.			
MOLLUSK	NAME OF CLASS	FEATURES	NUMBER OF SPECIES
	Bivalves (clams and relatives)	Shells in two parts, which hinge together	8,000
	Polyplacophorans (chitons)	Shell made of several plates	600
	Gastropods (slugs, snails, and relatives)	Mollusks with a muscular sucker-like foot	40,000
	Scaphopods (tusk shells)	Mollusks with tapering tubular shells	350
	Cephalopods (octopus, squid, cuttlefish)	Mollusks with a head and ring of tentacles	650

CUBAN LAND SNAILS

SCALLOP

TRITON

PACIFIC THORNY
OYSTER

MOLLUSK SHELLS

Mollusk shells have a huge variety of colors and shapes. They are formed from calcium carbonate, which is secreted by the mantle. Bivalves have a two-part shell with a hinge.

A sea star can grow a new arm to replace a damaged limb

SCARLET
SEA STAR

SEA STARS

A sea star is a typical echinoderm. It has a spiny-skinned body with five equal parts, tiny sucker feet, and an internal skeleton made from hard plates called ossicles. It lives in the sea. Sea stars pry open the shells of bivalves to eat the soft meat inside.

TYPES OF ECHINODERMS			
Echinoderms are a distinctive group of invertebrates that live in the sea. There are 7,000 species in six classes (four listed here.)			
ECHINODERM	NAME OF CLASS	FEATURES	NUMBER OF SPECIES
	Asteroids (sea stars)	Central mouth surrounded by arms	1,500
	Echinoids (sea urchins)	Body surrounded by a case bearing spines	1,000
	Crinoids (feather stars)	Mouth surrounded by feathery arms	625
	Holothuroidea (sea cucumbers)	Wormlike body with feeding tentacles	1,150

MOLLUSK FACTS

• The world's most venomous gastropod is the geographer cone in the Pacific Ocean. Its venom can kill a human.

• The largest land snail is the giant African land snail *Achatina achatina*. It can grow up to 15.4 in (39 cm) from head to tail.

ARTHROPODS

ARACHNIDS, CRUSTACEANS, and insects are part of the arthropod group of invertebrates. Insects are by far the largest of these three groups. All arthropods have a jointed body with a tough body case. The case is shed as the animal grows.

The egg is laid in a silk sac to protect it

Spiderlings resemble the adult spider

Spiderling molts

LIFE CYCLE OF A SPIDER
Arachnids such as spiders lay eggs that hatch into tiny versions of adults. They molt several times before they are mature.

Poison gland   IMPERIAL SCORPION   Pedipalps – a pair of pincers for feeding

Sting   Heart   Cephalothorax

Intestine

Abdomen

Spiracle – air hole

INSIDE AN ARACHNID
The body of an arachnid is divided into a front and middle part (cephalothorax) and a rear part (abdomen). Arachnids have four pairs of walking legs.

TYPES OF ARACHNIDS

The class Arachnida includes spiders, mites, and scorpions. It contains 73,000 species, which are grouped into 12 orders. Six orders are listed below.

ARACHNID	NAME OF ORDER	NUMBER OF SPECIES	ARACHNID	NAME OF ORDER	NUMBER OF SPECIES
	Scorpiones (scorpions)	1,200		Uropygi (whip scorpions)	100
	Solifugae (camel spiders)	900		Opiliones (harvestmen)	5,000
	Acari (mites and ticks)	30,000		Araneae (spiders)	35,000

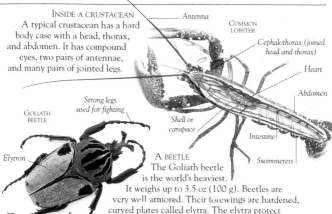

INSIDE A CRUSTACEAN
A typical crustacean has a hard
body case with a head, thorax,
and abdomen. It has compound
eyes, two pairs of antennae,
and many pairs of jointed legs.

Antenna

COMMON
LOBSTER

*Cephalothorax (joined
head and thorax)*

Heart

Abdomen

GOLIATH
BEETLE

*Strong legs
used for fighting*

*Shell or
carapace*

Intestine

Swimmerets

Elytron

A BEETLE
The Goliath beetle
is the world's heaviest.
It weighs up to 3.5 oz (100 g). Beetles are
very well armored. Their forewings are hardened,
curved plates called elytra. The elytra protect
the fragile hind wings that are used for flying.

TYPES OF CRUSTACEANS			
There are more than 50,000 species of crustaceans divided into eight classes. These include the four classes below.			
CRUSTACEAN	NAME OF CLASS	FEATURES	NUMBER OF SPECIES
	Branchiopods (fairy shrimp, water fleas)	Small animals of freshwater and salty lakes	1,000
	Cirripedia (barnacles)	Immobile animals with a boxlike case	1,000
	Copepods (cyclopoids and relatives)	Small animals often found in plankton	9,000
	Malacostracans (shrimp, crabs, lobsters)	Many-legged animals, often with pincers	20,000

*Mature
adult*

*Egg is fertilized
outside body*

*First
larval
stage*

*Post-
larval stage*

*Second
larval stage*

LIFE CYCLE OF A SHRIMP
Crustaceans usually lay
their eggs in water. Once
hatched, the egg begins
its first larval stage. After
two more larval stages,
there is a final post-larval
stage before adulthood.

CLASSIFICATION

BIOLOGISTS HAVE identified and classified most species of vertebrates (animals with backbones), although it is likely that new species of fish await discovery. Invertebrate animals have not been so well documented, and there are many species to be identified.

Springtails	Lice
Bristletails	Thrips
Diplurans	Booklice
Silverfish	Zorapterans
Mayflies	Bugs
Stoneflies	Beetles
Webspinners	Ants, bees, wasps
Dragonflies	Lacewings and
Grasshoppers and	antlions
crickets	Scorpionflies
Stick and leaf insects	Stylopids
Grylloblattids	Caddisflies
Earwigs	Butterflies and moths
Cockroaches	Flies
Praying mantids	Fleas
Termites	

INSECTS
(Insecta)
1,000,000 species

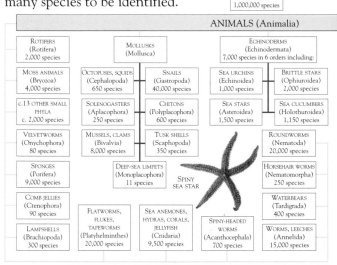

ANIMALS (Animalia)

ROTIFERS
(Rotifera)
2,000 species

MOSS ANIMALS
(Bryozoa)
4,000 species

c.13 OTHER SMALL
PHYLA
c. 2,000 species

VELVETWORMS
(Onychophora)
80 species

SPONGES
(Porifera)
9,000 species

COMB JELLIES
(Ctenophora)
90 species

LAMPSHELLS
(Brachiopoda)
300 species

MOLLUSKS
(Mollusca)

OCTOPUSES, SQUIDS
(Cephalopoda)
650 species

SOLENOGASTERS
(Aplacophora)
250 species

MUSSELS, CLAMS
(Bivalvia)
8,000 species

DEEP-SEA LIMPETS
(Monoplacophora)
11 species

FLATWORMS,
FLUKES,
TAPEWORMS
(Platyhelminthes)
20,000 species

SNAILS
(Gastropoda)
40,000 species

CHITONS
(Polyplacophora)
600 species

TUSK SHELLS
(Scaphopoda)
350 species

SEA ANEMONES,
HYDRAS, CORALS,
JELLYFISH
(Cnidaria)
9,500 species

ECHINODERMS
(Echinodermata)
7,000 species in 6 orders including:

SEA URCHINS
(Echinoidea)
1,000 species

SEA STARS
(Asteroidea)
1,500 species

BRITTLE STARS
(Ophiuroidea)
2,000 species

SEA CUCUMBERS
(Holothuroidea)
1,150 species

SPINY
SEA STAR

SPINY-HEADED
WORMS
(Acanthocephala)
700 species

ROUNDWORMS
(Nematoda)
20,000 species

HORSEHAIR WORMS
(Nematomorpha)
250 species

WATERBEARS
(Tardigrada)
400 species

WORMS, LEECHES
(Annelida)
15,000 species

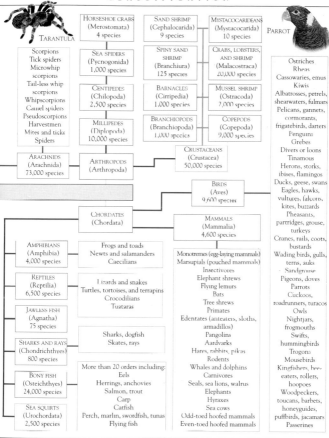

TARANTULA

PARROT

HORSESHOE CRABS (Merostomata)
4 species

SAND SHRIMP (Cephalocarida)
9 species

MYSTACOCARIDEANS (Mystacocarida)
10 species

Scorpions
Tick spiders
Microwhip scorpions
Tail-less whip scorpions
Whipscorpions
Camel spiders
Pseudoscorpions
Harvestmen
Mites and ticks
Spiders

SEA SPIDERS (Pycnogonida)
1,000 species

SPINY SAND SHRIMP (Branchiura)
125 species

CRABS, LOBSTERS, AND SHRIMP (Malacostraca)
20,000 species

CENTIPEDES (Chilopoda)
2,500 species

BARNACLES (Cirripedia)
1,000 species

MUSSEL SHRIMP (Ostracoda)
7,000 species

MILLIPEDES (Diplopoda)
10,000 species

BRANCHIOPODS (Branchiopoda)
1,000 species

COPEPODS (Copepoda)
9,000 species

ARACHNIDS (Arachnida)
73,000 species

ARTHROPODS (Arthropoda)

CRUSTACEANS (Crustacea)
50,000 species

Ostriches
Rheas
Cassowaries, emus
Kiwis
Albatrosses, petrels, shearwaters, fulmars
Pelicans, gannets, cormorants, frigatebirds, darters
Penguins
Grebes
Divers or loons
Tinamous
Herons, storks, ibises, flamingos
Ducks, geese, swans
Eagles, hawks, vultures, falcons, kites, buzzards
Pheasants, partridges, grouse, turkeys
Cranes, rails, coots, bustards
Wading birds, gulls, terns, auks
Sandgrouse
Pigeons, doves
Parrots
Cuckoos, roadrunners, turacos
Owls
Nightjars, frogmouths
Swifts, hummingbirds
Trogons
Mousebirds
Kingfishers, bee-eaters, rollers, hoopoes
Woodpeckers, toucans, barbets, honeyguides, puffbirds, jacamars
Passerines

BIRDS (Aves)
9,600 species

CHORDATES (Chordata)

MAMMALS (Mammalia)
4,600 species

AMPHIBIANS (Amphibia)
4,000 species

Frogs and toads
Newts and salamanders
Caecilians

Monotremes (egg-laying mammals)
Marsupials (pouched mammals)
Insectivores
Elephant shrews
Flying lemurs
Bats
Tree shrews
Primates
Edentates (anteaters, sloths, armadillos)
Pangolins
Aardvarks
Hares, rabbits, pikas
Rodents
Whales and dolphins
Carnivores
Seals, sea lions, walrus
Elephants
Hyraxes
Sea cows
Odd-toed hoofed mammals
Even-toed hoofed mammals

REPTILES (Reptilia)
6,500 species

Lizards and snakes
Turtles, tortoises, and terrapins
Crocodilians
Tuataras

JAWLESS FISH (Agnatha)
75 species

SHARKS AND RAYS (Chondrichthyes)
800 species

Sharks, dogfish
Skates, rays

BONY FISH (Osteichthyes)
24,000 species

More than 20 orders including:
Eels
Herrings, anchovies
Salmon, trout
Carp
Catfish
Perch, marlin, swordfish, tunas
Flying fish

SEA SQUIRTS (Urochordata)
2,500 species

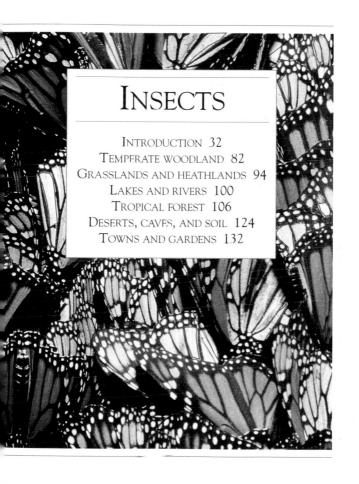

INSECTS

WHAT IS AN INSECT?

ABOUT ONE MILLION insect species are known – they are the most abundant animals on Earth. All insects have six legs, and their skeleton is on the outside of their body. This outer skeleton forms a hard, protective armor around the soft internal organs.

The antennae of insects can sense smells and vibrations in the air.

DISSECTED BEETLE

Eye

First part of thorax bears the front legs.

Jointed front leg

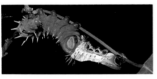

SHEDDING SKIN

An immature insect is called a nymph. As each nymph feeds and grows, it must shed its hard outer skin, which is also called an exoskeleton. When it grows too big for its skin, the skin splits, revealing a new, larger skin underneath.

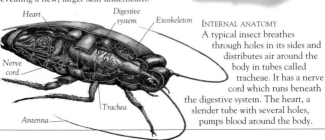

Heart

Digestive system

Exoskeleton

Nerve cord

Trachea

Antenna

INTERNAL ANATOMY

A typical insect breathes through holes in its sides and distributes air around the body in tubes called tracheae. It has a nerve cord which runs beneath the digestive system. The heart, a slender tube with several holes, pumps blood around the body.

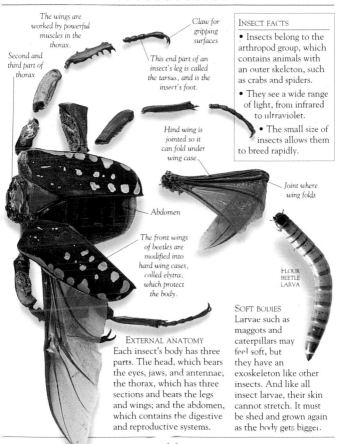

The wings are worked by powerful muscles in the thorax.

Claw for gripping surfaces

This end part of an insect's leg is called the tarsus, and is the insect's foot.

Second and third part of thorax

Hind wing is jointed so it can fold under wing case

Joint where wing folds

Abdomen

The front wings of beetles are modified into hard wing cases, called elytra, which protect the body.

INSECT FACTS

• Insects belong to the arthropod group, which contains animals with an outer skeleton, such as crabs and spiders.

• They see a wide range of light, from infrared to ultraviolet.

• The small size of insects allows them to breed rapidly.

FLOUR BEETLE LARVA

EXTERNAL ANATOMY
Each insect's body has three parts. The head, which bears the eyes, jaws, and antennae; the thorax, which has three sections and bears the legs and wings; and the abdomen, which contains the digestive and reproductive systems.

SOFT BODIES
Larvae such as maggots and caterpillars may feel soft, but they have an exoskeleton like other insects. And like all insect larvae, their skin cannot stretch. It must be shed and grown again as the body gets bigger.

THE FIRST INSECTS

INSECTS WERE the first animals to appear
on land, and also the first to fly. They
evolved at least 400 million years ago
– long before humans, and even
before dinosaurs. Fossils show that
some ancient species were similar to
modern dragonflies and cockroaches.

FLOWER FOOD
When flowering
plants evolved 100
million years ago,
insects gained two
important new foods –
pollen and nectar. Insects
thrived on these foods.
They pollinated the
flowers, and many new
species of plants and
insects evolved together.

INSECT IN AMBER
Amber is fossilized tree resin
from pine trees that grew
over 40 million years ago.
Well-preserved ancient
insects are sometimes
found in amber.
This sweat bee is
in fossilized copal,
a resin from certain
tropical trees.

FIRST INSECT FACTS

• The ancestors of insects
– and all other animals
alive on Earth today – were
wormlike marine creatures.

• Some of the earliest
insects seem to have had
three pairs of wings.

• The oldest known
butterfly or moth is
known from England
190 million years ago.

MODERN
EARWIG

*Fossil
earwig*

ROCK REMAINS
This fossil of an earwig
was found in 35-million-
year-old lake sediment in
Colorado. The fossil
shows how similar in
shape ancient earwigs
were to modern ones.

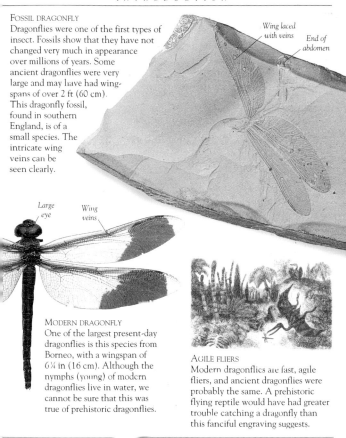

FOSSIL DRAGONFLY
Dragonflies were one of the first types of insect. Fossils show that they have not changed very much in appearance over millions of years. Some ancient dragonflies were very large and may have had wingspans of over 2 ft (60 cm). This dragonfly fossil, found in southern England, is of a small species. The intricate wing veins can be seen clearly.

Wing laced with veins

End of abdomen

Large eye

Wing veins

MODERN DRAGONFLY
One of the largest present-day dragonflies is this species from Borneo, with a wingspan of 6¼ in (16 cm). Although the nymphs (young) of modern dragonflies live in water, we cannot be sure that this was true of prehistoric dragonflies.

AGILE FLIERS
Modern dragonflies are fast, agile fliers, and ancient dragonflies were probably the same. A prehistoric flying reptile would have had greater trouble catching a dragonfly than this fanciful engraving suggests.

TYPES OF INSECT

SCIENTISTS ARE CONSTANTLY DISCOVERING new insects. They currently know of about one million species, but it is likely that there may be at least five million in total. Each belongs to one of about 30 groups, or orders, which are defined according to body structure and larval development.

Beetles, wasps, bees, and ants

About 350,000 species of beetles are described – they are the largest order of insects. Wasps, bees, and ants form the second largest order of insects, made up of about 125,000 species. The common feature in this order is a narrow "waist."

Jaws

STAG BEETLE

Hard wing cases meet in midline.

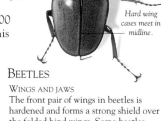

Fringed legs make swimming easier.

GREAT DIVING BEETLE

BEETLES

WINGS AND JAWS
The front pair of wings in beetles is hardened and forms a strong shield over the folded hind wings. Some beetles, such as stag beetles, have greatly enlarged jaws that look like horns.

DIFFERENT FOODS
Plants, fungi, insects, and dead animals are among the wide variety of beetle foods. The great diving beetle lives in ponds. It is a fierce predator which hunts tadpoles and small fish.

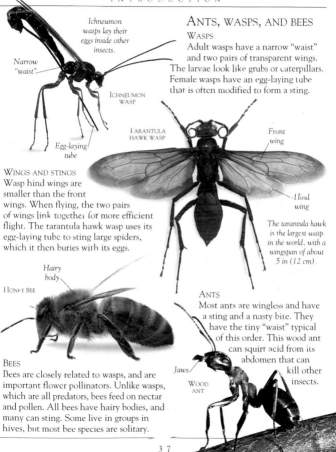

Ichneumon wasps lay their eggs inside other insects.

Narrow "waist"

ICHNEUMON WASP

Egg-laying tube

ANTS, WASPS, AND BEES

WASPS

Adult wasps have a narrow "waist" and two pairs of transparent wings. The larvae look like grubs or caterpillars. Female wasps have an egg-laying tube that is often modified to form a sting.

TARANTULA HAWK WASP

Front wing

Hind wing

The tarantula hawk is the largest wasp in the world, with a wingspan of about 5 in (12 cm).

WINGS AND STINGS

Wasp hind wings are smaller than the front wings. When flying, the two pairs of wings link together for more efficient flight. The tarantula hawk wasp uses its egg-laying tube to sting large spiders, which it then buries with its eggs.

Hairy body

HONEY BEE

BEES

Bees are closely related to wasps, and are important flower pollinators. Unlike wasps, which are all predators, bees feed on nectar and pollen. All bees have hairy bodies, and many can sting. Some live in groups in hives, but most bee species are solitary.

ANTS

Most ants are wingless and have a sting and a nasty bite. They have the tiny "waist" typical of this order. This wood ant can squirt acid from its abdomen that can kill other insects.

Jaws

WOOD ANT

Butterflies, moths, and flies

Two common insect orders are the two-winged flies and the moths
and butterflies. Flies are distinctive because their second pair of
wings is converted into balancing organs that resemble drumsticks.
Their young stages are maggots. Butterflies and moths have a coiled
proboscis (feeding tube), and their wings are covered in minute,
flattened scales. Butterfly and moth larvae are called caterpillars.

BUTTERFLIES AND MOTHS

CATERPILLARS

Although caterpillars' bodies are
soft, they have an exoskeleton
like other insects. Caterpillars
grow at a very fast rate. They
feed on leaves and have sharp
jaws for slicing vegetation.

Leaf-green coloring

Feathery antenna

MOTHS

There are 150,000 species of moth.
Most moth species fly only at
night. They are usually dull
in color and they often
have feathery antennae.
There are also many day-
flying species, and some of
these are brightly colored.

POLYPHEMUS MOTH

BUTTERFLIES

There are 15,000 species of butterfly.
Most butterflies fly by day, have club-
tipped antennae, and are brightly
colored. The scales that cover
moths and butterflies sometimes
produce colors by iridescence,
which is the effect of sunlight
shining on them to produce a
display of many different colors.

Club-tipped antenna

SWALLOWTAIL BUTTERFLY

FLIES

CRANE FLY

Crane flies live successfully all over the world. The larvae of some species of crane fly are known as "leather-jackets," because their skin is so tough.

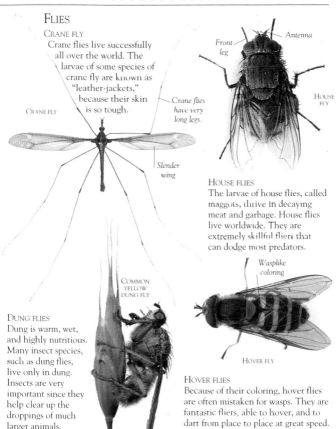

CRANE FLY

Crane flies have very long legs.

Slender wing

Front leg

Antenna

HOUSE FLY

HOUSE FLIES

The larvae of house flies, called maggots, thrive in decaying meat and garbage. House flies live worldwide. They are extremely skillful fliers that can dodge most predators.

DUNG FLIES

Dung is warm, wet, and highly nutritious. Many insect species, such as dung flies, live only in dung. Insects are very important since they help clear up the droppings of much larger animals.

COMMON YELLOW DUNG FLY

Wasplike coloring

HOVER FLY

HOVER FLIES

Because of their coloring, hover flies are often mistaken for wasps. They are fantastic fliers, able to hover, and to dart from place to place at great speed.

Bugs and other types

There are about 67,500 species of bug, the fifth-largest order of insects. Bugs have a feeding tube folded back between the legs, and most of them eat plant food. The other orders of insects contain fewer species. Some of these orders are well known, such as fleas, cockroaches, dragonflies, and locusts.

BUGS

FEEDING TUBES

The mandibles (jaws) found in most insects are modified in bugs into a needlelike tube called a rostrum. The bug pierces food with its rostrum and then sucks up juices.

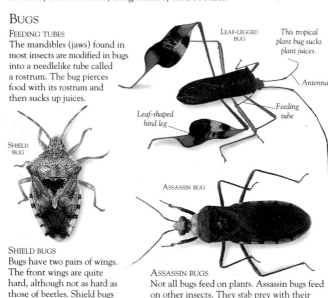

LEAF-LEGGED BUG

This tropical plant bug sucks plant juices.

Antenna

Leaf-shaped hind leg

Feeding tube

SHIELD BUG

ASSASSIN BUG

SHIELD BUGS

Bugs have two pairs of wings. The front wings are quite hard, although not as hard as those of beetles. Shield bugs are so called because when their wings are closed, they look like colorful shields.

ASSASSIN BUGS

Not all bugs feed on plants. Assassin bugs feed on other insects. They stab prey with their feeding tube and then suck out the victim's juices. Some South American assassin bugs feed on the blood of humans and transmit diseases.

DESERT LOCUST
NYMPH

Wing buds

OTHER INSECT ORDERS

GRASSHOPPERS

The desert locust belongs to the order that includes crickets and grasshoppers. These insects eat plants and have powerful back legs for leaping.

MANTID

MANTIDS

Adults and mantid nymphs look very similar. They both have very large eyes and grasping front legs. Many mantids are colored like leaves or flowers, so they can hide in them as they wait for their prey to come near.

STICK
INSECT

COCKROACH

COCKROACHES

There are many fossils of cockroaches, since they are one of the most ancient orders of insects. Their front wings overlap each other, instead of meeting in the middle, and the young stages look like the adults.

DRAGONFLY

STICK INSECTS

This order is usually found in the tropics. They look like sticks with their long, slender legs and bodies and feed only on leaves. Their sticklike disguise hides them from predators

Wings have many veins.

DRAGONFLIES

The ancestors of dragonflies and damselflies appeared at least 300 million years ago. The nymphs of these insects live in water. Like the adults, which catch their prey in flight, they are predators.

METAMORPHOSIS

INSECTS GO THROUGH several stages of growth before they become adults. This growing process is called metamorphosis. There are two types of metamorphosis: complete and incomplete. Complete metamorphosis has four growth stages – egg, larva, pupa, and adult. Incomplete metamorphosis involves three stages – egg, nymph, and adult.

Incomplete metamorphosis

This growing process is a gradual transformation. The insects hatch from their eggs looking like miniature adults. These young insects are called nymphs. As they grow, they shed their skin several times before they reach the adult stage.

Clawed feet hook onto stem.

Wing buds

Adult head

Adult head and thorax emerge.

1 DAMSELFLY NYMPH
A damselfly nymph lives underwater. Paddle-like plates on its tail help it swim and breathe. It sheds its skin several times as it grows toward adulthood.

2 HOLDING ON
When the nymph is ready to change into an adult it crawls out of the water up a plant stem.

3 BREAKING OUT
The skin along the back splits open and the adult head and thorax start to emerge.

Leg gripping stem

Eye

Crumpled wings

Old skin

5 FINAL STAGE
The young adult can fly weakly within two hours. The four wings become transparent and are crisscrossed with veins. It takes a few days for the bright green and black colors of the female damselfly to develop.

Blood pumps through veins in wings.

Long, slim abdomen

4 EMERGED
The soft bodied adult wriggles out of the old skin. Then it pumps blood into the crumpled wings to inflate them to full adult size.

Adult damselflies live for up to a month.

Complete metamorphosis

The four growth stages in a complete metamorphosis are egg,
larva, pupa, and adult. The larva bears no resemblance to the
adult it will become. During the pupa stage the larva makes the
amazing transformation into an adult. Insects such as wasps,
butterflies, beetles, and flies undergo complete metamorphosis.

1 LAYING EGGS
Butterflies lay eggs
near leaves that
caterpillars can
eat when they
hatch. Newly
hatched
caterpillars are
too small to
walk far to feed.

Egg

Eggshell

2 THE FIRST MEAL
When a caterpillar
emerges, the first meal it
eats is usually its own
eggshell. The eggshell
provides the caterpillar with
valuable nutrients before it
begins its diet of leaves.

*Strong
jaws slice
food.*

*A caterpillar
can increase its
body weight by
about 100 times in
a few weeks.*

3 GROWING
The caterpillar
chews up leaves and
grows much bigger, shedding
its skin several times. This growth
prepares the caterpillar for the pupal
stage of its life.

A butterfly pupa is also known as a chrysalis.

Silk thread holds pupa in place.

A butterfly pupa often looks like a leaf for camouflage.

4 PUPA ACTIVITY
A pupa is like a busy factory. From the outside it looks still, but inside there is a great deal of activity. The caterpillar's organs turn into a milky liquid, and new butterfly organs grow rapidly in their place.

5 CHANGE COMPLETED
Once the metamorphosis is complete, the butterfly emerges from its pupa. It stretches its wet, crumpled wings. Before the butterfly is ready to fly, it must wait a couple of hours for its wings to expand and harden.

Empty pupa

Antenna

Wet, crumpled wings

Blood is pumped into the veins in the wings to expand them.

SWALLOWTAIL BUTTERFLY

It takes about eight weeks for this swallowtail butterfly to grow from egg to adult.

6 BUTTERFLY
The fully developed butterfly leads a totally different life from the caterpillar. While caterpillars eat leaves in order to grow, butterflies spend their time sipping nectar from flowers and seeking a mate.

4 5

HOW INSECTS MOVE

INSECTS MOVE using muscles which are attached
to the inner surfaces of their hard outer skeleton.
Many insects walk, but some larvae have no legs so
they crawl or wriggle along. Some insects swim,
others jump, but most adult insects can fly and in
this way they may travel long distances.

Legs

Insects use their legs for walking,
running, jumping, and swimming.
Many insects have legs modified
for a number of other purposes.
These include catching prey,
holding a female when mating,
producing songs, digging, fighting,
and camouflage.

LEGS FOR SWIMMING
The backswimmer has long, oar-
shaped back legs, allowing the insect
to "row" rapidly through water. The
legs have flattened ends and a fringe
of thick hairs. The front legs are short
to grasp prey on the water's surface.

MOVEMENT FACTS

• Fairyflies use
their wings to "fly"
underwater.

• Many butterflies walk
on four legs; the front
pair are used for tasting.

• The legless larvae of
some parasitic wasps
hitch a ride on a
passing ant in order to
enter an ant's nest.

1 PREPARING TO JUMP
The back legs of locusts are swollen and packed
with strong muscles for jumping. Before leaping, a
locust holds its back legs tightly under its body, near its
center of gravity. This is the best position for the legs
to propel the insect
high into the air.

Long back
legs

Wing

Shorter
front legs

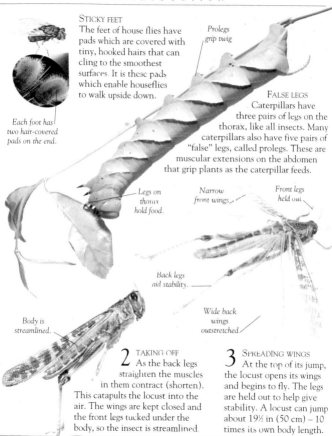

STICKY FEET
The feet of house flies have pads which are covered with tiny, hooked hairs that can cling to the smoothest surfaces. It is these pads which enable houseflies to walk upside down.

Prolegs grip twig

Each foot has two hair-covered pads on the end.

FALSE LEGS
Caterpillars have three pairs of legs on the thorax, like all insects. Many caterpillars also have five pairs of "false" legs, called prolegs. These are muscular extensions on the abdomen that grip plants as the caterpillar feeds.

Legs on thorax hold food.

Narrow front wings

Front legs held out

Back legs aid stability.

Body is streamlined.

Wide back wings outstretched

2 TAKING OFF
As the back legs straighten the muscles in them contract (shorten). This catapults the locust into the air. The wings are kept closed and the front legs tucked under the body, so the insect is streamlined.

3 SPREADING WINGS
At the top of its jump, the locust opens its wings and begins to fly. The legs are held out to help give stability. A locust can jump about 19½ in (50 cm) – 10 times its own body length.

Wings and scales

Insect wings are a wide variety of shapes and sizes. They are used not just for flying, but also for attracting a mate or hiding from predators. Most insects have two pairs of wings, each with a network of veins to give strength. Flies have only one pair of wings – the second pair is modified into small balancing organs called halteres. Small insects have few wing veins since their wings are so tiny.

EXPERT FLIERS
Dragonflies are among the most accomplished fliers in the insect world. They can hover, fly fast or slow, change direction rapidly, and even fly backward. As they maneuver, their two pairs of wings beat independently of each other.

WING FACTS
• The scales of butterflies and moths contain waste products from the pupal stage.

• There is a hearing organ in one of the wing veins of green lacewings for hearing the shrieks of bats.

• Scientists still have a lot to learn about how insects fly and control their flight once airborne.

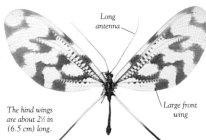

Long antenna

The hind wings are about 2½ in (6.5 cm) long.

Large front wing

LACEWINGS
The hind wings of ribbon-tail lacewings are modified into long graceful streamers. Scientists are not sure what these are for, but they may act as stabilizers in flight, or even divert predators from attacking the lacewing's body. The lacewing's mottled patterns probably help to conceal it in the dry, sandy places where it lives.

Eyespot on
front wing

Antenna

Large
wings

Eyespot on
hind wing

PEACOCK
BUTTERFLY

BUTTERFLY

CRANE FLY

Balancing
organ called
a haltere

WASP

Hind wings are
slightly smaller
than front wings.

BEETLE

Wing
case

Large hind
wing

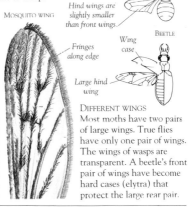

EYESPOTS

Insects sometimes use their wings to play tricks on
their enemies. Many butterflies and moths have
eyespots on their wings. These are probably used to
startle predators when flashed suddenly. This gives
the butterfly or moth a little more time to escape.

SCALES

The wings of
moths and
butterflies are
covered in scales,
which overlap like the tiles on
a roof. Some butterflies have
special scent scales.

MOSQUITO WING

Fringes
along edge

FRINGED WINGS

Many insect wings, such as this wing
from a mosquito, have hairy fringes
around the edge. The fringes may
aid flight by smoothing the flow
of air over the wings. In some
tiny insects, the fringes are
longer than the wings.

DIFFERENT WINGS

Most moths have two pairs
of large wings. True flies
have only one pair of wings.
The wings of wasps are
transparent. A beetle's front
pair of wings have become
hard cases (elytra) that
protect the large rear pair.

Flight

The ability to fly is one of the main reasons insects have survived for millions of years, and continue to flourish. Flight helps insects escape from danger. It also makes it easier to find food and new places to live. Sometimes insects fly thousands of miles to reach fresh food or warmer weather.

FLYING GROUPS
This African grasshopper has broad hind wings which allow it to glide for long distances. Locusts are a type of grasshopper that fly in huge groups when they need new food. Sometimes as many as 100 million locusts fly together for hundreds of miles.

WARMING UP
An insect's flight muscles must be warm before the wings can be moved fast enough for flight. On cool mornings, insects such as bumblebees have to vibrate their wings to warm themselves up.

Elytra protect body.

1 PREPARING TO FLY
This cockchafer beetle prepares for flight by climbing to the top of a plant and facing into the wind. It may open and shut its elytra (wing cases) several times while warming up.

2 OPENING THE WINGS
The hardened elytra, which protect the fragile hind wings, begin to open. The antennae are spread so the beetle can monitor the wind direction.

ACROBATS OF THE AIR

Hoverflies are capable of incredible acrobatics in the air. They can move like a helicopter – forward, backward, sideways, and directly upward or downward. They can also hover, a flight maneuver that very few insects are capable of.

Wings are fully open and have begun to beat.

Outstretched legs help stabilize beetle as it steers through the air.

Antenna can sense air movements.

Elytra held out to provide lift

Leading edge of wing

4 IN FLIGHT

The cockchafer leaps into the air, legs outstretched to aid stability. The hind wings are beating, driving the insect forward. On the upbeat, the leading edge of the wing is pulled upward and backward. On the downbeat it travels downward and forward.

Wings have a joint which unfolds.

3 ALMOST OFF

The elytra are opened wide and the hind wings rapidly unfold. The hind wings provide propulsion during flight, and the elytra assist by providing lift, like the wings of an airplane.

INSECT SENSES

INSECTS NEED to be fully aware of the world around them in order to survive. Although insects are tiny, some have keener senses than many larger animals. They can see colors and hear sounds that are undetectable to humans, as well as being able to detect smells from many miles away.

Sight

There are two types of insect eyes – simple and compound. Simple eyes can probably detect only light and shade. Compound eyes have hundreds of lenses, giving their owner excellent vision.

HEAD OF COMMON
DARTER DRAGONFLY

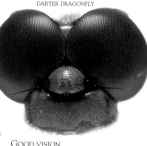

SIMPLE EYES
Caterpillars never need to look far for their plant food – they are constantly surrounded by it. Because of this, they do not need sharp eyesight. They can manage perfectly well with a group of simple eyes.

GOOD VISION
The eyes of dragonflies take up most of their head. This allows them to see what's in front, above, below, and behind them all at the same time. Dragonflies use their excellent sight and agile flight to catch prey.

Simple
eyes

COMMON DARTER
DRAGONFLY

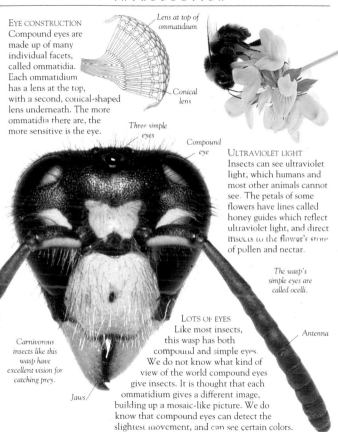

EYE CONSTRUCTION
Compound eyes are made up of many individual facets, called ommatidia. Each ommatidium has a lens at the top, with a second, conical-shaped lens underneath. The more ommatidia there are, the more sensitive is the eye.

Lens at top of ommatidium

Conical lens

Three simple eyes

Compound eye

ULTRAVIOLET LIGHT
Insects can see ultraviolet light, which humans and most other animals cannot see. The petals of some flowers have lines called honey guides which reflect ultraviolet light, and direct insects to the flower's store of pollen and nectar.

The wasp's simple eyes are called ocelli.

Carnivorous insects like this wasp have excellent vision for catching prey.

Antenna

Jaws

LOTS OF EYES
Like most insects, this wasp has both compound and simple eyes. We do not know what kind of view of the world compound eyes give insects. It is thought that each ommatidium gives a different image, building up a mosaic-like picture. We do know that compound eyes can detect the slightest movement, and can see certain colors.

Smelling, hearing, and touching

The bodies of insects are covered in short hairs which are connected to the nervous system. These hairs can feel, or "hear," vibrations in the air due to either sound or movement. Some hairs are modified to detect smells and flavors. Sensory hairs are often found on the antennae, but also occur on the feet and mouthparts.

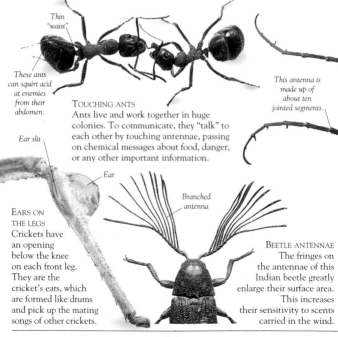

Thin "waist"

These ants can squirt acid at enemies from their abdomen.

This antenna is made up of about ten jointed segments.

TOUCHING ANTS
Ants live and work together in huge colonies. To communicate, they "talk" to each other by touching antennae, passing on chemical messages about food, danger, or any other important information.

Ear slit

Ear

Branched antenna

EARS ON THE LEGS
Crickets have an opening below the knee on each front leg. They are the cricket's ears, which are formed like drums and pick up the mating songs of other crickets.

BEETLE ANTENNAE
The fringes on the antennae of this Indian beetle greatly enlarge their surface area. This increases their sensitivity to scents carried in the wind.

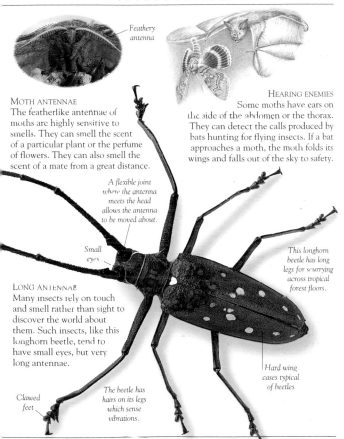

MOTH ANTENNAE
The featherlike antennae of moths are highly sensitive to smells. They can smell the scent of a particular plant or the perfume of flowers. They can also smell the scent of a mate from a great distance.

Feathery antenna

HEARING ENEMIES
Some moths have ears on the side of the abdomen or the thorax. They can detect the calls produced by bats hunting for flying insects. If a bat approaches a moth, the moth folds its wings and falls out of the sky to safety.

A flexible joint where the antenna meets the head allows the antenna to be moved about.

Small eyes

LONG ANTENNAE
Many insects rely on touch and smell rather than sight to discover the world about them. Such insects, like this longhorn beetle, tend to have small eyes, but very long antennae.

This longhorn beetle has long legs for scurrying across tropical forest floors.

Hard wing cases typical of beetles

Clawed feet

The beetle has hairs on its legs which sense vibrations.

Jaws chew leaf.

Caterpillar holds leaf with its legs.

HOW INSECTS FEED

INSECTS HAVE complex mouthparts. The insects that chew their food have a pair of strong jaws for chopping, a smaller pair of jaws for holding food, and two pairs of sensory organs, called palps, for tasting. Some insects drink only liquid food and have special tubular mouthparts like a straw.

Chewing

Predatory, chewing insects need sharp, pointed jaws for stabbing, holding, and chopping up their struggling prey. Insects that chew plants have blunter jaws for grinding their food.

PLANT CHEWER
A caterpillar needs powerful jaws to bite into plant material. Their jaws are armed with teeth that overlap when they close. Some caterpillars' jaws are modified into grinding plates for mashing up the toughest leaves.

THRUSTING JAWS
Dragonfly larvae have pincers at the end of a hinged plate folded under the head. When catching prey, the plate unfolds, shoots forward, and the pincers grab the prey. Toothed jaws in the head reduce the victim to mincemeat.

BULLDOG ANT

Ants have many different jaw shapes, reflecting the variety of food they eat. Harvester ants have broad, toothless jaws for crushing seeds. Some predatory ants have long, pointed jaws for killing prey; others have simple jaws for feeding on soft-bodied insects and honeydew. This formidable bulldog ant has very large, spiky jaws for chopping up other insects.

Spikes along jaws stick into prey, giving a better grip.

Jaws cut up caterpillar.

Ends of jaws overlap.

CHOPPING JAWS

The massive jaws of ground beetles act like a pair of scissors to cut up worms, slugs, and caterpillars. A smaller pair of jaws is used to shovel the dismembered prey into the mouth.

Mantis uses its jaws to cut up a fly.

Spiny front legs hold the fly.

STRONG GRIP

The praying mantis holds its prey in a viselike grip with its spiny front legs. The strong, sharp jaws of the mantis easily slice through the prey's body, and the mantis devours the meal within a few minutes.

Drinking

For many insects, the main way of feeding is by drinking. The most nutritious foods to drink are nectar and blood. Nectar is rich in sugar, and blood is packed with proteins. Some insects drink by sucking through strawlike mouthparts. Others have spongelike mouthparts with which they mop up liquids.

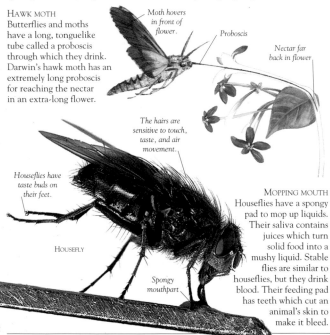

HAWK MOTH
Butterflies and moths have a long, tonguelike tube called a proboscis through which they drink. Darwin's hawk moth has an extremely long proboscis for reaching the nectar in an extra-long flower.

Moth hovers in front of flower.

Proboscis

Nectar far back in flower

The hairs are sensitive to touch, taste, and air movement.

Houseflies have taste buds on their feet.

HOUSEFLY

Spongy mouthpart

MOPPING MOUTH
Houseflies have a spongy pad to mop up liquids. Their saliva contains juices which turn solid food into a mushy liquid. Stable flies are similar to houseflies, but they drink blood. Their feeding pad has teeth which cut an animal's skin to make it bleed.

Rostrum injects saliva into victim

Assassin bug

Antenna

ROSTRUM

Assassin bugs use their rostrum to pierce their prey. Inside the rostrum are two tubes. One tube pumps saliva into the prey to dissolve its innards. The other tube sucks up the resulting mush.

COILED PROBOSCIS

When the proboscis of butterflies and moths is not in use it is coiled beneath the head. Different species have different lengths of proboscis. The longest known proboscis belongs to a Madagascan moth, and is about 13 in (33 cm) long.

Long proboscis

Coiled proboscis

HORSEFLIES

Most horseflies have knifelike jaws to make animals bleed. But this curious oriental horsefly has short, stout mouthparts to feed on blood, and a long slender proboscis to collect nectar from flowers.

COURTSHIP, BIRTH, AND GROWTH

REPRODUCTION is hazardous for insects. A female must first mate with a male of her own species and lay eggs where the newly hatched young can feed. The larvae must shed their skin several times as they grow. All this time the insects must avoid being eaten.

Courtship and mating

Males and females use special signals to ensure that their chosen mate is the right species. Courtship usually involves using scents, but may include color displays, dancing, caressing, and even gifts.

The light is produced by a chemical reaction.

GUIDING LIGHT
Glowworms are the wingless females of certain beetle species. They attract males by producing a light near the tip of their abdomen. Some species flash a distinctive code to attract the correct males.

COURTSHIP FLIGHTS
Butterflies may recognize their own species by sight, but scent is more reliable. Butterfly courtship involves dancing flights with an exchange of scented chemical signals specific to each species.

Butterflies find the scented chemicals, called pheromones, very attractive.

MATING DANGER
Mating between some insect species may last for several hours, with the male gripping the female's abdomen with claspers. This keeps other males away, but the pair are vulnerable to predators at this time.

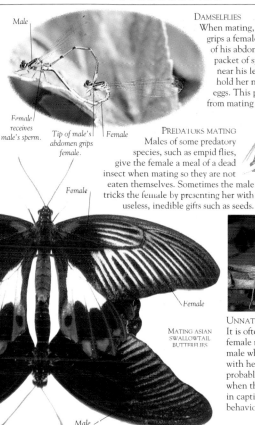

Male

Female receives male's sperm.

Tip of male's abdomen grips female.

Female

DAMSELFLIES

When mating, a male damselfly grips a female's neck with the tip of his abdomen. She receives a packet of sperm from a pouch near his legs; he continues to hold her neck while she lays eggs. This prevents other males from mating with her.

PREDATORS MATING

Males of some predatory species, such as empid flies, give the female a meal of a dead insect when mating so they are not eaten themselves. Sometimes the male tricks the female by presenting her with useless, inedible gifts such as seeds.

Female

Female

MATING ASIAN
SWALLOWTAIL
BUTTERFLIES

Male

UNNATURAL BEHAVIOR

It is often said that a female mantis eats the male while he is mating with her. But this probably happens only when the mantises are in captivity and their behavior is not natural.

Eggs and egg-laying

Insects use up a lot of energy producing eggs. To make sure this energy is not wasted, insects have many ways of protecting their eggs from predators. A few species of insect stay with their eggs to protect them until the larvae hatch. Some insects lay their eggs underground with a supply of food waiting for the newly hatched larvae. Most insects lay their eggs either in or near food, so the young larvae do not have to travel far to eat.

The egg-laying tube, also known as an ovipositor, drills into the wood.

The ovipositor is longer than the ichneumon's body.

ICHNEUMON WASP
The larvae of ichneumon wasps are parasites, which means they feed on other living creatures. When finding a host for its egg, an adult ichneumon detects the vibrations of a beetle grub gnawing inside a tree trunk. The wasp drives its egg-laying tube into the trunk until it finds the grub. An egg is laid on the grub, which then provides food for the wasp larva when it hatches.

SUITABLE FOOD

Butterflies desert their eggs once they are laid. Different butterflies lay their eggs on different plants, depending on what the larvae eat. The Malay lacewing butterfly lays its eggs on vine tendrils.

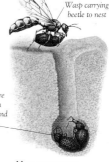

Wasp carrying beetle to nest

Beetles are stored in underground nest.

CARING EARWIGS

A female earwig looks after her eggs, licking them regularly to keep them clean. When the nymphs hatch, she feeds them until they are big enough to leave the nest.

Earwig eggs

HUNTING WASPS

Most species of hunting wasp collect soft-bodied prey, such as caterpillars or spiders, for their grubs. But the weevil-hunting wasp collects adult beetles, which it stings and then stores in a tunnel as food for its larvae.

Vertical main tunnel

Beetles mold dung into balls.

Beetle fills tunnel with dung as food for newly hatched grubs.

DUNG BEETLES

The males and females of some dung beetle species work together to dig an underground tunnel with smaller tunnels branching off it. A female lays an egg in each of the smaller tunnels and fills them with animal dung, which the beetle grubs will feed on.

INSECT EGG FACTS

• Whitefly eggs have stalks that extract water from leaves.

• Tsetse flies develop their eggs internally and lay mature larvae.

• Green lacewing eggs have long stalks, making them difficult for predators to eat.

Birth and growth

Newborn aphid

As an insect grows from egg to adult it sheds its skin several times to produce a larger exoskeleton. While this new skin hardens the insect is soft and vulnerable. Insects have many life-cycle adaptations to protect their soft young stages.

EGGS LARVA PUPA ADULT LADYBUG

LADYBUG GROWTH
Ladybugs and all other beetles go through a complete metamorphosis. An adult ladybug lays its eggs on a plant where small insects called aphids feed. Ladybug larvae eat aphids and shed their skin three times as they grow. The colorful adult emerges from the dull resting stage, or pupa.

APHIDS
Female aphids can reproduce without mating. They give birth to live young rather than lay eggs, and each female may have about 100 offspring. The newborn aphids can give birth after only a few days.

FROTHY PROTECTION
Spittlebugs are soft-bodied bugs like aphids. A spittlebug nymph produces frothy liquid excrement from its anus. The froth protects the nymph from drying out, and also hides it from predators.

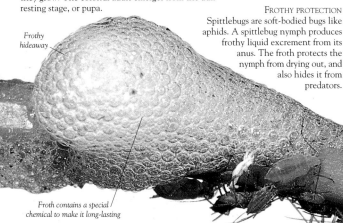

Frothy hideaway

Froth contains a special chemical to make it long-lasting

PARENTAL CARE

The females of some species of shield bug stay with their eggs and young nymphs to protect them. If touched, the parent produces a powerful smell, giving these bugs the alternative name of stinkbugs.

SHIELD BUG
NYMPHS WITH
PARENT

Hopper
burrowing
to surface

Eggs

BURROWING NYMPHS

A female locust can extend her abdomen to almost twice its length when laying eggs. The eggs are placed deep in the soil for protection. The newborn nymphs, called hoppers, must burrow to the surface to feed.

*Nymph was removed
from its froth for this
photograph*

SPITTLEBUG
NYMPH

Adult
mayfly

LEAVING WATER

Unlike all other insects, mayflies have two adult stages. The first stage, the subadult, crawls out of the water where it lived as a nymph. It flies weakly and is dull colored. It soon molts to produce the true adult, which then mates.

*Subadult emerging
from water*

Nymph

Survival of the young

Predators eagerly hunt insect larvae since many are slow-moving, soft, and nutritious. To ensure survival, most insect species produce large numbers of young which grow rapidly. Most insect larvae are defenseless and have developed special ways of hiding from predators. But many insect larvae are fierce predators themselves, consuming other creatures for nourishment as they grow.

Grub in pupal cell

Eyespots make front of thorax resemble a fearsome face

WELL HIDDEN
The larvae of chafer beetles live underground, safely hidden from most predators. The larvae, or grubs, may take many weeks to develop. They then produce a cell of hardened soil in which they will change into an adult.

Real head

Sharp spines

True legs

Proleg

SPINY LARVA
Mexican bean beetle larvae eat leaves and develop rapidly. They are covered with long, branched spines which may deter birds and other predators from attacking them.

SCARY DISPLAY
Caterpillars are a favorite food of birds. Some caterpillars try to hide to stay safe. But if the puss moth caterpillar is threatened, it puts on a startling display which can frighten off birds.

WATER LARVA
Stonefly larvae live in cold water and grow slowly, spending about three years as a larva. They are slow-moving and hide from predators under rocks and among plants.

NIGHT FEEDER
The mormon butterfly caterpillar feeds in the dark of night to avoid being seen by predators. In less than eight hours it will chew away a leaf which is more than twice its own length. During the day it rests as inconspicuously as possible.

SOFT BODIES
Young mantids are fierce predators. The body of some species resembles a flower. This disguise helps them to go unnoticed by prey, and also by predators such as birds.

For a more frightening display, the caterpillar waves these "tails" as if they were stings

Eye

Pink, flowerlike body

Leg

Legs are striped pink and green.

NESTS AND SOCIETIES

MOST INSECTS lead solitary lives, but some, particularly wasps, ants, bees, and termites, live in societies which are sometimes very ordered. There are queens, kings, workers, and soldiers. Each of these has particular jobs to do. Social insects live in nests which are often elaborate, where they protect each other and rear their young.

TROPICAL WASP NEST MADE OF CHEWED-UP PLANT FIBERS

Wasps, ants, and bees

The nest is cemented together with wasp saliva.

These insects produce a wide range of nests. Some are small with only a few dozen members, but larger nests may contain thousands or even millions of insects. Most have a single queen, and all the nest members are her offspring.

ANTS
A species of African tree ant builds its nest from fragments of plants and soil to produce a substance like dark cement. The ants live on a diet of honeydew that they get from aphids. The aphids feed on the sap of leaves in the tree tops and discharge the honeydew from their rear ends.

BEES
A bumblebee queen starts her nest alone in spring in a hole in the ground. She makes cells for her eggs out of wax. She also makes a wax pot which she fills with honey for food.

The queen uses her antennae to measure the cells as she builds them.

1 A NEW START
European wasp colonies die out each winter. In spring a queen begins a new nest of "paper" made with chewed-up wood. She makes a few cells for her eggs, building walls around the cells to shield them.

Entrance hole

2 PROTECTIVE LAYERS
The queen builds more and more paper layers around the cells. The layers will protect the larvae from cold winds as well as from predators. The queen leaves an entrance hole at the bottom.

Finished nest

3 HARD-WORKING FAMILY
The first brood the queen rears become workers, gathering food for more larvae and expanding the nest. By summer, a nest may have 500 wasps, all collecting caterpillars for the larvae. A large nest may be as much as 18 in (45 cm) in diameter.

INSIDE THE NEST
The queen lays a single egg in each cell. When the larvae hatch they stay in their cell and the queen feeds them with pieces of chewed-up caterpillar.

Termite nests

Termites have the most complex insect societies. Their elaborate nests, which may be in wood or underground, last for several years. Each nest has a single large queen and king, which are served by specialized small workers and large soldiers. Termites feed and protect each other, and one generation will help raise the next generation of offspring.

QUEEN TERMITE
In a termite society; the queen lays all the eggs. She is too fat to move, so the workers bring food to her. The queen lays 30,000 eggs each day and, as she lays them, the workers carry them off to special chambers for rearing.

Layers of "umbrellas"

NEST DEFENDERS
Termite soldiers fight enemies that attack the nest. Most termite species have soldiers with enlarged heads and powerful jaws. In some species, each soldier's head has a snout that squirts poison at invaders.

UMBRELLA NEST
The curved layers on this African termite nest act like umbrellas and protect the nest from heavy rain. If an "umbrella" is damaged, it does not get repaired, but a new one may be built.

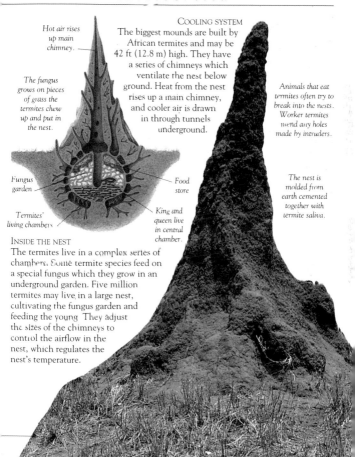

Hot air rises up main chimney.

The fungus grows on pieces of grass the termites chew up and put in the nest.

COOLING SYSTEM
The biggest mounds are built by African termites and may be 42 ft (12.8 m) high. They have a series of chimneys which ventilate the nest below ground. Heat from the nest rises up a main chimney, and cooler air is drawn in through tunnels underground.

Animals that eat termites often try to break into the nests. Worker termites mend any holes made by intruders.

Fungus garden

Food store

Termites' living chambers

King and queen live in central chamber.

The nest is molded from earth cemented together with termite saliva.

INSIDE THE NEST
The termites live in a complex series of chambers. Some termite species feed on a special fungus which they grow in an underground garden. Five million termites may live in a large nest, cultivating the fungus garden and feeding the young. They adjust the sizes of the chimneys to control the airflow in the nest, which regulates the nest's temperature.

HUNTING AND HIDING

SOME INSECT SPECIES are deadly hunters, killing prey with poisonous stings and sharp jaws. Insects are also hunted by a huge number of animals. To hide from predators, many insects have developed special disguises and patterns of behavior.

Hunting insects

About one-third of insect species are carnivorous (they eat meat). Some species eat decaying meat and dung, but most carnivorous insects hunt for their food.

KILLER BEETLE
Some insects are easily recognized as predators. The large jaws of this African ground beetle indicate that it is a hunter, and its long legs show that it can run fast after its insect prey.

KILLER WASPS
There are many types of hunting wasp. Most adult hunting wasps are vegetarians – they hunt prey only as food for their larvae. Each hunting wasp species hunts a particular type of prey. The weevil-hunting wasp hunts only a type of beetle called a weevil.

ESSENTIAL INSECTS

Ants are the most important
carnivores on Earth. They eat
more animal tissue (flesh) than all the
big carnivores put together. Without
ants, the numbers of insects would soar. Ants in
turn are eaten by birds, lizards, and other animals.

*Wasp
cocoons*

PARASITES

The larvae of many species of wasp are
parasites, which means they feed and
grow inside another insect's body. This
caterpillar has had about 50 wasp larvae
feeding inside it. The larvae are pupating
on the caterpillar's back. Soon they will
hatch as adult wasps.

*Wasp uses its
antennae and
sight to find
cockroaches*

SPECIALIST HUNTER

Many predatory insects specialize
on one particular type of prey.
This jewel wasp hunts only
cockroaches, which it uses as
food for its larvae. The adult
wasp is not carnivorous – it
feeds on the nectar
in flowers.

ROVE BEETLE

Some rove beetles
specialize in feeding on
springtails. To catch
such elusive prey the
beetle can flick out a
long, sticky "tongue"
to pull an unwary
springtail into
its mouth.

*Beetle raises
tail before
attacking prey.*

Camouflage

Insects whose body coloring matches their background are almost impossible to see. This method of hiding is known as camouflage. One of the first rules of successful camouflage is to keep still, since movement can betray an insect to a sharp-eyed predator. Some insects use another type of camouflage called disruptive coloration. They disguise their body by breaking up its shape with stripes and blocks of color.

GRASSY DISGUISE
The stripe-winged grasshopper can be heard singing in meadow grasses, but its camouflaged body is very hard to spot.

Grasshopper kicks any attackers with its back legs.

DISRUPTIVE COLORATION
This tropical moth has disruptive coloration. The patterns on the wings break up their shape. A predator might notice the patterns, but not the whole moth.

BLENDING IN
This tropical bush cricket's color and shape help it to blend in with the foliage of the plants on which it lives in the rainforest.

This bush cricket lives in the Peruvian Amazon rainforest.

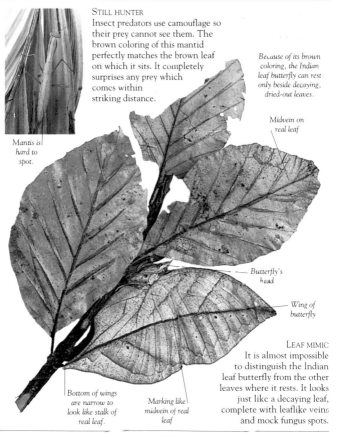

STILL HUNTER
Insect predators use camouflage so their prey cannot see them. The brown coloring of this mantid perfectly matches the brown leaf on which it sits. It completely surprises any prey which comes within striking distance.

Mantis is hard to spot.

Because of its brown coloring, the Indian leaf butterfly can rest only beside decaying, dried-out leaves.

Midvein on real leaf

Butterfly's head

Wing of butterfly

LEAF MIMIC
It is almost impossible to distinguish the Indian leaf butterfly from the other leaves where it rests. It looks just like a decaying leaf, complete with leaflike veins and mock fungus spots.

Bottom of wings are narrow to look like stalk of real leaf.

Marking like midvein of real leaf

Warning coloration

Birds, mammals, and other intelligent predators learn through experience that some insects are poisonous or harmful. Such insects do not camouflage themselves. Instead they have brightly colored bodies which warn predators that they have an unpleasant taste or a nasty sting. The most common warning colors are red, yellow, and black. Any insect with those colors is probably poisonous.

BASKER MOTH
Moths that fly by day are often brightly colored, particularly when they taste unpleasant. The red, yellow, and black coloring of this basker moth tells birds that it is not a tasty meal.

PAINFUL REMINDER
The saddle-back caterpillar is eye-catching with its vivid coloring and grotesque appearance. No young bird would ever forget the caterpillar if it tried a mouthful of the poisonous, stinging spines.

Poisonous spines

Vivid green coloring across back

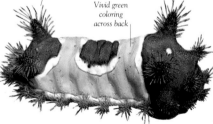

Bright spot

WARNING SPOTS
This assassin bug is easily seen because of the two bright spots on its back. These bold markings warn predators that there is a reason for them to stay away. The bug's weapon is a needle-sharp beak which can give a very painful bite.

EYESPOTS

This silk moth is camouflaged when its wings are closed. But when attacked by a predator, the moth flashes the eyespots on its hind wings. This startles the attacker briefly, and may give the moth time to escape.

Camouflaged front wings

Eyespot

POISONOUS BODY

This grasshopper tastes horrible. It gets its terrible flavor from eating poisonous plants and storing the poisons in its body. The yellow and black stripes advertise its unpleasantness to birds and other predators.

Grasshopper uses the spines on its legs for defense.

Eyes are black to blend with rest of coloring.

Mimicry

Predators usually avoid preying on dangerous animals. Many harmless insects take advantage of this by mimicking harmful creatures. Mimicking insects copy a dangerous animal's body shape and coloring. They also behave like the animal they're copying to make the disguise more convincing. Inedible objects, such as twigs and thorns, are also mimicked by insects.

The treehoppers move only when they need a fresh source of food.

Wasp has two wings, but the hover fly has four.

Wasp has a narrower waist than hover fly.

Hover fly resembles wasp in color, size, and shape.

WASP MIMIC
Hover flies cannot sting, so they find protection by mimicking the warning colors of wasps. They even hover like wasps. Although the disguise is not perfect, it is enough to persuade most animals to leave them alone.

HOVER FLY

WASP

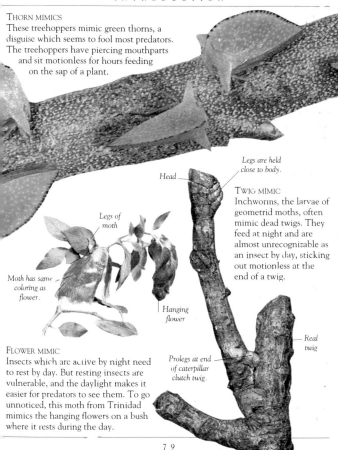

THORN MIMICS
These treehoppers mimic green thorns, a
disguise which seems to fool most predators.
The treehoppers have piercing mouthparts
and sit motionless for hours feeding
on the sap of a plant.

*Legs are held
close to body.*

Head

TWIG MIMIC
Inchworms, the larvae of
geometrid moths, often
mimic dead twigs. They
feed at night and are
almost unrecognizable as
an insect by day, sticking
out motionless at the
end of a twig.

*Legs of
moth*

*Moth has same
coloring as
flower.*

*Hanging
flower*

*Real
twig*

FLOWER MIMIC
Insects which are active by night need
to rest by day. But resting insects are
vulnerable, and the daylight makes it
easier for predators to see them. To go
unnoticed, this moth from Trinidad
mimics the hanging flowers on a bush
where it rests during the day.

*Prolegs at end
of caterpillar
clutch twig.*

WHERE INSECTS LIVE

INSECTS LIVE everywhere there is warmth and moisture. Many of the one million or more species have specialized habitat requirements. They can live only in particular places, and easily become extinct when humans change or destroy their surroundings. Other species are able to adapt to changing conditions; these adaptable insects often become pests.

NORTH AMERICA

SOUTH AMERICA

TEMPERATE WOODLAND
The varied plant life and complex structure of temperate woodland provides insects with many different habitats. Trees, shrubs, and herbs all have flowers, fruits, and buds for insects to feed on, as well as stems and roots for insects to bore into.

GRASSLANDS AND HEATHLANDS
These habitats offer little shelter from bad weather. But they warm up quickly in the sun, and have a rich variety of flowering plants.

TOWNS AND GARDENS
Hundreds of insect species take advantage of human habitats. Insects find food and shelter in our roofs, cellars, food stores, kitchens, garbage cans, farms, and in our flower-filled gardens.

ARCTIC

EUROPE

ASIA

AFRICA

AUSTRALASIA

ANTARCTIC

DESERTS, SOIL, AND CAVES
Food and water are scarce in deserts. Dense soil makes it hard for insects to communicate and move. Caves are dark and may be very cold or hot and humid.

TROPICAL FORESTS
This is the richest habitat for insect species. Thousands of species of plants provide countless niches for insects to live in, from treetop fruits to dead leaves and twigs on the ground.

LAKES AND RIVERS
Freshwater insects are highly specialized. Their bodies have modified to allow them to swim and breathe underwater.

TEMPERATE WOODLAND

FIELD SCABIOUS FLOWER

TEMPERATE WOODLANDS are often
dominated by one tree species,
such as oak, which is
deciduous (the trees lose
their leaves in winter).
The types of insect found,
and their numbers, will vary
with the seasons, as well
as with the types of tree
species in the woodlands.

DRAINING
Forests in
wetlands have
many different plant
species. But people often
drain this habitat because
it is good for farming.
Draining kills plants such
as milk-parsley, the only
plant the English
swallowtail butterfly
will breed on. This
beautiful insect is
now rarely seen.

+1.4

*Although the
English swallowtail will
lay eggs only on milk-parsley,
adults eat a variety of flowers.*

WOODLAND FACTS

• The woodland edge supports the greatest number of insect species.

• Each pair of blue tits needs about 5,000 caterpillars to feed their chicks.

• In Britain, over 280 species of insect live on native oak trees.

• Temperate rainforests in the northwestern United States are disappearing faster than tropical rainforests.

Bumblebees are very common in woodlands.

Q_{+2}

FLOWERS
Woodlands contain many types of flower. These attract various species of insect, such as bumblebees, which nest in the ground in animal burrows and pollinate many woodland flowers.

Vaporer moth caterpillar is covered with tufts of hair.

VAPORER MOTH CATERPILLAR
This attractive caterpillar eats the leaves of many different trees in Europe and North America. It will also attack rosebushes and heather plants.

Processionary caterpillars are covered in poisonous hairs.

PROCESSIONS
Conifer forests have fewer types of plant and animal than deciduous forests, although some, such as processionary moth caterpillars, can be common. These are named for their habit of following each other head to tail.

OAK TREE

IN NORTH AMERICA and Europe, oak
trees support a rich variety of insects.
There are insects living on every part
of the oak tree – the leaves,
buds, flowers, fruits, wood,
bark, and on decaying
leaves and branches. All
these insects provide food
for the many birds and other
animals found in oak woodland.

OAK TREE

GREEN OAK
TORTRIX MOTH

CATERPILLAR

GREEN OAK TORTRIX
The green wings of the green
oak tortrix moth camouflage
the moth when it rests on a
leaf. Green oak tortrix
caterpillars are extremely
common on oak trees.
The caterpillars hide from
hungry predators by rolling
themselves up in a leaf.

+2

+1.25

Leaf rolled
around green
oak tortrix
caterpillar

MAKING A TUNNEL
The caterpillars of some small
moths tunnel between the
upper and lower surfaces of a
leaf. They eat the green tissues
between these surfaces as they
tunnel, and leave a see-
through trail called a mine.

Mine

+12

Chalcid wasp larvae have eaten the gall wasp larvae

GALLS

Oak trees have many tiny growths called galls. Galls are grown by the tree around eggs laid by gall wasps. When the eggs hatch, the gall provides food and shelter for up to 30 wasp larvae. Parasitic wasps called chalcid wasps sometimes burrow inside galls and lay their eggs beside the gall wasp eggs. When the chalcid larvae hatch they eat the gall wasp larvae.

CHALCID WASP ON GALL

NUT WEEVILS

Acorns are used as food by nut weevils. They drill a hole in an acorn with their long, thin snout, and then lay their eggs inside. The larvae feed inside the acorn, and this turns the acorn black.

Black acorn

ACORNS

Long, thin snout

Antenna

+4

NUT WEEVIL

TREE CANOPY

THE UPPER BRANCHES and leaves of a tree are like a living green umbrella, forming a canopy over the lower plants. Countless insects find their food in the canopy and they are food for many different birds.

Inchworm on leaf

Silken thread suspends inchworm.

INCHWORMS
Some young birds like to feed on inchworms, the caterpillars of Geometrid moths. When in danger, inchworms can drop from a leaf and hang below by a silken thread.

Very long antennae help the cricket find its way in the dark. They also alert the cricket to the approach of an enemy.

Compound eye

OAK BUSH CRICKETS
At night, male oak bush crickets drum on leaves with their feet so that a female oak bush cricket, like this one, knows where to find a mate. The cricket's green body blends in well with its leafy surroundings.

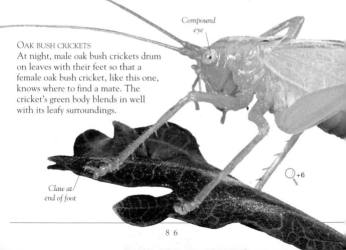

Claw at end of foot

+6

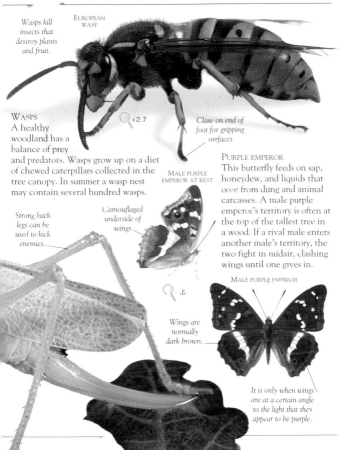

Wasps kill insects that destroy plants and fruit.

EUROPEAN WASP

WASPS

A healthy woodland has a balance of prey and predators. Wasps grow up on a diet of chewed caterpillars collected in the tree canopy. In summer a wasp nest may contain several hundred wasps.

×2.7

Claw on end of foot for gripping surfaces

MALE PURPLE EMPEROR AT REST

Strong back legs can be used to kick enemies.

Camouflaged underside of wings

×6

PURPLE EMPEROR

This butterfly feeds on sap, honeydew, and liquids that ooze from dung and animal carcasses. A male purple emperor's territory is often at the top of the tallest tree in a wood. If a rival male enters another male's territory, the two fight in midair, clashing wings until one gives in.

MALE PURPLE EMPEROR

Wings are normally dark brown.

It is only when wings are at a certain angle to the light that they appear to be purple.

WOODLAND BUTTERFLIES

THE RICH VARIETY of habitats in woodlands supports many butterfly species. Some live in the canopy; others feed on low shrubs. But most butterflies need sunshine and can be found on flowers in sunny clearings.

🔍 –.5

SILVER-WASHED FRITILLARY
This butterfly lays its eggs in cracks in the bark of mossy tree trunks, close to where violets are growing. The caterpillars feed on the leaves of these plants.

Brown upperside

🔍 –.7

Green underside

GREEN HAIRSTREAK
Whether it is sitting on a branch or resting on a leaf, the green hairstreak butterfly is well camouflaged. Its upperside is a woody brown while its underside is a leafy green.

PURPLE HAIRSTREAK BUTTERFLY

Female

Male

PURPLE HAIRSTREAK
High in the canopy of oak trees the caterpillars of the purple hairstreak butterfly feed on flowers and young leaves. Adult purple hairstreaks spend most of their lives in the treetops, feeding and sunbathing with their wings open.

Eyespots on underwings

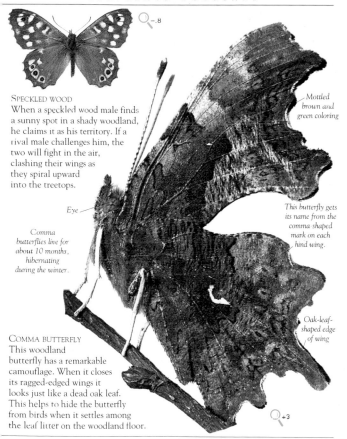

Q −.8

SPECKLED WOOD
When a speckled wood male finds
a sunny spot in a shady woodland,
he claims it as his territory. If a
rival male challenges him, the
two will fight in the air,
clashing their wings as
they spiral upward
into the treetops.

Mottled
brown and
green coloring

Eye

Comma
butterflies live for
about 10 months,
hibernating
during the winter.

This butterfly gets
its name from the
comma-shaped
mark on each
hind wing.

Oak-leaf-
shaped edge
of wing

COMMA BUTTERFLY
This woodland
butterfly has a remarkable
camouflage. When it closes
its ragged-edged wings it
looks just like a dead oak leaf.
This helps to hide the butterfly
from birds when it settles among
the leaf litter on the woodland floor.

Q +3

TREE TRUNKS AND BRANCHES

CRACKS IN THE bark of trees provide a hiding place for many species of insect. Some burrow into the wood and live completely concealed from predators. Many insects also live and feed among the different plant life that grows on tree trunks and branches.

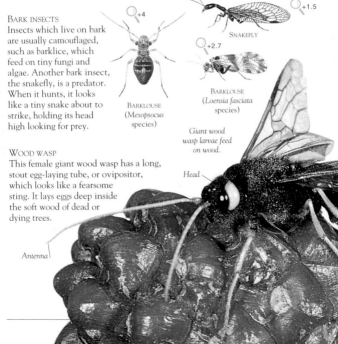

BARK INSECTS

Insects which live on bark are usually camouflaged, such as barklice, which feed on tiny fungi and algae. Another bark insect, the snakefly, is a predator. When it hunts, it looks like a tiny snake about to strike, holding its head high looking for prey.

+4

BARKLOUSE
(*Mesopsocus*
species)

SNAKEFLY

+1.5

+2.7

BARKLOUSE
(*Loensia fasciata*
species)

*Giant wood
wasp larvae feed
on wood.*

WOOD WASP

This female giant wood wasp has a long, stout egg-laying tube, or ovipositor, which looks like a fearsome sting. It lays eggs deep inside the soft wood of dead or dying trees.

Head

Antenna

ELM BARK BEETLE

A female elm bark beetle lays eggs along a tunnel which she bores in the bark of an elm tree. The larvae feed on the inner surface of the bark, creating radiating tunnels as they feed and grow.

ELM BARK
BEETLE

+5

ELM BARK
BEETLE
TUNNELS

Moth
camouflaged
on lichen

Tunnels
which larvae
have created

Eggs are laid
in central
tunnel.

The merveille
du jour moth is
easy to see when
not on lichen.

+3

Ovipositor bores
into wood where
it deposits eggs.

MERVEILLE MOTH

The patterns on the front wings of the merveille du jour moth help to camouflage it when it rests on lichens growing on a tree trunk. The moth is active at night and rests during the day. Its camouflage has to be good to hide it in bright daylight from predators such as birds and lizards.

GROUND LEVEL

THE WOODLAND floor does not get much sunlight, so few plants grow there. Most insects at ground level feed on plant and animal debris falling from the canopy, or, if they are carnivorous, eat other insects.

ANT NEST
The wood ant is a voracious predator. Colonies build huge nests of plant debris, with a network of tunnels below ground providing a home for thousands of ants.

WOOD CRICKET
Most crickets are nocturnal (active at night). But the wood cricket is active on sunny days when it can be heard chirping loudly. It is unable to fly because of its short wings.

Strong jaws bite into prey.

WOOD ANT
Wood ants forage out from their nest for hundreds of yards, making distinct paths on the woodland floor. They catch huge numbers of insects and bring them to the nest in pieces as food for their young.

Ant can squirt poison from abdomen.

Q+8

VIOLET GROUND BEETLE
This beetle can run fast on its long legs, catching other insects among the leaf litter. It hunts mainly at night and grips its prey with powerful jaws.

–1

WHITE ADMIRALS
On sunny days, white admiral butterflies can be spotted near the ground feeding on the nectar of bramble flowers. They can often be seen in the morning sipping water from puddles. They spend much of their time in the tree canopy, basking in the sunshine.

+2.5

UPPERSIDE OF
WHITE ADMIRAL

UNDERSIDE OF
WHITE ADMIRAL

STAG BEETLE
The larvae of stag beetles spend about three years feeding on rotting wood inside a dead tree. These handsome beetles are now becoming rare because dead wood is often cleared away and burned.

Antenna

Only male
stag beetles
have enlarged
jaws.

+3

GRASSLANDS AND HEATHLANDS

HERE, THE LACK OF PROTECTIVE tree canopy results in quick changes in the weather. Grassland and heathland habitats provide fewer dwelling places for insects than forest or woodland, since there is little wood to burrow into and hardly any leaf litter to dwell in.

This grass is called cocks-foot.

FIELD CHAFER

+1.2

FOOD SOURCE
Plant roots are an important food for insects in these habitats. Field chafer larvae eat roots, while the adults fly from plant to plant seeking a mate.

SPRINGTAILS
Cultivated grass fields, such as sports fields, support few insect species. But they do contain vast numbers of tiny insects called springtails. An area the size of a tennis court might be home to up to three hundred million springtail

OXFORD RAGWORT

A weed called the Oxford ragwort is a common invader of neglected pasture in Europe. The cinnabar moth lays its eggs on this weed, and its caterpillars eat the leaves.

CINNABAR MOTH

GRASSLAND FACTS

• The grasslands of Argentina are called Pampas, or "plains" in the language of the native people.

• Long grasses grow on the prairies of the US.

• The Steppes (prairie-like lands) of Siberia have short grasses.

The moth has warning coloration because it tastes unpleasant.

An Oxford ragwort is often stripped of its leaves by feeding caterpillars.

RICH IN PLANT LIFE

Natural grassland and heathland have a huge variety of grasses and flowering plants. These rich habitats buzz with insect life in the summer months.

CRANESBILL

RARE BUTTERFLY

The English large copper butterfly was once common in fenland but is now extinct. This is a result of intensive land development for agriculture, which destroyed the butterfly's food plant, the great water dock.

GRASSLAND INSECTS

MOST INSECT species cannot survive in cultivated grasslands, such as garden lawns, since they usually contain only one type of grass. Also, weedkillers and other chemicals harm many insects. But natural grasslands, with their variety of plants, support thousands of insect species that have adapted to this open, windy habitat.

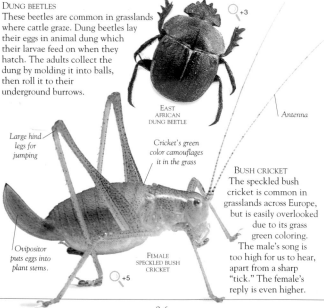

DUNG BEETLES
These beetles are common in grasslands where cattle graze. Dung beetles lay their eggs in animal dung which their larvae feed on when they hatch. The adults collect the dung by molding it into balls, then roll it to their underground burrows.

+3

EAST AFRICAN DUNG BEETLE

Antenna

Large hind legs for jumping

Cricket's green color camouflages it in the grass

BUSH CRICKET
The speckled bush cricket is common in grasslands across Europe, but is easily overlooked due to its grass green coloring. The male's song is too high for us to hear, apart from a sharp "tick." The female's reply is even higher.

Ovipositor puts eggs into plant stems.

FEMALE SPECKLED BUSH CRICKET

+5

ANTEATER

There are so many ants in the grasslands of South America and Africa that specialized ant-eating mammals have evolved. They have powerful claws to break open ant nests, and long sticky tongues to collect the ants.

ANTEATER

LARGE BLUE BUTTERFLY

This butterfly lays its eggs on the wild thyme plant, and the newly hatched caterpillars feed on thyme flowers. The caterpillars attract red ants with a special milk. The ants are deceived into carrying the caterpillars into their nest, where the caterpillars eat the ant eggs and larva.

Ragwort flowers

Mating soldier beetles

MARBLED WHITE BUTTERFLY

This butterfly can be found in a variety of grassland habitats, including grassy areas inside woodland. Marbled whites often gather in groups to bask in the early morning and early evening sunshine.

SOLDIER BEETLES

Some insects feed on one particular flower, while others, such as soldier beetles, eat pollen from various flowers. These feeding sites are also good places for insects to find a mate.

HEATHLAND INSECTS

MANY BURROWING insects live in heathland, since the soil is loose and easy to dig into. Heathland occurs in parts of the world with a climate of rainy winters and warm, dry summers. It has a rich mixture of plants, and the soil, which is often sandy, warms up quickly in the sunshine.

Butterfly is hard to spot in the grass.

GRAYLING BUTTERFLY
The tops of the wings of the grayling butterfly are brightly colored, while their underside is mottled gray for camouflage on the ground. When resting, it folds back its wings and sometimes leans toward the sun so it casts no shadow.

COMMON
YELLOW
DUNG FLY

+4

Dung flies eat other insects, which they kill with piercing mouthparts.

DUNG FLY
Wherever cattle are grazing, insects will be found breeding in the cattle's nutritious dung. Dung flies lay their eggs on freshly deposited cow pats. The maggots hatch a few hours later and start eating the dung.

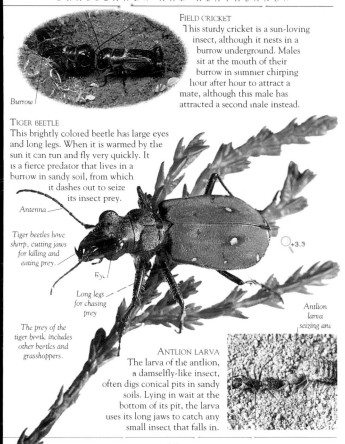

FIELD CRICKET

This sturdy cricket is a sun-loving insect, although it nests in a burrow underground. Males sit at the mouth of their burrow in summer chirping hour after hour to attract a mate, although this male has attracted a second male instead.

Burrow

TIGER BEETLE

This brightly colored beetle has large eyes and long legs. When it is warmed by the sun it can run and fly very quickly. It is a fierce predator that lives in a burrow in sandy soil, from which it dashes out to seize its insect prey.

Antenna

Tiger beetles have sharp, cutting jaws for killing and eating prey.

Eye

Long legs for chasing prey

The prey of the tiger beetle includes other beetles and grasshoppers.

+3.3

Antlion larva seizing ant

ANTLION LARVA

The larva of the antlion, a damselfly-like insect, often digs conical pits in sandy soils. Lying in wait at the bottom of its pit, the larva uses its long jaws to catch any small insect that falls in.

LAKES AND RIVERS

INSECTS CAN be found in all sorts of freshwater habitats: lakes, fast-flowing streams, ponds, puddles, damp moss, and wet leaf litter. These insects have many adaptations for surviving in their watery homes.

This case is made of a mixture of leaves and stones.

Q +3

The stony case is held together by silk woven by the larva.

Head

Legs hold onto plant.

CADDISFLY LARVAE
Insects can be swept away by fast-flowing water. Caddisfly larvae build a case around their body for protection. Some cases have long twigs sticking out sideways to prevent fish from swallowing them.

Flowers attract nectar-eating insects.

The flat leaves have a water-repellent waxy covering so they don't get waterlogged.

FRINGED WATERLILY
The tangled stems of the fringed waterlily are a good hiding place for pond insects. Dragonflies also find the leaves and stems a safe place on which to lay their eggs.

Leg

Breathing tube

Head of caddisfly larva

Case made of leaves

○+2

GILLS
A caddisfly larva has gills for taking oxygen from the water. The larva undulates its body to create a flow of oxygen-rich water over its gills inside the case.

SPRING TAILS
In corners of ponds sheltered from the wind, swarms of springtails sometimes gather on the surface of the water. They feed on organic debris that has blown into the pond.

FAST STREAMS
Insects that live in fast flowing streams have streamlined bodies and strong claws to help them cling to stones. The water that passes over their gills is always rich in oxygen, but cool temperatures mean that larvae develop more slowly than they would in a shallow, sun-warmed pond.

WATER SCORPION
The water scorpion has a breathing tube on its rear end so it can breathe the outside air while it is underwater. Insects with breathing tubes can survive in warm ponds or polluted waters that are low in oxygen.

LAKES AND RIVERS FACTS
• Fish populations depend on plenty of insects as food.

• Dragonfly larvae are considered a delicacy in New Guinea.

• Swarms of nonbiting midges are sometimes so dense over African lakes that fishermen have been suffocated.

WATER SURFACE INSECTS

A WATER SURFACE behaves like a skin due to a force called surface tension. This force enables certain insects to walk on the "skin," and others to hang just beneath it. Many of these insects are predators, and much of their food comes from the constant supply of flying insects which have fallen into the water.

+6

WHIRLIGIG

The whirligig beetle swims around and around very fast on the water surface. It hunts insects trapped on the surface tension. The whirligig's eyes are divided into two halves, allowing it to see both above and below the water surface at the same time.

BACKSWIMMER

Using its oar-shaped back legs, this water bug swims along upside down as it patrols in search of insects trapped on the water's surface. The backswimmer is a hungry hunter and will even attack fish and young frogs.

Piercing mouthparts inject poison into prey and suck out the prey's body fluids.

Large, compound eyes for spotting prey

+5

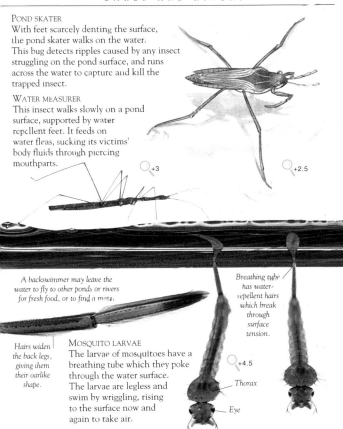

POND SKATER
With feet scarcely denting the surface, the pond skater walks on the water. This bug detects ripples caused by any insect struggling on the pond surface, and runs across the water to capture and kill the trapped insect.

WATER MEASURER
This insect walks slowly on a pond surface, supported by water repellent feet. It feeds on water fleas, sucking its victims' body fluids through piercing mouthparts.

+3

+2.5

A backswimmer may leave the water to fly to other ponds or rivers for fresh food, or to find a mate.

Breathing tube has water-repellent hairs which break through surface tension.

Hairs widen the back legs, giving them their oarlike shape.

MOSQUITO LARVAE
The larvae of mosquitoes have a breathing tube which they poke through the water surface. The larvae are legless and swim by wriggling, rising to the surface now and again to take air.

+4.5

Thorax

Eye

UNDERWATER INSECTS

MANY OF THE insects that live underwater are
carnivorous, either hunting their prey or
scavenging. Some of these insects are fierce,
sometimes killing prey larger than themselves.

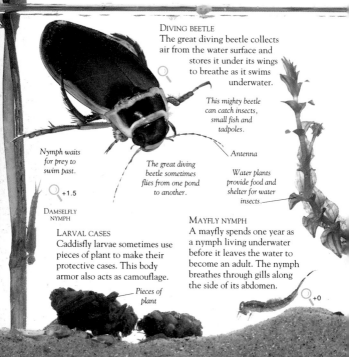

DIVING BEETLE
The great diving beetle collects
air from the water surface and
stores it under its wings
to breathe as it swims
underwater.

*This mighty beetle
can catch insects,
small fish and
tadpoles.*

*Nymph waits
for prey to
swim past.*

*The great diving
beetle sometimes
flies from one pond
to another.*

+1.5

DAMSELFLY
NYMPH

Antenna

*Water plants
provide food and
shelter for water
insects.*

LARVAL CASES
Caddisfly larvae sometimes use
pieces of plant to make their
protective cases. This body
armor also acts as camouflage.

MAYFLY NYMPH
A mayfly spends one year as
a nymph living underwater
before it leaves the water to
become an adult. The nymph
breathes through gills along
the side of its abdomen.

*Pieces of
plant*

+0

ADULT DRAGONFLY
Male darter dragonflies perch
on plants that emerge from the
water. They fiercely attack and
drive away any rival males of
the same species, but attempt
to mate with any female darter
dragonfly that flies past.

Q –.7

DRAGONFLY EGGS
Darter dragonflies scatter their
eggs in the water. The eggs are
surrounded by a sticky, jelly-
like substance, and hatch
after a few days.

Jelly holds
eggs in place.

Q –.7

BEETLE LARVA
The larva of the great diving beetle
injects juices into prey with its jaws.
The juices turn the prey's insides
into liquid for the larva to suck out.

DRAGONFLY NYMPH
Dragonfly nymphs breathe by
pumping water in and out of their
rear end, where they have
complex gills.

Q +1.5

TROPICAL FOREST

INSECTS THRIVE in the humid heat and flourishing plant life of tropical forests. These forests have a complex structure that provides many habitats for insects. Trees vary in shape and size; vines and dead branches are everywhere, and thick leaf litter covers the ground.

ORCHID

ORCHIDS

Tropical forests contain a spectacular variety of plants – there are about 25,000 species of orchid alone. It is quite dark beneath the forest canopy and orchids are strongly scented to help insects find them.

EPIPHYTES

Many plants grow on the trunks and branches of trees where birds have wiped seeds from their beaks. These tree-dwelling plants, called epiphytes, provide extra habitats for insects.

INSECT PREDATORS

A tropical forest is a rich habitat for birds as well as insects. Tropical birds feed on countless insects each day. This high rate of predation is a major reason for the evolution of camouflage and mimicry in tropical insects.

FRUITY NOURISHMENT

Some tropical butterflies live for several months. An important source of fuel for their continued activity is rotting fruit and dung on the forest floor. This gives them not only sugars for energy, but also amino acids and vitamins needed for survival.

Until recently, this insect was known only from dull brown museum specimens.

Blue face

Red eye

TROPICAL FORESTS

Bright colors are typical of tropical forests, and they can be seen in both the plant and animal life. This Central American grasshopper looks as if it would be easy to spot with its multicolored body, but it is camouflaged among the shining leaves of the forest trees.

The bright colors of this grasshopper surprised even entomologists.

Bright green abdomen

+2

The cricket loses its blue color when it dies.

TROPICAL FOREST FACTS

• Tropical forests cover about five percent of the Earth's land surface.

• They contain over half of all living species.

• Around 1,200 species of butterfly have been recorded in one forest in southern Peru.

• Over half the world's rainforest has been cut since 1945.

IN THE CANOPY

THERE IS WARMTH, light, and plenty of food to eat in the canopy of tropical trees. The canopy provides living space for thousands of insect species. In one day 3,000 different species were collected from a single tree in a forest in Borneo.

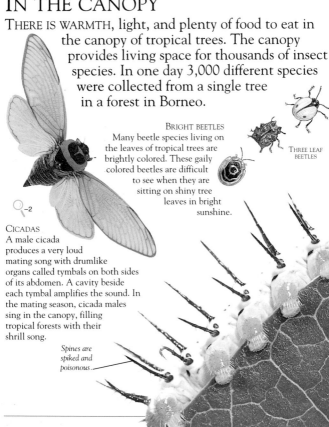

BRIGHT BEETLES
Many beetle species living on the leaves of tropical trees are brightly colored. These gaily colored beetles are difficult to see when they are sitting on shiny tree leaves in bright sunshine.

THREE LEAF BEETLES

CICADAS
A male cicada produces a very loud mating song with drumlike organs called tymbals on both sides of its abdomen. A cavity beside each tymbal amplifies the sound. In the mating season, cicada males sing in the canopy, filling tropical forests with their shrill song.

Spines are spiked and poisonous

FROG BEETLE

This vividly colored jeweled frog beetle is probably less noticeable in the bright sunshine of its leafy habitat. Despite its name, the froglike hind legs are not used for jumping, but for holding onto a female while mating.

Froglike hind leg

VIOLIN BEETLE

Little is know about the curious violin beetle, which got its name because of its violin-like shape. It is very flat, and has been found living between layers of shelf fungi on tree trunks in Indonesian forests.

Six simple eyes on either side of the head can sense whether it is light or dark.

PASSIONFLOWER

POISON SPINES

The body of the postman butterfly caterpillar contains poisons. It gets the poisons from chemicals in the leaves of the passionflower vines that it eats. The prickly spines remind birds to avoid it.

NESTS IN THE CANOPY

WITH SO MANY insects feeding in the
forest canopy, it is not surprising that
the insect-eating ants and wasps
build their nests there. But these
ants and wasps are in turn hunted
by mammals and lizards, so their
nests must give protection.

*Nest is made
of paperlike
material.*

GREEN WEAVER ANTS

Each green weaver ant colony has several nests
made of leaves. To make a nest, the ants join
forces to pull leaves together and sew the edges.
They sew using silk which the larvae produce
when they are squeezed by the adult ants. These
carnivorous ants hunt through the tree canopy,
catching other insects and carrying the
prey in pieces back to
the ants' nests.

WASP NESTS

Each wasp species makes a
different type of nest. This nest
from South America has been
cut in half to reveal the "floors"
which house the larvae. There is
one small opening at the bottom
where the wasps defend the nest
from invading ants.

*Ants pulling
leaves together.*

*This nest hangs
from a branch
of a tree.*

*There may be
half a million ants
in one weaver
ant colony.*

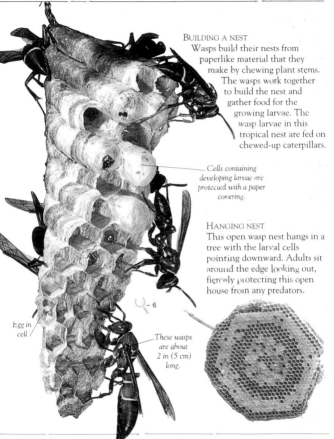

BUILDING A NEST

Wasps build their nests from paperlike material that they make by chewing plant stems. The wasps work together to build the nest and gather food for the growing larvae. The wasp larvae in this tropical nest are fed on chewed-up caterpillars.

Cells containing developing larvae are protected with a paper covering.

HANGING NEST

This open wasp nest hangs in a tree with the larval cells pointing downward. Adults sit around the edge looking out, fiercely protecting this open house from any predators.

Egg in cell

These wasps are about 2 in (5 cm) long.

BRILLIANT BUTTERFLIES

MANY TROPICAL butterflies are large and brilliantly colored, which ought to make it easy for predators to catch them. But they fly rapidly and erratically, flash their bright colors in the sun, and then seem to disappear, darting into the deep shade of the forest.

BLUE MORPHO
The iridescent blue of South American morpho butterflies is so vivid it can be seen from a great distance. But its underwings are a muddy brown for camouflage when feeding on the ground.

—.3

SOUTHEAST ASIAN MOTH
The vivid colors of this southeast Asian moth shows that some day-flying moths can be as colorful as butterflies. The bright colors warn predators that this moth is poisonous.

—.5

+2

NERO BUTTERFLY
The bright yellow Nero butterfly drinks from streams and puddles near mammal dung. This habit is common in butterflies of tropical forests, and supplies them with nutrients that are not available in flowers.

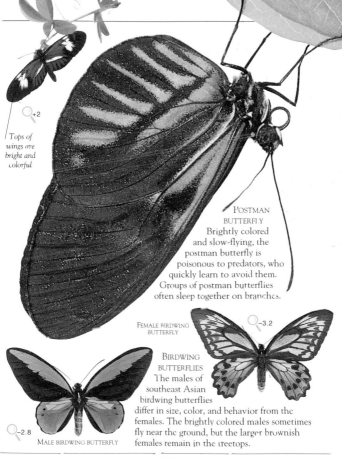

Q +2

Tops of wings are bright and colorful

POSTMAN
BUTTERFLY
Brightly colored
and slow-flying, the
postman butterfly is
poisonous to predators, who
quickly learn to avoid them.
Groups of postman butterflies
often sleep together on branches.

FEMALE BIRDWING
BUTTERFLY

Q –3.2

BIRDWING
BUTTERFLIES
The males of
southeast Asian
birdwing butterflies
differ in size, color, and behavior from the
females. The brightly colored males sometimes
fly near the ground, but the larger brownish
females remain in the treetops.

Q –2.8

MALE BIRDWING BUTTERFLY

TROPICAL BUTTERFLIES

THOUSANDS OF butterfly species live in tropical forests. Each butterfly has to recognize members of its own species among all the others in order to mate. They find each other by sight – butterflies have a good sense of color – and by smell.

-.6

Tail brush

USING SCENTS
Striped blue crow butterfly males have a yellow brush at the end of their abdomen. When a male has found a female, he uses his brush to dust scented scales on her. The arousing scent encourages the female to mate with him.

SCENT DETECTORS
Butterflies and moths detect smells with their antennae. Each antenna has thousands of microscopic sensory organs. These respond to airborne scent molecules, triggering nerve cells in the antennae to send signals to the insect's brain.

MOTH ANTENNA

Scent chemicals stimulate nerves in the antennae.

-2.5

SITTING TOGETHER
At sunny spots in the forest, butterflies gather at muddy puddles to drink water and salts. Butterflies of the same species usually sit together, so that white-colored species form one group, blue another, and so on.

Postman butterflies and small postman butterflies are two different species. But they share the same wing patterns in different parts of South America.

SMALL POSTMAN BUTTERFLY
FROM SOUTHERN ECUADOR

POSTMAN BUTTERFLY
FROM SOUTHERN ECUADOR

SMALL POSTMAN BUTTERFLY
FROM SOUTHERN BRAZIL

POSTMAN BUTTERFLY
FROM SOUTHERN BRAZIL,

SMALL POSTMAN BUTTERFLY
FROM WESTERN BRAZIL

POSTMAN BUTTERFLY
FROM WESTERN BRAZIL

COPYING PATTERNS

Sometimes two or more different species of poisonous butterfly – such as the postman and the small postman – share the same wing pattern. This type of mimicry protects both species, because birds only need to learn that one species is poisonous to avoid the other.

HORNED BEETLES

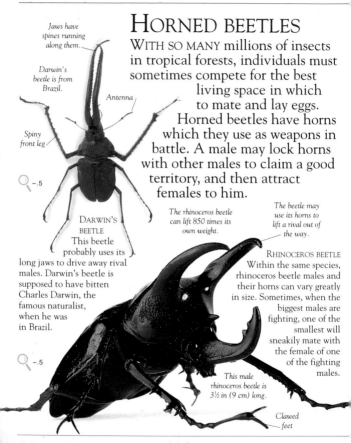

WITH SO MANY millions of insects in tropical forests, individuals must sometimes compete for the best living space in which to mate and lay eggs. Horned beetles have horns which they use as weapons in battle. A male may lock horns with other males to claim a good territory, and then attract females to him.

Jaws have spines running along them.

Darwin's beetle is from Brazil.

Antenna

Spiny front leg

–.5

DARWIN'S BEETLE
This beetle probably uses its long jaws to drive away rival males. Darwin's beetle is supposed to have bitten Charles Darwin, the famous naturalist, when he was in Brazil.

–.5

The rhinoceros beetle can lift 850 times its own weight.

The beetle may use its horns to lift a rival out of the way.

RHINOCEROS BEETLE
Within the same species, rhinoceros beetle males and their horns can vary greatly in size. Sometimes, when the biggest males are fighting, one of the smallest will sneakily mate with the female of one of the fighting males.

This male rhinoceros beetle is 3½ in (9 cm) long.

Clawed feet

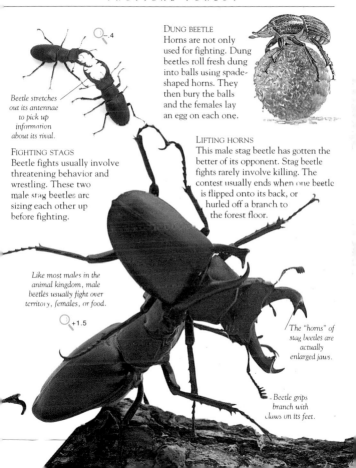

Beetle stretches out its antennae to pick up information about its rival.

.4

FIGHTING STAGS

Beetle fights usually involve threatening behavior and wrestling. These two male stag beetles are sizing each other up before fighting.

DUNG BEETLE

Horns are not only used for fighting. Dung beetles roll fresh dung into balls using spade-shaped horns. They then bury the balls and the females lay an egg on each one.

LIFTING HORNS

This male stag beetle has gotten the better of its opponent. Stag beetle fights rarely involve killing. The contest usually ends when one beetle is flipped onto its back, or hurled off a branch to the forest floor.

Like most males in the animal kingdom, male beetles usually fight over territory, females, or food.

+1.5

The "horns" of stag beetles are actually enlarged jaws.

Beetle grips branch with claws on its feet.

THE LARGEST INSECTS

SOME OF THE largest insects live in tropical forests, where the warm temperatures and abundance of food allow them to grow quickly. But insects cannot grow very large, since their simple breathing system could not cope with a large body. Also, big insects would be easy prey for birds and mammals.

ATLAS MOTH
With a wingspan of 6 in (15 cm), the atlas moth has the largest wing area of all insects. Silvery patches on each wing shine like mirrors.

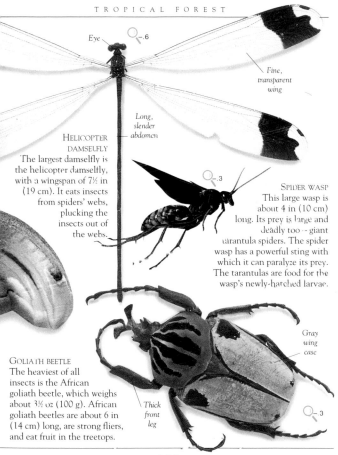

Eye

O—.6

Fine,
transparent
wing

Long,
slender
abdomen

**HELICOPTER
DAMSELFLY**
The largest damselfly is
the helicopter damselfly,
with a wingspan of 7½ in
(19 cm). It eats insects
from spiders' webs,
plucking the
insects out of
the webs.

O—.3

SPIDER WASP
This large wasp is
about 4 in (10 cm)
long. Its prey is large and
deadly too – giant
tarantula spiders. The spider
wasp has a powerful sting with
which it can paralyze its prey.
The tarantulas are food for the
wasp's newly-hatched larvae.

Gray
wing
case

GOLIATH BEETLE
The heaviest of all
insects is the African
goliath beetle, which weighs
about 3½ oz (100 g). African
goliath beetles are about 6 in
(14 cm) long, are strong fliers,
and eat fruit in the treetops.

Thick
front
leg

O—.3

119

STICK AND LEAF INSECTS

A TROPICAL FOREST is alive with animals, most of which eat insects. To survive, insects adopt many strategies. Stick and leaf insects hide from predators by keeping still and resembling their background of leaves and sticks.

STICK INSECTS
Some stick insects are slender, brown, or green, just like the twigs and leaf stalks they sit on. Other species are shorter and fatter, with spines and other projections. These often look like curled dead leaves.

Winged male of Macleay's spectre

Wingless female of Macleay's spectre

Indian stick insect

Spiny green nymph

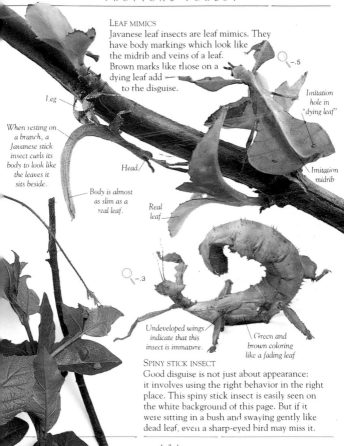

LEAF MIMICS

Javanese leaf insects are leaf mimics. They have body markings which look like the midrib and veins of a leaf. Brown marks like those on a dying leaf add to the disguise.

Leg

When resting on a branch, a Javanese stick insect curls its body to look like the leaves it sits beside.

Head

Body is almost as slim as a real leaf.

Real leaf

⊖ –.5

Imitation hole in "dying leaf"

Imitation midrib

⊖ –.3

Undeveloped wings indicate that this insect is immature.

Green and brown coloring like a fading leaf

SPINY STICK INSECT

Good disguise is not just about appearance: it involves using the right behavior in the right place. This spiny stick insect is easily seen on the white background of this page. But if it were sitting in a bush and swaying gently like dead leaf, even a sharp-eyed bird may miss it.

ARMIES ON THE GROUND

ANTS ARE THE dominant creatures of tropical forests.
They live in colonies made up of any number from
20 individuals to many thousands. Ants are mostly
carnivorous. Some species make slaves of other ant
species by invading their
nest and killing their queen.

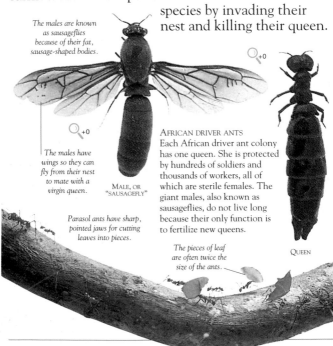

*The males are known
as sausageflies
because of their fat,
sausage-shaped bodies.*

*The males have
wings so they can
fly from their nest
to mate with a
virgin queen.*

MALE, OR
"SAUSAGEFLY"

*Parasol ants have sharp,
pointed jaws for cutting
leaves into pieces.*

AFRICAN DRIVER ANTS
Each African driver ant colony
has one queen. She is protected
by hundreds of soldiers and
thousands of workers, all of
which are sterile females. The
giant males, also known as
sausageflies, do not live long
because their only function is
to fertilize new queens.

*The pieces of leaf
are often twice the
size of the ants.*

QUEEN

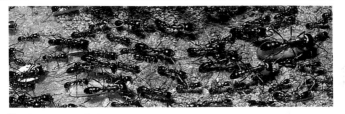

DRIVER ANTS MARCHING
These ants get their name from the way a colony sweeps through an area catching all the insects it can find. They move their nests from place to place regularly, unlike most ants which have a permanent nest and territory.

+3

Beetle pupae are among the prey of driver ants.

CARRYING PREY
Ants in a column collaborate to cut large insects they have caught into smaller pieces. This is so they can carry their food back to the nest. Smaller prey can be carried whole.

ATTENTIVE SOLDIER
Driver ant soldiers have very large jaws. Often they can be seen standing beside a marching column of ants with their jaws wide open, waiting to attack intruders such as parasitic flies.

Ant returning for more leaves

PARASOL ANTS
These South American ants are not carnivorous. They feed on fungus which they cultivate in huge underground nests. The fungus is grown on pieces of leaf which the ants bring to the nest.

DESERTS, CAVES, AND SOIL

SOME INSECTS flourish in habitats where it is difficult for living things to survive. Desert habitats, for example, lack water and have very high temperatures. Caves are dark and lack plant life for food. Life in soil makes communication, by both scent and sight, difficult for insects.

+4

A spike on the larva's back anchors it to the wall of the burrow.

HIDING IN SOIL

Life in the soil is only a passing phase for some insect species. This tiger beetle larva hides underground by day. At night it waits in its vertical tunnel with its jaws projecting at the ground surface, and snatches passing insects to devour in its burrow.

CAVE DWELLER

This cockroach lives all its life in the dark. Like other cave creatures, it feeds on debris from the outside world. Bat dung, dead animals, and pieces of plants washed into the cave provide the cockroach with its nourishment.

DESERT BEETLE
The lack of water in deserts forces insects to find ingenious ways of obtaining moisture. This darkling beetle lives in the Namib Desert, where sea winds bring mists each night. The beetle holds its abdomen high to catch the moisture, which then runs down into its mouth.

DESERT HEAT
The hot and dry days in deserts can lead to rapid water loss and death for animals. Most living creatures hide under stones or in the sand to avoid drying out. These animals are active at night when it is much cooler.

DESERT FACTS
• The Sahara Desert is spreading at a rate of 3 miles (5 km) per year.

• In deserts the temperature may range from 90°F (30°C) in the day to below 32°F (0°C) at night.

• Caves are a nearly constant temperature throughout the year.

• 20% of the Earth's land surface is desert.

CACTUS FLOWER

DESERT PLANTS
Rain may not fall in a desert for months, or even years. Most desert plants store water so they can survive, and some desert animals rely on these plants for food. But many animals, including some insects, migrate in search of rain and the plant growth it produces.

DESERT INSECTS

HOT, DRY DESERTS are dangerous places in which to live. Animals often die from sunstroke and dehydration (drying out). To prevent this, insects avoid the sun by staying in the shade or burrowing in the sand. Some insects have special methods of collecting water. Many feed only at night, because the surface of the sand is too hot for them to walk on during the day.

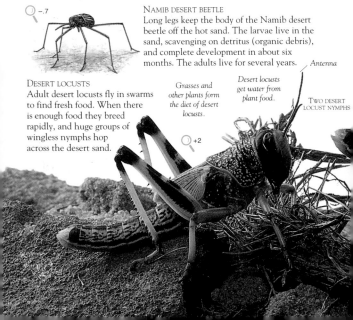

−.7

NAMIB DESERT BEETLE
Long legs keep the body of the Namib desert beetle off the hot sand. The larvae live in the sand, scavenging on detritus (organic debris), and complete development in about six months. The adults live for several years. *Antenna*

DESERT LOCUSTS
Adult desert locusts fly in swarms to find fresh food. When there is enough food they breed rapidly, and huge groups of wingless nymphs hop across the desert sand.

Grasses and other plants form the diet of desert locusts.

Desert locusts get water from plant food.

+2

TWO DESERT LOCUST NYMPHS

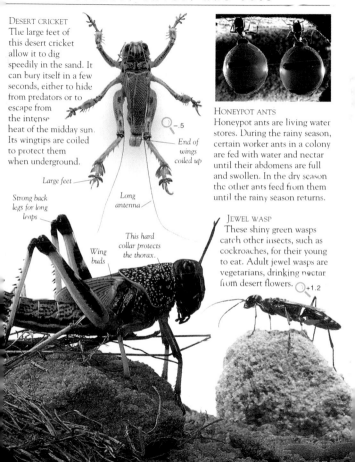

DESERT CRICKET
The large feet of this desert cricket allow it to dig speedily in the sand. It can bury itself in a few seconds, either to hide from predators or to escape from the intense heat of the midday sun. Its wingtips are coiled to protect them when underground.

–.5

End of wings coiled up

Large feet

Strong back legs for long leaps

Long antenna

This hard collar protects the thorax.

Wing buds

HONEYPOT ANTS
Honeypot ants are living water stores. During the rainy season, certain worker ants in a colony are fed with water and nectar until their abdomens are full and swollen. In the dry season the other ants feed from them until the rainy season returns.

JEWEL WASP
These shiny green wasps catch other insects, such as cockroaches, for their young to eat. Adult jewel wasps are vegetarians, drinking nectar from desert flowers. +1.2

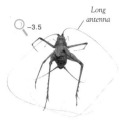

Long antenna

🔍 −3.5

AFRICAN CRICKET
Some insects have
developed very long
antennae to make up
for lack of vision in
dark caves. This African
cricket has the longest
antennae for its body
size of any insect.

CAVE INSECTS
No plants can grow in the dark,
inhospitable depths of caves,
where the Sun's rays cannot reach.
Despite this, cave-dwelling insects
still manage to find enough food.
Bat droppings, material
washed in by floods, and
the fungi that often grow
on this decaying material
all provide nourishment.

*Long back legs
for jumping out
of danger*

FEMALE
AFRICAN
CAVE
CRICKET

*Two sensitive spines,
called cerci, can detect
enemies approaching
from behind.*

*Cricket uses its
ovipositor (egg-
laying tube) to lay
eggs in soil.*

🔍 +2.5

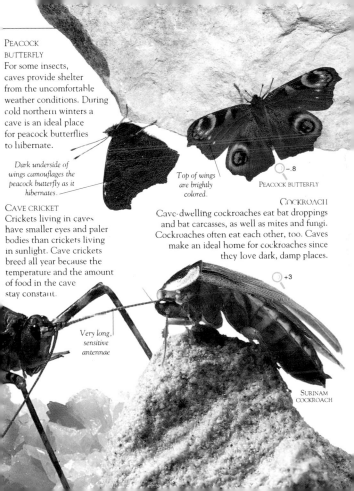

PEACOCK BUTTERFLY

For some insects, caves provide shelter from the uncomfortable weather conditions. During cold northern winters a cave is an ideal place for peacock butterflies to hibernate.

Dark underside of wings camouflages the peacock butterfly as it hibernates.

Top of wings are brightly colored.

–.8

PEACOCK BUTTERFLY

CAVE CRICKET

Crickets living in caves have smaller eyes and paler bodies than crickets living in sunlight. Cave crickets breed all year because the temperature and the amount of food in the cave stay constant.

Very long, sensitive antennae

COCKROACH

Cave-dwelling cockroaches eat bat droppings and bat carcasses, as well as mites and fungi. Cockroaches often eat each other, too. Caves make an ideal home for cockroaches since they love dark, damp places.

+3

SURINAM COCKROACH

SOIL INSECTS

WHEN PLANTS and animals die, their remains usually get absorbed into the soil. Insects that live in soil are among the most important creatures on Earth because they help to recycle these remains, releasing their nutrients and so helping new crops and forests to grow. Soil insects are also an important food for many mammals and birds.

BEETLE LARVA
Roots and decaying tree trunks provide food for many types of insect larva, such as this beetle grub. The grub breathes through holes called spiracles, which are along the side of its body. Although there is not very much air underground, there is enough for insects.

Spiracle

Pupa

GOOD HABITAT
Living in soil has advantages. Insects are unlikely to dehydrate, and there is plenty of food in plant roots and decaying plants. This spurge hawk-moth pupa has sharp plates on its abdomen which help it climb to the surface just before the adult emerges.

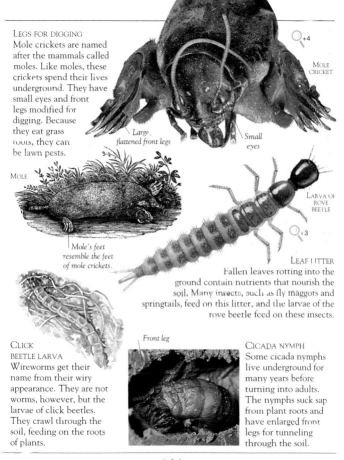

LEGS FOR DIGGING
Mole crickets are named
after the mammals called
moles. Like moles, these
crickets spend their lives
underground. They have
small eyes and front
legs modified for
digging. Because
they eat grass
roots, they can
be lawn pests.

*Large,
flattened front legs*

*Small
eyes*

+4

MOLE
CRICKET

MOLE

*Mole's feet
resemble the feet
of mole crickets.*

LARVA OF
ROVE
BEETLE

+3

LEAF LITTER
Fallen leaves rotting into the
ground contain nutrients that nourish the
soil. Many insects, such as fly maggots and
springtails, feed on this litter, and the larvae of the
rove beetle feed on these insects.

CLICK
BEETLE LARVA
Wireworms get their
name from their wiry
appearance. They are not
worms, however, but the
larvae of click beetles.
They crawl through the
soil, feeding on the roots
of plants.

Front leg

CICADA NYMPH
Some cicada nymphs
live underground for
many years before
turning into adults.
The nymphs suck sap
from plant roots and
have enlarged front
legs for tunneling
through the soil.

TOWNS AND GARDENS

SINCE INSECTS HAVE managed to make homes for themselves in practically every natural habitat, it is not surprising that they have turned human habitats into their homes, too. Insects live in our houses, feeding in our furniture, clothes, foodstores, and garbage dumps. Our gardens and farms are also teeming with insect life, nourished by the abundance of flowers, fruits and vegetables.

Colorado beetle

−1.4

POTATO PESTS
When potatoes were brought to Europe from South America, the Colorado beetle came with them. This insect eats potato plant leaves, and can cause great damage to crops.

Leaves of potato plant

Potato

CABBAGE EATERS
Cabbage white butterflies lay eggs on cabbage plants so the larvae can eat the leaves. Farms provide acres of cabbages, and the butterflies become pests since they breed at an unnaturally high rate because of the abundance of food.

INSECT INFESTATIONS

Pests such as cockroaches are quick to make use of any food which we waste. Uncovered or spilled food in kitchens allows these insects to thrive, and can cause an infestation that is hard to eliminate.

WASPS IN OUR HOMES

The roofs of our houses keep us warm and dry, but they also provide ideal conditions for wasps' nests. Wasps are useful to us in summer since they catch our garden insect pests to feed to their young.

Nest hangs from rafters.

GREENHOUSES

In temperate countries, tropical insects often thrive in greenhouses, which reproduce tropical conditions. Butterfly farms use this principle to breed exotic insects for us to look at and enjoy.

TOWNS AND GARDENS FACTS

• More than 1,800 insect species were found in a typical English garden.

• Fewer than one percent of cockroach species are considered to be pests.

• Peacock butterflies often spend the winter in garden sheds.

The monarch butterfly is bred on butterfly farms.

HOUSEHOLD INSECTS

SINCE PREHISTORIC times, insects have lived in human homes, attracted by warmth, shelter, and food. These insects eat our food, our furniture, and some even eat our carpets. Parasitic insects also live in our homes, feeding on the human inhabitants.

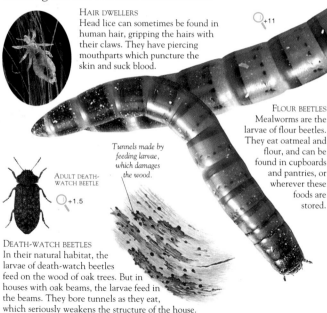

HAIR DWELLERS
Head lice can sometimes be found in human hair, gripping the hairs with their claws. They have piercing mouthparts which puncture the skin and suck blood.

Q +11

FLOUR BEETLES
Mealworms are the larvae of flour beetles. They eat oatmeal and flour, and can be found in cupboards and pantries, or wherever these foods are stored.

ADULT DEATH-
WATCH BEETLE
Q +1.5

Tunnels made by feeding larvae, which damages the wood.

DEATH-WATCH BEETLES
In their natural habitat, the larvae of death-watch beetles feed on the wood of oak trees. But in houses with oak beams, the larvae feed in the beams. They bore tunnels as they eat, which seriously weakens the structure of the house.

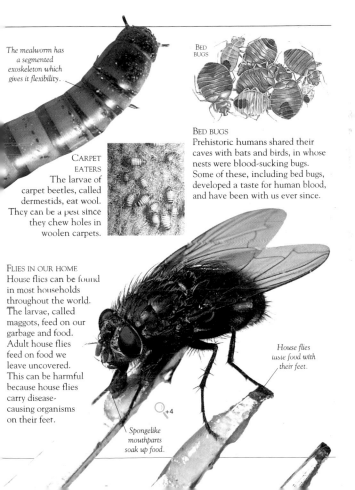

The mealworm has a segmented exoskeleton which gives it flexibility.

BED BUGS

BED BUGS
Prehistoric humans shared their caves with bats and birds, in whose nests were blood-sucking bugs. Some of these, including bed bugs, developed a taste for human blood, and have been with us ever since.

CARPET EATERS
The larvae of carpet beetles, called dermestids, eat wool. They can be a pest since they chew holes in woolen carpets.

FLIES IN OUR HOME
House flies can be found in most households throughout the world. The larvae, called maggots, feed on our garbage and food. Adult house flies feed on food we leave uncovered. This can be harmful because house flies carry disease-causing organisms on their feet.

House flies taste food with their feet.

+4

Spongelike mouthparts soak up food.

GARDEN INSECTS

A GARDEN IS a good place to watch and study insects. Many different insects are attracted into gardens to feed on the flowers, vegetables, and other plants. Some predatory insects come to eat the plant-eating insects. But most garden insects are just tourists, feeding on flower nectar as they pass through.

ROVE BEETLES
Rove beetles hunt at night, scouring the garden for insects to eat. These large beetles are common in compost piles, scurrying away from the daylight when the compost is turned.

+2.5

GARDENER'S FRIENDS
Hover flies hover in front of flowers on hot, sunny days as they feed on nectar. They are particularly attracted to thistle flowers. Hover fly larvae are the gardener's friends, feeding voraciously on plant-damaging aphids.

+3

Eye

Antenna

HAWK MOTH
The caterpillars of hawk moths can be recognized by their short, erect "tail." Most adult hawk moths fly at night, hovering in front of flowers to gather nectar with their long tongues.

SILVER-STRIPED HAWK MOTH CATERPILLAR

"Tail"

+0

Caterpillar has eyespots to frighten off predators.

Eyespot

Fuchsia flower

GARDEN GRASSHOPPER
The common field grasshopper is widespread in Europe on short grass in sunny places, and often finds a home in gardens. Like tropical locusts, common field grasshoppers sometimes migrate in swarms, but on a much smaller scale.

RED ADMIRAL

–.3

FOOD FOR BUTTERFLIES
The flower border of a garden is like a filling station for passing butterflies. They feed on nectar to give them energy as they search for suitable mates or plants on which to lay eggs.

Butterflies often stop to sunbathe for a while.

PEACOCK

–.6

SILVER-SPOTTED SKIPPER

–.3

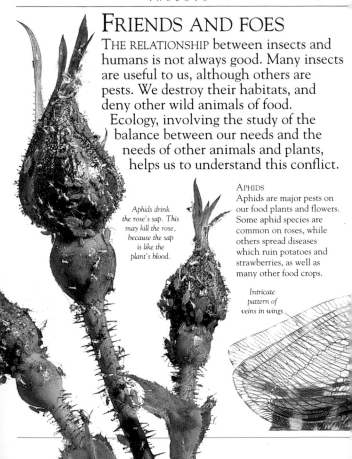

FRIENDS AND FOES

THE RELATIONSHIP between insects and humans is not always good. Many insects are useful to us, although others are pests. We destroy their habitats, and deny other wild animals of food.
Ecology, involving the study of the balance between our needs and the needs of other animals and plants, helps us to understand this conflict.

Aphids drink the rose's sap. This may kill the rose, because the sap is like the plant's blood.

APHIDS
Aphids are major pests on our food plants and flowers. Some aphid species are common on roses, while others spread diseases which ruin potatoes and strawberries, as well as many other food crops.

Intricate pattern of veins in wings

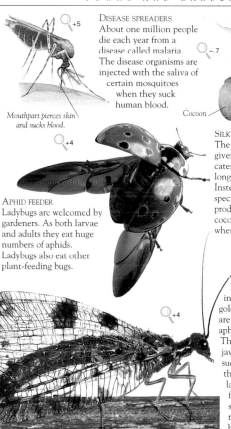

DISEASE SPREADERS
About one million people die each year from a disease called malaria. The disease organisms are injected with the saliva of certain mosquitoes when they suck human blood.

Mouthpart pierces skin and sucks blood.

Moth

Cocoon

SILK PROVIDERS
The silk we use in clothes is given to us by silk moth caterpillars. Silk moths no longer occur in the wild. Instead, they are bred in special farms. The caterpillars produce the silk to form cocoons that protect them when they pupate.

APHID FEEDER
Ladybugs are welcomed by gardeners. As both larvae and adults they eat huge numbers of aphids. Ladybugs also eat other plant-feeding bugs.

PEST EATERS
Lacewings are delicate insects, often with shining golden eyes. Their larvae are voracious predators of aphids and other plant lice. They have long, tubular jaws through which they suck the body contents of their prey. Lacewing larvae hide themselves from predators by sticking the remains of their prey onto small hairs on their back.

BEES AND POLLINATION

BEES AND PLANTS depend on each other.
Plants need bees to carry pollen
between flowers to produce seeds.
Bees collect pollen and nectar
from flowers to feed their larvae.
Nectar in a hive is made into
honey for winter food.

BEE-KEEPING
For thousands of years people have
kept bees for their honey. Modern
hives have racks of frames, each with a
ready-made comb of cells. Individual frames
can be removed and the honey drained.

POLLINATION
Other insects, such as butterflies, also
pollinate flowers. Many flowers are a
special color or shape to attract
particular insects. These insects
receive pollen and nectar in
the process of carrying pollen
to another flower.

+2

+6

POLLEN BASKETS

Bees carry pollen back to their nest in special pollen baskets on their back legs. The baskets are made from curved bristles. A bee uses its front legs to comb pollen from its furry body and put it in the baskets.

Shape of dance shows bees direction of flowers.

BEE COMMUNICATION

When a honeybee finds flowers with nectar it tells other bees in the hive by dancing. The bee conveys the distance of the flowers by how fast it shakes its abdomen, and the direction by the angle of its dance.

Pollen basket

FISH

WHAT IS A FISH?

THE FIRST FISH appeared in the seas 500 million years ago. Today, there are about 25,000 known species. Fish live in water, breathe through gills, have a scaly body, and maneuver themselves using fins. All fish are vertebrates, which means that they have a backbone or similar structure, and an internal skeleton. The three main fish groups are bony fish, cartilaginous fish, and jawless fish.

Caudal fin or tail moves fish through water

Lateral line helps fish feel vibrations

BONY FISH FINS
Most bony fish have a dorsal fin, paired pectoral and pelvic fins, and a tail for movement. In some fish, fins have become specialized as lifting foils, walking legs, suckers for holding on, or poisoned spines for protection.

Anal fin

Pelvic fin for maneuvering

WHALE SHARK

CARTILAGINOUS FISH
Sharks are cartilaginous fish, which means that they have skeletons made of strong, flexible cartilage, rather than bone. The world's biggest fish is the whale shark, which grows to 49 ft (15 m) in length.

WHAT IS NOT A FISH?
Some animals are confused with "fish" just because they live in water. Fish-shaped dolphins and seals are mammals, and come to the surface to breathe. Shellfish like mussels and cuttlefish are in fact mollusks.

ATLANTIC CUTTLEFISH

BOTTLE-NOSED DOLPHIN

Skin

Vibrations

Fluid-filled tube

Pore

Hairs turn vibrations into nerve messages

Sensory nerves to brain

GOOD VIBRATIONS
Fish do not have ears, but sense sound vibrations in water using the lateral line, a fluid-filled tube that runs along each side of the body, under the skin. Vibrations that pass into this tube via pores in the skin stimulate nerve endings, sending messages to the brain.

Dorsal fin

Overlapping scales on body

Nostril

Right pectoral fin

Operculum (bony covering for gills)

SCALY COAT
Most fish have a covering of backward-facing scales that help to streamline them. Rather than scales, sharks have toothlike structures buried in the skin.

FRESH OR SALT?
Most fish spend their whole lives in either freshwater, or saltwater. Some, however, like the salmon, leave the sea and swim up rivers to breed in fresh water.

FISH ANATOMY

FISH HAVE MANY of the same internal organs found in reptiles, birds, and mammals, such as a heart, brain, lungs, and liver. However, in order to live and "breathe" underwater, a fish also needs some unique body parts.

BREATHING AND GILLS
Fish "breathe" in water using their gills. Oxygen passes from the water through the thin gill membranes into the fish's blood, and is then distributed around the body, to power the muscles.

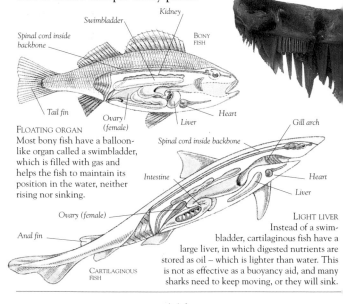

Swimbladder

Kidney

BONY FISH

Spinal cord inside backbone

Tail fin

Ovary (female)

Liver

Heart

FLOATING ORGAN
Most bony fish have a balloon-like organ called a swimbladder, which is filled with gas and helps the fish to maintain its position in the water, neither rising nor sinking.

Gill arch

Spinal cord inside backbone

Intestine

Heart

Liver

Ovary (female)

Anal fin

CARTILAGINOUS FISH

LIGHT LIVER
Instead of a swim-bladder, cartilaginous fish have a large liver, in which digested nutrients are stored as oil – which is lighter than water. This is not as effective as a buoyancy aid, and many sharks need to keep moving, or they will sink.

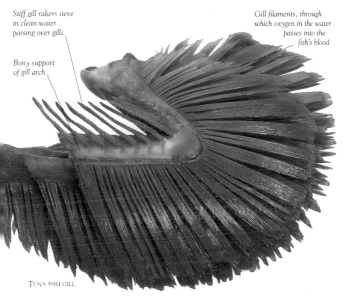

Stiff gill rakers sieve in clean water passing over gills

Gill filaments, through which oxygen in the water passes into the fish's blood

Bony support of gill arch

TUNA FISH GILL

WATER FLOW
To obtain oxygen, the fish takes in a mouthful of water, while the gill cover shuts flat to stop water from escaping. The fish then closes its mouth, forcing the water inside to flow past the gills. On its way out, the water pushes open the flaplike gill cover.

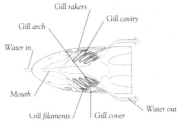

Gill rakers

Gill arch

Gill cavity

Water in

Mouth

Gill filaments

Gill cover

Water out

FISH BONES

ALL FISH HAVE internal skeletons.
Sharks, rays, and jawless fish have
skeletons made of cartilage,
but most fish have
skeletons made
of bone.

First dorsal fin

*Cranium – supports
and protects
the brain*

*Upper
jaw*

Pectoral fin

*Opercular bones form
the gill covers and protect
the delicate gills*

Lower jaw

Pelvic fin

SKELETON PARTS

There are three main parts of a fish skeleton: the skull, which
contains the brain and suspends the jaw and gill arches; the
backbone or vertebral column, which bears spines and ribs,
and the "fin skeleton," the bones and rods which support
fins and tails.

SLOW SWIMMER

The trunkfish's backbone has long supporting rods for
its dorsal fin, which is near its tail. The trunkfish swims
slowly with its fins and tail, as its rigid, scaly body
makes it too stiff to flex in the normal way.

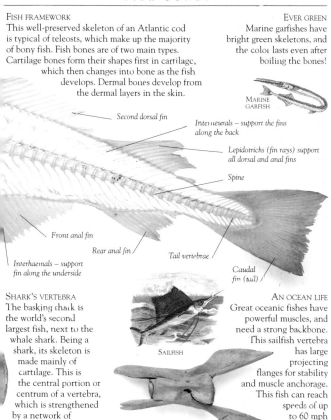

FISH FRAMEWORK
This well-preserved skeleton of an Atlantic cod is typical of teleosts, which make up the majority of bony fish. Fish bones are of two main types. Cartilage bones form their shapes first in cartilage, which then changes into bone as the fish develops. Dermal bones develop from the dermal layers in the skin.

EVER GREEN
Marine garfishes have bright green skeletons, and the color lasts even after boiling the bones!

MARINE GARFISH

Second dorsal fin

Intermeurals – support the fins along the back

Lepidotrichs (fin rays) support all dorsal and anal fins

Spine

Front anal fin

Rear anal fin

Tail vertebrae

Caudal fin (tail)

Interhaemals – support fin along the underside

SHARK'S VERTEBRA
The basking shark is the world's second largest fish, next to the whale shark. Being a shark, its skeleton is made mainly of cartilage. This is the central portion or centrum of a vertebra, which is strengthened by a network of mineral-laced fibers.

SAILFISH

AN OCEAN LIFE
Great oceanic fishes have powerful muscles, and need a strong backbone. This sailfish vertebra has large projecting flanges for stability and muscle anchorage. This fish can reach speeds of up to 60 mph (96 km/h).

Large projecting flanges

COLOR FOR SURVIVAL

MANY FISH USE color for survival tactics, and have
evolved almost every imaginable hue and pattern,
for various reasons. Color is an excellent means of
camouflage or defense, or of advertising a territory,
whether it be in the open
ocean, in rivers or lakes,
or on a coral reef.

*Barbels for finding
way in muddy water*

CLOWN LOACH

HIDING IN SHADOWS
The clown loach's
dark stripes camouflage it in
plants at the bottom of lakes.

*Long, thin mouth
for nibbling
in crevices*

NOW YOU SEE IT...
The forceps fish has a false
eyespot near its tail base, so that
when a predator tries to attack
its "head," it is able to swim away.

False eyespot

FORCEPS
FISH

FRENCH
ANGELFISH

*Eye hidden
in a stripe*

ZEBRA PIPEFISH

A COLORFUL ANGEL
As this young French angelfish grows
older, the four vertical bars on its body
will deepen to a bright yellow, and the
rest of its body color will deepen.

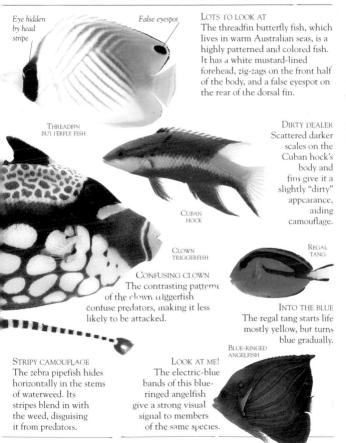

Eye hidden by head stripe

False eyespot

LOTS TO LOOK AT
The threadfin butterfly fish, which lives in warm Australian seas, is a highly patterned and colored fish. It has a white mustard-lined forehead, zig-zags on the front half of the body, and a false eyespot on the rear of the dorsal fin.

THREADFIN BUTTERFLY FISH

DIRTY DEALER
Scattered darker scales on the Cuban hock's body and fins give it a slightly "dirty" appearance, aiding camouflage.

CUBAN HOCK

CLOWN TRIGGERFISH

REGAL TANG

CONFUSING CLOWN
The contrasting patterns of the clown triggerfish confuse predators, making it less likely to be attacked.

INTO THE BLUE
The regal tang starts life mostly yellow, but turns blue gradually.

BLUE-RINGED ANGELFISH

STRIPY CAMOUFLAGE
The zebra pipefish hides horizontally in the stems of waterweed. Its stripes blend in with the weed, disguising it from predators.

LOOK AT ME!
The electric-blue bands of this blue-ringed angelfish give a strong visual signal to members of the same species.

SKATES AND RAYS

IT IS HARD TO BELIEVE that flat, slow-moving skates and rays, which live on the bed of the ocean, are related to fast, streamlined sharks. However, the anatomy of rays and sharks is very similar: for example, both have cartilaginous skeletons, and up to seven gill slits.

Underside is pale in colour, while upper surface is camouflaged

SEABED FEEDER
Rays feed mainly on sand-living creatures, so their mouths are on the underside of their bodies. There is a hole called a spiracle on the upper side, through which clean water for breathing is taken in and passed over the gills.

MOLLUSKS
Rays feed on hard-shelled animals, such as sea snails, that live in the sand.

Grinding teeth crush the armor of prey

POISON GLAND
Some rays have sharp, sawlike stings on their tails. These are good protection against their enemies.

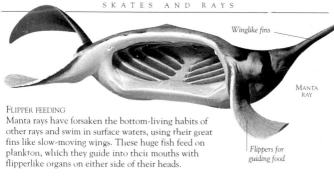

Winglike fins

MANTA RAY

Flippers for guiding food

FLIPPER FEEDING

Manta rays have forsaken the bottom-living habits of
other rays and swim in surface waters, using their great
fins like slow-moving wings. These huge fish feed on
plankton, which they guide into their mouths with
flipperlike organs on either side of their heads.

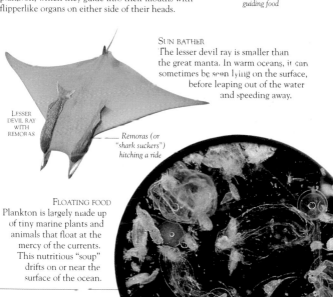

SUN BATHER

The lesser devil ray is smaller than
the great manta. In warm oceans, it can
sometimes be seen lying on the surface,
before leaping out of the water
and speeding away.

LESSER
DEVIL RAY
WITH
REMORAS

*Remoras (or
"shark suckers")
hitching a ride*

FLOATING FOOD

Plankton is largely made up
of tiny marine plants and
animals that float at the
mercy of the currents.
This nutritious "soup"
drifts on or near the
surface of the ocean.

AMBHIBIANS

WHAT IS AN AMPHIBIAN?

AMPHIBIANS ARE DIVIDED into frogs and toads, salamanders, sirens, and the wormlike caecilians. They are vertebrates, and are cold-blooded, which means that their body temperature varies with their surroundings. Amphibians have no hair, feathers, or surface scales on their skin, and can breathe through their skin, as well as their lungs.

Smooth, slimy skin of frog is typical

EUROPEAN
COMMON FROG

FIRE SALAMANDER

FROG FEATURES
Frogs and toads have a distinctive body shape – a large head and wide mouth, prominent eyes, no tail, and back legs longer than the front ones.

NOT AMPHIBIANS
Lizards and snakes are
reptiles, although
they look similar to
some amphibians.
Reptiles can be easily
distinguished by their dry, scaly skin.
Some tadpoles may look like small fish,
but the lack of scales and body fins
shows that they are quite different.

TEGU LIZARD

Typical dry, scaly
skin of a reptile

AMPHIBIAN ODDITY
The body rings on a caecilian
make it look like a worm, but
the sharklike head and
needle-sharp teeth
show it is not!

The smooth
damp skin of a
salamander is
typical of many
amphibians

A SPECIFIC SHAPE
Newts and salamanders have
narrower heads with smaller eyes and
mouths than frogs and toads. The body is
also longer and more lizard-shaped,
and there is always a well-developed tail.

EARLY AMPHIBIANS

THE FIRST AMPHIBIANS appeared some 360 million years ago. They evolved from fishes with fleshy fins that looked like legs, and had fishlike features. These amphibians may have been attracted onto land by a good food supply, and relatively few enemies to prey on them. Most amphibians had become extinct by the Triassic period, leaving only a few to evolve into modern amphibians.

SKELETON OF *ICHTHYOSTEGA*

FISH-LIKE AMPHIBIAN
Ichthyostega was an early amphibian from the Devonian period in Greenland. It had some fishlike features, but also had legs suitable for walking.

RECONSTRUCTION OF
ICHTHYOSTEGA

SWAMP DWELLER
This skeleton is of *Eryops*, a crocodile-like amphibian that lived in swamps in Texas about 270 million years ago. These terrestrial creatures used their strong limbs to move around.

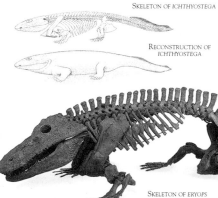

SKELETON OF ERYOPS

Wide, flat skull, like modern frogs

FOSSIL SANDWICH

This fossil is the only known specimen of *Triadobatrachus*, which was found in France, dating from the Triassic period about 210 million years ago. It has a wide, flat, froglike skull, but contains more vertebrae than modern frogs do, and also has a bony tail and short hind legs.

Short tail

KEEPING WELL

Well-preserved fossil frog skeletons like *Rana pueyoi* show how little some groups have changed in the last 25 million years.

Body shape of fossil salamander is like that of modern hellbender

Short, stout legs supporting heavy body

LONG LOST RELATIVE

This fossil salamander was found in Switzerland and is about eight million years old. It is a close relative of the hellbender salamander, the only living member now found in the southeastern US.

SKELETONS AND BONES

AMPHIBIANS HAVE SIMPLE SKELETONS with fewer bones than other modern vertebrates and many fewer than their fishy ancestors. This shows an evolutionary trend in amphibians – toward reducing the number of bones in the skull and spine (backbone).

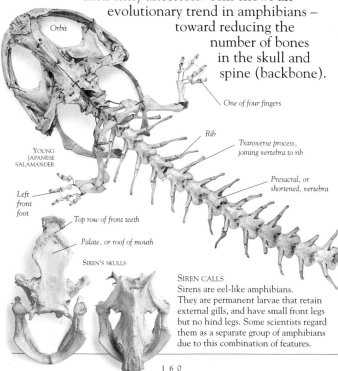

Orbit

One of four fingers

Rib

Transverse process, joining vertebra to rib

Presacral, or shortened, vertebra

YOUNG JAPANESE SALAMANDER

Left front foot

Top row of front teeth

Palate, or roof of mouth

SIREN'S SKULLS

SIREN CALLS
Sirens are eel-like amphibians. They are permanent larvae that retain external gills, and have small front legs but no hind legs. Some scientists regard them as a separate group of amphibians due to this combination of features.

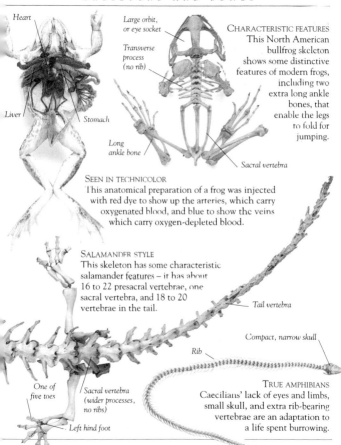

Heart

Large orbit, or eye socket

Transverse process (no rib)

CHARACTERISTIC FEATURES
This North American bullfrog skeleton shows some distinctive features of modern frogs, including two extra long ankle bones, that enable the legs to fold for jumping.

Liver

Stomach

Long ankle bone

Sacral vertebra

SEEN IN TECHNICOLOR
This anatomical preparation of a frog was injected with red dye to show up the arteries, which carry oxygenated blood, and blue to show the veins which carry oxygen-depleted blood.

SALAMANDER STYLE
This skeleton has some characteristic salamander features – it has about 16 to 22 presacral vertebrae, one sacral vertebra, and 18 to 20 vertebrae in the tail.

Tail vertebra

Compact, narrow skull

Rib

One of five toes

Sacral vertebra (wider processes, no ribs)

Left hind foot

TRUE AMPHIBIANS
Caecilians' lack of eyes and limbs, small skull, and extra rib-bearing vertebrae are an adaptation to a life spent burrowing.

AMPHIBIAN SENSES

AMPHIBIANS HAVE THE FIVE basic senses of touch, taste, sight, hearing, and smell. But they can also detect ultraviolet and infrared light, and the Earth's magnetic field. Through touch, amphibians can feel temperature and pain, and respond to irritants, such as acids in the environment. As cold-blooded animals with porous skin, amphibians need to respond quickly to external changes.

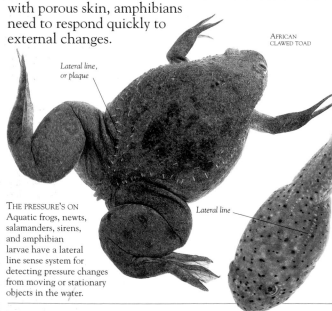

AFRICAN CLAWED TOAD

Lateral line, or plaque

Lateral line

THE PRESSURE'S ON
Aquatic frogs, newts, salamanders, sirens, and amphibian larvae have a lateral line sense system for detecting pressure changes from moving or stationary objects in the water.

PAINTED REED
FROG

RED-EYED
TREEFROG

ORIENTAL FIRE-
BELLIED TOAD

FEELING HOT?
In hot or drying conditions, amphibians
lose body water by evaporation. They
control their body temperature by
basking in the sun if too cold, or going
into the shade if too hot. By tucking in
its legs, the painted reed frog reduces the
amount of body area exposed to the sun.

EYE SEE
Eye color and pupil shape are
variable in frogs. The red-eyed treefrog
has vertical, catlike pupils for night
vision or quick response to rapidly
changing light conditions. The fire-
bellied toad has heart-shaped pupils.

Ear of American
bullfrog

AMERICAN
BULLFROG
TADPOLE

LISTEN UP
Hearing is one of
the most important
senses in frogs. The size
of, and distance between,
a frog's ears are related
to the wavelength and
frequency of the sound
of the male's call.

TAILED AMPHIBIANS

SALAMANDERS, NEWTS, AND SIRENS make up a group of about 360 species of tailed amphibians, which, like frogs and toads, have adopted a wide range of lifestyles. Some live on land in damp areas, although they may go into the water to breed. Some lungless salamanders even live in trees. Others spend their whole lives in water. Caecilians are found only in the tropics, and burrow in soft earth or mud, often near water, or else swim in rivers and streams.

Short hind legs – toes more equal in size than in frogs

Longer body than frogs and toads

Well-developed tail

TIGER SALAMANDER

Tip of crest on male's tail only grows during mating season

SHY AWAY
"Salamander" is a term generally used to refer to land-based amphibians with tails, although newts and sirens are also members of this family. Land-dwelling salamanders are shy and live mostly in damp, hidden areas.

Narrower head than
frogs and toads

A LIFE IN THE WATER
Sirens are distinct from
salamanders – they have
lungs as well as gills and are
permanent aquatic larvae
(they never leave the water.)

One of four toes
on front foot

LESSER SIREN

Gills

One of five
toes on
hind foot

Newts are
semi-aquatic
salamanders,
that return to
the water to breed

MALE GREAT
CRESTED NEWT

REPTILES

PAINTING OF MEDUSA

WHAT IS A REPTILE?

LIKE FISH, amphibians, birds, and mammals, reptiles are vertebrates (have backbones). But what makes them different from fish and amphibians is that they are basically land animals – they do not have to live in or keep returning to water. And unlike birds and mammals, they are cold-blooded. That is, their bodies remain at the same temperature as their surroundings.

MEDUSA
Throughout history, reptiles have been feared. Medusa, a monster from Greek mythology, had snakes for hair.

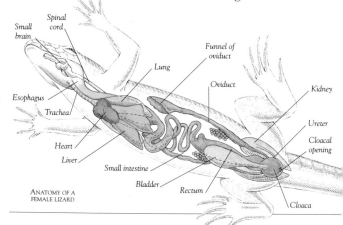

Small brain

Spinal cord

Esophagus

Trachea

Heart

Liver

Lung

Funnel of oviduct

Oviduct

Kidney

Ureter

Cloacal opening

Small intestine

Bladder

Rectum

Cloaca

ANATOMY OF A FEMALE LIZARD

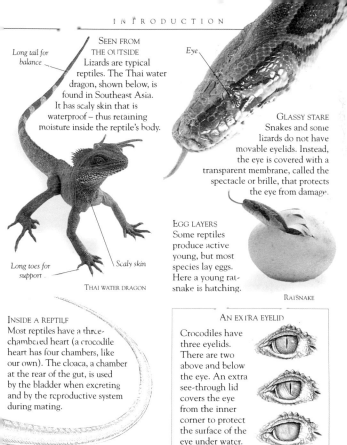

SEEN FROM
THE OUTSIDE
Lizards are typical
reptiles. The Thai water
dragon, shown below, is
found in Southeast Asia.
It has scaly skin that is
waterproof – thus retaining
moisture inside the reptile's body.

Long tail for
balance

Long toes for
support

Scaly skin

THAI WATER DRAGON

Eye

GLASSY STARE
Snakes and some
lizards do not have
movable eyelids. Instead,
the eye is covered with a
transparent membrane, called the
spectacle or brille, that protects
the eye from damage.

EGG LAYERS
Some reptiles
produce active
young, but most
species lay eggs.
Here a young rat-
snake is hatching.

RATSNAKE

INSIDE A REPTILE
Most reptiles have a three-
chambered heart (a crocodile
heart has four chambers, like
our own). The cloaca, a chamber
at the rear of the gut, is used
by the bladder when excreting
and by the reproductive system
during mating.

AN EXTRA EYELID
Crocodiles have
three eyelids.
There are two
above and below
the eye. An extra
see-through lid
covers the eye
from the inner
corner to protect
the surface of the
eye under water.

REPTILE GROUPS

REPTILES FIRST APPEARED about 340 million years ago, during the Carboniferous period (see diagram). Their ancestors were amphibians, but the first reptiles could breed without having to return to water. Today, four main groups, or orders, remain: turtles and tortoises (chelonians), snakes and lizards, crocodilians, and tuataras.

GIANT SEASNAKE

PALAEOPHIS
Snakes first appeared in the late Jurassic. *Palaeophis* was an ancient seasnake.

MODERN PYTHON
These vertebrae are from a python that is four times smaller than *Palaeophis*.

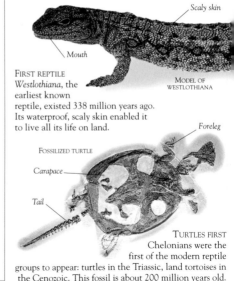

Scaly skin

Mouth

MODEL OF WESTLOTHIANA

FIRST REPTILE
Westlothiana, the earliest known reptile, existed 338 million years ago. Its waterproof, scaly skin enabled it to live all its life on land.

Foreleg

FOSSILIZED TURTLE

Carapace

Tail

TURTLES FIRST
Chelonians were the first of the modern reptile groups to appear: turtles in the Triassic, land tortoises in the Cenozoic. This fossil is about 200 million years old.

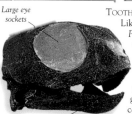

TOOTHLESS TURTLE
Like modern turtles, *Puppigerus*, a Cenozoic sea turtle, had toothless jaws. It used its beak to feed on plants such as seagrass in shallow coastal waters.

Large eye sockets

Toothless jaws

REPTILE GROUP FACTS
• Rhynchocephalians were common in the Triassic. Today, the only ones left are tuataras.
• Mammal-like reptiles appeared in the Permian. During the Triassic they gave rise to the first mammals.

Semi-sprawling stance

Five-toed feet

REPTILE EVOLUTION
This diagram shows the evolution of reptiles. The column on the left shows when they existed and how many millions of years ago that was.

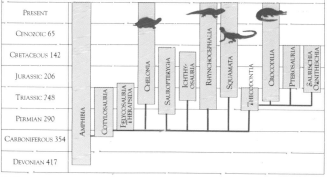

PRESENT	
CENOZOIC 65	
CRETACEOUS 142	
JURASSIC 206	
TRIASSIC 248	
PERMIAN 290	
CARBONIFEROUS 354	
DEVONIAN 417	

AMPHIBIA · COTYLOSAURIA · PELYCOSAURIA THERAPSIDA · CHELONIA · SAUROPTERYGIA · ICHTHYOSAURIA · RHYNCHOCEPHALIA · SQUAMATA · THECODONTIA · CROCODILIA · PTEROSAURIA · SAURISCHIA ORNITHISCHIA

PREHISTORIC REPTILES

THE FIRST REPTILES encountered no competition for the wide range of land habitats available. Over millions of years they adapted to every possible type of lifestyle and diet. Some of them even learned to fly. Others returned to living in the sea.

The "sail" was probably used to help control body temperature

DIMETRODON

SAIL BACK
Dimetrodon was a mammal-like reptile of the Permian period. Its relatives were the ancestors of modern mammals.

Fangs and sharp cheek-teeth for eating flesh

CYNOGNATHUS

Sharp claws

REPTILE DOG
Cynognathus lived in the early Triassic period. It was about 7 ft (2 m) long and looked like a large dog. Scientists have discovered that it probably had hair.

BACK TO THE SEA
In the Jurassic and Cretaceous periods, some reptiles returned to living in water, but this time they chose the sea; there were invertebrates and fish to eat. Plesiosaurs had long necks and their limbs had become paddles.

REPTILE DOLPHINS
Ichthyosaurs were the most fishlike of reptiles. They were the same size – and ate the same food – as modern dolphins. Like many of today's fish, they used their tail to propel themselves and steered with their fins.

PLESIOSAUR

Dolphinlike snout

Powerful tail for swimming

ICHTHYOSAUR

Paddles for steering and braking

GIANT SEA LIZARDS
Mosaurs were huge, measuring about 49 ft (15 m) in length. They preyed on fish and ammonites (a type of shellfish), crushing the shells in their powerful jaws.

MOSASAUR

More prehistoric reptiles

During the Jurassic and Cretaceous periods, reptiles ruled the land. Among these reptiles were the dinosaurs ("terrible lizards"). Some dinosaurs were gentle herbivores; others were ferocious carnivores. At the same time, a number of reptiles adapted to life in the air, 100 million years before flying birds appeared.

RHAMPHORHYNCIDS
The first flying reptiles, or pterosaurs, appeared during the Triassic period. *Rhamphorhynchus* and its relatives were Jurassic pterosaurs. They had long tails, curved snouts, and jaws with teeth. *Rhamphorynchus* may have used its teeth for spearing fish.

Claws on wings

Vane on tail for steering

Hairy body

RHAMPHORHYNCHUS

Throat pouch – possibly for holding fish

Tail may have aided balance while eating

PTERANODON AND HANG-GLIDER

GLIDERS ANCIENT AND MODERN
Pterosaurs probably could not fly like birds. Instead, they launched themselves from cliffs and glided through the air, using updrafts – just like modern hang-gliders. The largest pterosaurs, such as *Pteranodon*, had wingspans of 26 ft (8 m) or more.

Strong neck to support
the huge head

Skin stretched
between elongated
fingers and the body,
forming wings

Tyrannosaurus
moved around on its
massive hind legs

TYRANNOSAURUS

LIZARD TYRANT
Standing taller than a
giraffe and weighing about
98 tons (100 tonnes),
Tyrannosaurus was a two-
legged carnivore with teeth up
to 7 in (18 cm) long.

Tough hide
helped protect
against predators

Bony club to
deter predators

EUOPLOCEPHALUS

EUOPLOCEPHALUS
Ankylosaurs, such as *Euoplocephalus*, needed
protection from their carnivorous relatives. The
tanklike ankylosaurs developed an armoured
covering of bony plates and knobs. Some
of them had clublike tails.

GENTLE GIANTS
Brachiosaurus
and its relatives
were huge but only
ate vegetation. Its long
neck, balanced by a
long tail, enabled it to
reach into high branches
inaccessible to other creatures.

Massive legs to
support the body's
great weight

PREHISTORIC FACTS

• *Brachiosaurus* would
have eaten 882 lb
(400 kg) of food a day.

• Large carnivorous
dinosaurs may have
been warm-blooded.

• The fastest dinosaurs
could run at up to
50 mph (80 km/h).

BRACHIOSAURUS

SCALY SKIN

REPTILES TYPICALLY have skins covered in overlapping, horny scales. They act as a waterproof covering and help retain precious body moisture. In some reptiles, the scales form an armored protection. As a reptile grows, its old skin becomes too small and starts to wear out. A new skin replaces it.

ARMORED ALLIGATOR
Like all crocodilians, this Chinese alligator is covered in large, tough, partly ossified (turned into bone) scales. As it grows, the scales flake off and are replaced by new ones.

SECTION THROUGH SKIN

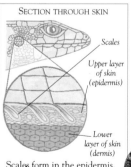

Scales

Upper layer of skin (epidermis)

Lower layer of skin (dermis)

Scales form in the epidermis. They are made mostly of keratin – the same substance found in hair and nails.

The new segments are added where the tail joins the rattle

End segments may break off if the rattle gets very long

WARNING RATTLE
A rattlesnake's rattle is made up of hollow pieces of keratin formed at the end of the tail. A new segment is added when the snake sheds its skin.

The rattle warns off attackers

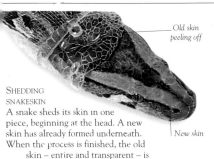

Old skin peeling off

New skin

SHEDDING SNAKESKIN

A snake sheds its skin in one piece, beginning at the head. A new skin has already formed underneath. When the process is finished, the old skin – entire and transparent – is left behind.

A SHED SNAKESKIN

SCALY SKIN FACTS

• A reptile grows throughout its life.

• The crests and spines sported by some lizards are formed from scales.

• Turtle shells are made of bony plates covered in horny material.

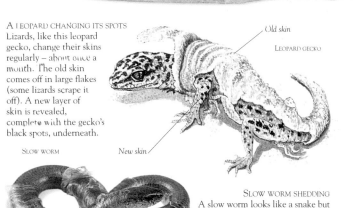

A LEOPARD CHANGING ITS SPOTS

Lizards, like this leopard gecko, change their skins regularly – about once a month. The old skin comes off in large flakes (some lizards scrape it off). A new layer of skin is revealed, complete with the gecko's black spots, underneath.

Old skin

LEOPARD GECKO

New skin

SLOW WORM

SLOW WORM SHEDDING

A slow worm looks like a snake but is actually a legless lizard. It sheds either large flakes, like other lizards, or almost the entire skin, like snakes.

COLD-BLOODED CREATURES

REPTILES ARE DESCRIBED as cold-blooded. This does not mean that their blood is always cold. But, unlike birds and mammals, they do not make their own heat by using the chemical reactions in their bodies. Instead, a reptile relies on heat from the outside, and its body temperature goes up or down with the surrounding temperature.

CHILLING OUT
To cool, a reptile finds shade, or angles its body to expose the smallest possible area to the sun.

Reptiles warm up by basking in the sun

AGAMA LIZARD

COLD-BLOODED FACTS

• Scientists call "cold-blooded" animals poikilotherms or ectotherms.

• Reptiles need a high body temperature for digestion to take place. If a snake eats when it is not warm enough, it has to regurgitate its meal.

WARMING UP
When a reptile starts to get too cold, it warms itself by basking in the sun, presenting as much of its body as possible to the sun's rays. By moving regularly between sun and shade, a reptile is able to maintain an almost constant body temperature.

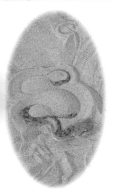

DIGGING IN
Shade is difficult to find in the desert. A sand viper solves this problem by wriggling its body down into the sand. If it did not do this it would literally fry in the heat.

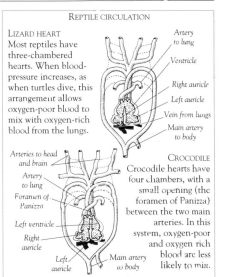

REPTILE CIRCULATION

LIZARD HEART
Most reptiles have three-chambered hearts. When blood-pressure increases, as when turtles dive, this arrangement allows oxygen-poor blood to mix with oxygen-rich blood from the lungs.

Artery to lung

Ventricle

Right auricle

Left auricle

Vein from lungs

Main artery to body

Arteries to head and brain

Artery to lung

Foramen of Panizza

Left ventricle

Right auricle

Left auricle

Main artery to body

CROCODILE
Crocodile hearts have four chambers, with a small opening (the foramen of Panizza) between the two main arteries. In this system, oxygen-poor and oxygen rich blood are less likely to mix.

Open-mouthed cooling is called gaping

Like all reptiles, the crocodile cannot sweat to lose heat

Water evaporates from mouth

OPEN-MOUTHED COOLING
One way of cooling is to let water evaporate from the body. A crocodile lies with its mouth open to let water evaporate from its mouth. American crocodiles lie in burrows when they get too hot. Other species cool down in water.

SENSES

MOST REPTILES have eyes and ears. Snakes and lizards also "taste" their surroundings using their tongues. The tuatara, and many lizards, also have a light-sensitive organ on their heads, which may be important to temperature regulation and to reproduction.

Scaly skin contains sensors that detect touch, pain, heat, and cold

Notched iris with vertical slit

Heat-sensitive pit helps snake to calculate direction and distance of prey

SLIT EYES
A gecko is active mostly at night and its eyes are very sensitive. In daylight, the iris of each eye closes to a slit, stopping too much light from reaching the retina. Notches in the iris allow the animal to see.

HEAT SENSITIVE
On each side of its head, a pit viper has a heat-sensitive pit that can detect the body heat given off by warm-blooded prey. The pits can sense temperature changes as small as 0.002°F (0.001°C), enabling the snake to strike accurately, even at night.

TEGU SENSES

A tegu lizard's well-developed eyes are designed for use in daylight and are protected by movable eyelids. Its eardrums are visible as small patches on the sides of its head behind the jaws. Its flicking, forked tongue is used, in conjunction with its Jacobson's organ, to "taste" the air.

SWIVELING EYES

To see without being seen, a chameleon remains perfectly still, while swiveling its eyes to see in almost any direction. The eyes swivel independently of each other.

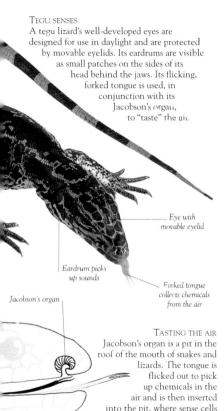

Eye with movable eyelid

Eardrum picks up sounds

Forked tongue collects chemicals from the air

Jacobson's organ

TASTING THE AIR

Jacobson's organ is a pit in the roof of the mouth of snakes and lizards. The tongue is flicked out to pick up chemicals in the air and is then inserted into the pit, where sense cells detect the nature of the chemicals.

SENSES FACTS

• A chameleon can use one eye to hunt and the other to watch out for predators.

• Most snakes "hear" by feeling vibrations through the ground; however, most lizards hear airborne sounds.

MOVEMENT

THE LEGS OF A typical reptile,
such as a lizard, protrude sideways
from its body. Heavier reptiles may
require considerable physical effort to
lift their bodies off the ground. Larger,
land-based reptiles tend to move
slowly, but smaller, lighter ones can
be fast-moving and agile. Some
reptiles, notably snakes, have
dispensed with legs altogether.

GECKO

STICKY FEET
Geckos are small
and light, and able to
move rapidly. Pads on
their feet have millions
of tiny hooks that enable
them to cling to smooth
surfaces, even glass.

*Fringelike
scales on feet*

SANDFISH

SWIMMING IN SAND
A sandfish (a type of skink)
has fringelike scales on its feet
to help it move on sand. It
can also dive into the sand,
wriggling like a snake.

SIDEWINDING
Some desert snakes move
over the sand by looping
their bodies sideways and
moving in a series of sideway
steps, known as sidewinding.

SIDEWINDER

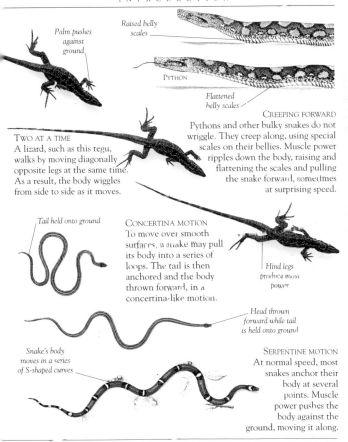

Raised belly scales

PYTHON

Palm pushes against ground

Flattened belly scales

CREEPING FORWARD
Pythons and other bulky snakes do not wriggle. They creep along, using special scales on their bellies. Muscle power ripples down the body, raising and flattening the scales and pulling the snake forward, sometimes at surprising speed.

TWO AT A TIME
A lizard, such as this tegu, walks by moving diagonally opposite legs at the same time. As a result, the body wiggles from side to side as it moves.

Tail held onto ground

CONCERTINA MOTION
To move over smooth surfaces, a snake may pull its body into a series of loops. The tail is then anchored and the body thrown forward, in a concertina-like motion.

Hind legs produce most power

Head thrown forward while tail is held onto ground

Snake's body moves in a series of S-shaped curves

SERPENTINE MOTION
At normal speed, most snakes anchor their body at several points. Muscle power pushes the body against the ground, moving it along.

Flying reptiles

Reptiles have never learned to fly like bats or birds. The first "flying" reptiles, the pterosaurs of the Triassic period, were gliding animals rather than fliers, and the same is true of the modern species that have taken to the air. Nevertheless, the ability to glide can be very useful in escaping quickly from predators or simply moving swiftly from one tree branch to the next in the search for food.

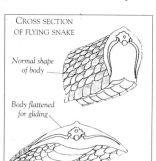

CROSS SECTION
OF FLYING SNAKE

*Normal shape
of body*

*Body flattened
for gliding*

A flying snake turns itself into a wing by pushing out its ribs and holding in its belly, so that the body becomes flattened.

*Six or seven pairs of
ribs support skin flaps*

FLYING DRAGON
The "wings" of the flying dragon of Southeast Asia are flaps of skin supported by elongated ribs. They normally lie folded against the body, but can be spread out wide for gliding flights.

*Limbs spread
out to help
steering*

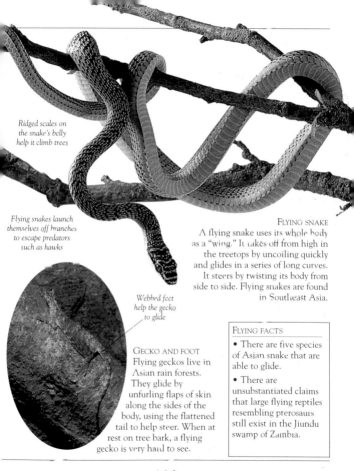

Ridged scales on the snake's belly help it climb trees

Flying snakes launch themselves off branches to escape predators such as hawks

Webbed feet help the gecko to glide

FLYING SNAKE

A flying snake uses its whole body as a "wing." It takes off from high in the treetops by uncoiling quickly and glides in a series of long curves. It steers by twisting its body from side to side. Flying snakes are found in Southeast Asia.

GECKO AND FOOT

Flying geckos live in Asian rain forests. They glide by unfurling flaps of skin along the sides of the body, using the flattened tail to help steer. When at rest on tree bark, a flying gecko is very hard to see.

FLYING FACTS

• There are five species of Asian snake that are able to glide.

• There are unsubstantiated claims that large flying reptiles resembling pterosaurs still exist in the Jiundu swamp of Zambia.

COURTSHIP

LIKE ALL ANIMALS, reptiles need to attract members of the opposite sex in order to reproduce. They do this in various ways: by signals, colourful displays, or eye-catching ornaments, such as frills or crests.

Male's head

SNAKES MATING

Mating may take several hours

SNAKE CHARMERS
Once a male snake has attracted a female he stimulates her into mating by rubbing his chin along her back. She then allows him to intertwine her body with his. This enables their cloacal openings to meet so that the pair can mate.

Tails intertwined

A CLASH OF SHELLS
Tortoise mating, especially in large species such as these Galápagos tortoises, is a laborious affair. The males roar during mating.

All anoles have very long tails

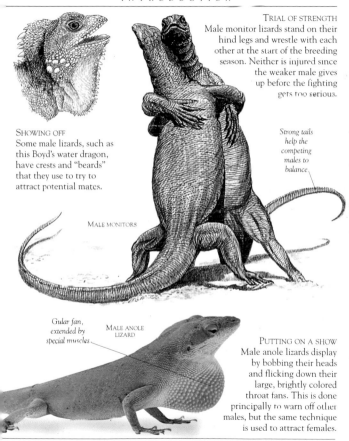

TRIAL OF STRENGTH
Male monitor lizards stand on their
hind legs and wrestle with each
other at the start of the breeding
season. Neither is injured since
the weaker male gives
up before the fighting
gets too serious.

SHOWING OFF
Some male lizards, such as
this Boyd's water dragon,
have crests and "beards"
that they use to try to
attract potential mates.

*Strong tails
help the
competing
males to
balance*

MALE MONITORS

*Gular fan,
extended by
special muscles*

MALE ANOLE
LIZARD

PUTTING ON A SHOW
Male anole lizards display
by bobbing their heads
and flicking down their
large, brightly colored
throat fans. This is done
principally to warn off other
males, but the same technique
is used to attract females.

NESTS AND EGGS

ANIMALS THAT TAKE CARE of their young usually have fewer offspring than those that leave their young to fend for themselves. Some reptiles, such as the marine turtles, lay thousands of eggs, but because they abandon them, only a few hatchlings reach maturity. A crocodile, on the other hand, guards not only her eggs but also her young for some time after they hatch. So a higher percentage of eggs and young survive.

ALLIGATOR NEST

ROTTEN NEST

A female American alligator builds a mound of mud and decaying vegetation, in which she lays 15 to 80 eggs. The heat produced by the rotting material incubates the eggs for two to three months.

The mother uncovers the eggs when they hatch

ON GUARD

The estuarine, or saltwater, crocodile of Southeast Asia and northern Australia builds a mound of leaves for her eggs. She builds her nest near water and shade so she can keep cool as she guards her offspring against predators, including lizards, herons, mongooses, turtles, and other crocodiles.

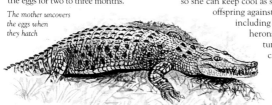

The female covers the nest with her body

SAFE IN MOTHER'S MOUTH
After baby Nile
crocodiles have
hatched, their mother
gathers as many as she
can in her mouth and
carries them to the
safety of a pool,
making several trips
to complete the task.
She remains to
defend her offspring.

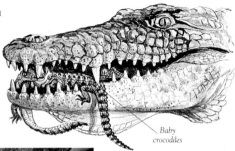

*Baby
crocodiles*

GREEN TURTLE LAYING EGGS

NO SAFETY IN NUMBERS
A marine turtle lays up to 200
eggs, burying them in a nest in
the sand. If the nest remains
undiscovered, the eggs hatch
6 to 10 weeks later, but the
hatchlings fall prey to crabs,
seabirds, and other predators
on the way to the sea.

LIVE BIRTH
A rattlesnake keeps her
eggs inside her body
until they hatch, which
greatly improves their
chances of survival.
Approximately 10 to 20
young are born, measuring
about 11¼ in (30 cm) in
length. The mother abandons
them soon after birth.

RATTLESNAKE AND YOUNG

More nests and eggs

Reptile eggs have shells that retain moisture so they can be laid on land. Most reptile eggs have soft, leathery shells, but some, such as a crocodile's, have hard shells. In most cases the eggs hatch outside the mother's body, although a few reptiles produce live young. In some cases the eggs hatch just before laying; in others, the embryos obtain nourishment from their mother through a placenta.

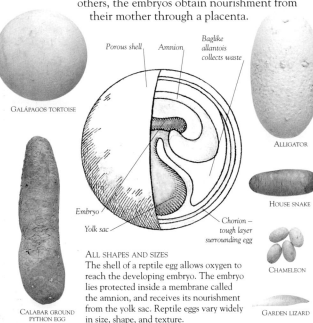

GALÁPAGOS TORTOISE

Porous shell *Amnion*

Baglike allantois collects waste

ALLIGATOR

HOUSE SNAKE

Embryo

Yolk sac

Chorion – tough layer surrounding egg

CHAMELEON

CALABAR GROUND PYTHON EGG

GARDEN LIZARD

ALL SHAPES AND SIZES
The shell of a reptile egg allows oxygen to reach the developing embryo. The embryo lies protected inside a membrane called the amnion, and receives its nourishment from the yolk sac. Reptile eggs vary widely in size, shape, and texture.

EGG TOOTH
As it grows inside the egg, a young lizard or snake develops a sharp "egg tooth" on the tip of its upper jaw. When the time for hatching arrives, the animal escapes from the shell by using the egg tooth to cut its way out.

Egg tooth

HOW A SNAKE HATCHES

Just before a snake hatches, the yolk sac is drawn into the snake's body and the remaining yolk is absorbed into its intestine. Then, using its egg tooth, the snake cuts a slit large enough to push its head through. It may remain like this for up to two days before finally emerging from the egg. When it is fully hatched, the snake may be up to seven times longer than the egg from which it came.

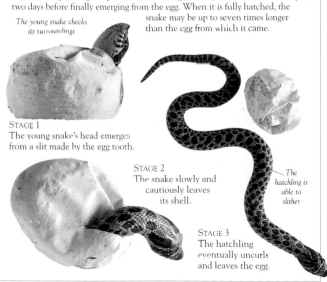

The young snake checks its surroundings

STAGE 1
The young snake's head emerges from a slit made by the egg tooth.

STAGE 2
The snake slowly and cautiously leaves its shell.

The hatchling is able to slither

STAGE 3
The hatchling eventually uncurls and leaves the egg.

DEADLY ENEMIES

MOST REPTILES are predators, but they are also preyed upon by other animals. Sometimes reptiles eat other reptiles. Eggs and young are especially vulnerable and in many cases adults, too, have their enemies. Even the largest and most dangerous reptiles may fall victim to human hunters.

The secretary bird tramples its reptile prey to death

SECRETARY BIRD
This African bird hunts tortoises, snakes, and lizards, flushing them from grass by stamping its feet. It uses its wings as a shield against venomous snakes.

The mongoose has lightning reactions

ENEMY FACTS
• When they are away from water, Nile crocodiles are vulnerable to attack by lions.
• The giant tortoises of Mauritius and Reunion Island were wiped out by hunters in the late 1700s.

Faced with a mongoose, a cobra looks fierce but its chances are slim

LEGENDARY ENEMIES
The mongoose is the only mammal that includes poisonous snakes in its diet. Although smaller than some of its prey, it is very courageous and is immune to snake venom. When tackling a snake, such as a spitting cobra, it bites the head of its prey with lightning speed.

SNAKE EATS SNAKE

Kingsnakes, some of which are also known as milk snakes, feed on small mammals, lizards, frogs, and other snakes. Kingsnakes, which squeeze their prey, are not afraid to tackle venomous snakes, such as copperheads.

Copperhead   Kingsnake

A kingsnake swallows a copperhead

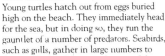

A gull has easy pickings when a turtle nest hatches

GULL GAUNTLET

Young turtles hatch out from eggs buried high on the beach. They immediately head for the sea, but in doing so, they run the gauntlet of a number of predators. Seabirds, such as gulls, gather in large numbers to feast on the hatchlings, and many of them never reach the safety of the water.

HATCHLINGS AND GULL

HUMANS AND REPTILES

Humans hunt reptiles for various reasons – for food, for their skins, or simply because they are poisonous. Humans have also reduced the natural habitat of many species. A combination of these factors has brought some species to extinction and made others very rare.

Cobras are protected in India, but they are still caught so that that their venom can be collected (see page 97)

SOUTH INDIAN VILLAGERS DISPLAY A LIVE COBRA

BATTLE FOR SURVIVAL

SURVIVAL IN THE ANIMAL WORLD means not only being able to find something to eat but also avoiding being eaten by other animals. Large reptiles deter predators by their sheer size, but smaller species have to use a range of strategies, including camouflage, warning colors, mimicry, and bluff.

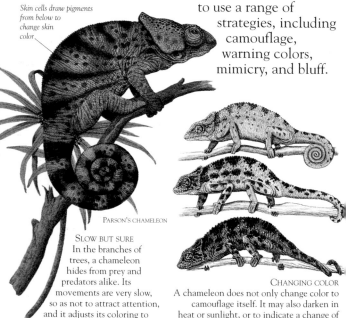

Skin cells draw pigments from below to change skin color

PARSON'S CHAMELEON

SLOW BUT SURE
In the branches of trees, a chameleon hides from prey and predators alike. Its movements are very slow, so as not to attract attention, and it adjusts its coloring to blend in with its surroundings.

CHANGING COLOR
A chameleon does not only change color to camouflage itself. It may also darken in heat or sunlight, or to indicate a change of mood – an angry chameleon turns black.

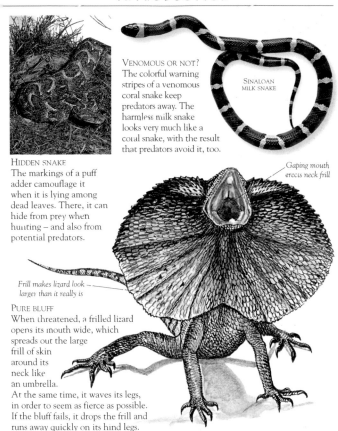

VENOMOUS OR NOT?
The colorful warning stripes of a venomous coral snake keep predators away. The harmless milk snake looks very much like a coral snake, with the result that predators avoid it, too.

SINALOAN MILK SNAKE

HIDDEN SNAKE
The markings of a puff adder camouflage it when it is lying among dead leaves. There, it can hide from prey when hunting – and also from potential predators.

Gaping mouth erects neck frill

Frill makes lizard look larger than it really is

PURE BLUFF
When threatened, a frilled lizard opens its mouth wide, which spreads out the large frill of skin around its neck like an umbrella.
At the same time, it waves its legs, in order to seem as fierce as possible. If the bluff fails, it drops the frill and runs away quickly on its hind legs.

Defense strategies

Reptiles have evolved many ways to avoid being eaten. Small lizards often use speed to escape, and many species retreat into underground burrows or rock crevices. Some use water as a means of escape. When cornered, many lizards, particularly large ones like monitors, will turn to face their attackers. Two lizards, the Gila monster and the beaded lizard, are venomous.

The snake lies absolutely still

Mouth gapes and tongue hangs out

PLAYING DEAD
When it cannot escape, a grass snake turns over, curls up, then lies still. It is playing dead, hoping its attacker will go away.

STINKING STINKPOT
The stinkpot turtle is the reptile equivalent of the skunk. It produces such an unpleasant smell that predators avoid it.

As it loses speed, the basilisk drops into the water and must swim

BASILISK

SURVIVAL FACTS

• Horned lizards squirt blood at their attackers from their eyes.

• Some skinks have a bright blue tail that attracts predators away from vital body parts.

LOSING A TAIL TO SAVE A LIFE
In many cases a lizard can shed
its tail if it is grabbed by an
attacker. The tail is equipped with
special breaking points in the vertebrae,
and the shed tail usually twitches for a
while after it breaks off, distracting the
attacker long enough for the lizard to
make good its escape. A new tail grows.

Tail recently shed

New tail after eight months

Growing the new tail uses up energy

TREE SKINK

Tail can only break in the old part, where there are still breakable vertebrae

Tail helps basilisk balance as it runs

RUNNING ON WATER
Basilisks have long hind legs for running,
and their feet have broad soles
with a fringe of scales
around the toes.
This enables
them to run across water in order to
escape from potential predators.

LIVING IN WATER

ALTHOUGH REPTILES EVOLVED as land animals, many species have become adapted to living in water, where food is often plentiful. For these species, swimming is more important than walking, and many are equipped with paddles instead of feet. But they are still air-breathing animals and so have special adaptations enabling them to cope with a watery environment.

GOGGLE EYES
Crocodilians, like this caiman, lie submerged in the water, waiting for prey. The eyes and nostrils are placed high on the head so that only these parts show above the water.

The spectacled caiman has a bony ridge between its eyes, resembling the frame of a pair of glasses

SNORKELING TURTLE
The matamata turtle of Brazil waits for its prey on the river bed. It pokes its nostrils out of the water to breathe, without moving – thus it avoids disturbing the fish.

WATER FACTS

• Sea turtles excrete salt absorbed in sea water from their eyes, which is why they seem to cry.

• To prevent water from getting into its lung, a seasnake closes off its nostrils with a spongelike tissue.

Seasnakes are highly venomous

Powerful tail moves the snake forward

PADDLE TAIL
A seasnake is virtually helpless on land but is an excellent swimmer. Its tail is flattened vertically to form a powerful, oarlike paddle.

The four paddles propel the turtle

WEB-FOOTED SLIDER
Freshwater chelonians, such as terrapins, have webbed feet for swimming. The red-eared slider has a habit of sliding back into the water if disturbed.

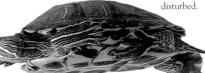

PADDLE FEET
A marine turtle can tolerate high levels of carbon dioxide in its blood and so can swim under water for long periods.

CHELONIAN ANATOMY

CHELONIANS are reptiles whose bodies are protected by shells. The shells are made up of the plastron which protects the belly, and the carapace, which covers the back. There are between 250 and 300 species of chelonian. Some live in salt water, others in fresh water, and yet others on land. Water dwellers are usually called turtles or terrapins, while land dwellers are known as tortoises.

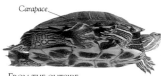

Carapace

FROM THE OUTSIDE
The red-eared terrapin is a typical chelonian. It has a carapace made up of several layers. The outer layer consists of horny shields, known as scutes.

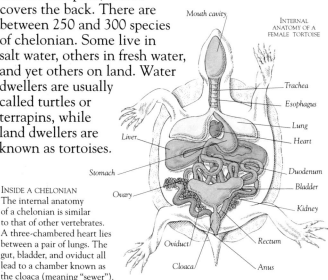

INTERNAL ANATOMY OF A FEMALE TORTOISE

Mouth cavity

Trachea

Esophagus

Lung

Liver

Heart

Stomach

Duodenum

Ovary

Bladder

Kidney

Oviduct

Rectum

Cloaca

Anus

INSIDE A CHELONIAN
The internal anatomy of a chelonian is similar to that of other vertebrates. A three-chambered heart lies between a pair of lungs. The gut, bladder, and oviduct all lead to a chamber known as the cloaca (meaning "sewer").

FUSED VERTEBRAE

The carapace is made up of about 50 bony plates formed in the skin. The shell has an outer layer of horny shields and an inner one of bone. The vertebrae, with the ribs and the two limb girdles, are fused to the carapace. This has resulted in the limb girdles being inside the ribs.

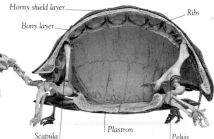

Horny shield layer

Bony layer

Ribs

Scapula

Plastron

Pelvis

SKELETON OF A TURTLE

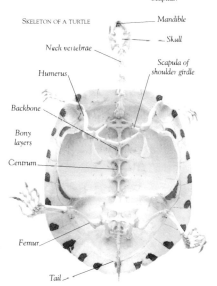

Mandible

Skull

Neck vertebrae

Scapula of shoulder girdle

Humerus

Backbone

Bony layers

Centrum

Femur

Tail

FLEXIBLE NECK

Inside the horny outer layer, the carapace is made of several layers of bone. The eight neck vertebrae are very flexible. The upper limb bones are short, with enlarged ends to take the weight of the animal's body and shell.

CHELONIAN FACTS

• Some female turtles produce eggs four years after mating.

• All chelonians lay eggs on land, even the marine turtles.

• Some turtles can live for more than a year without food.

MARINE TURTLES

TURTLES INVADED the world's seas and oceans during the Triassic period, some 200 million years ago. Today there are seven species, six of which are grouped together in the one family, the Chelonidae. The leatherback turtle is classified by itself in another family, called the Dermochelyidae.

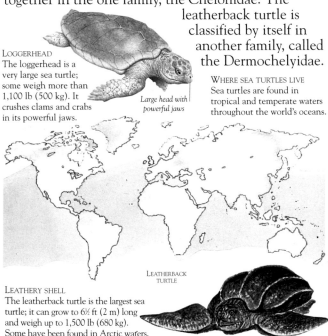

LOGGERHEAD
The loggerhead is a very large sea turtle; some weigh more than 1,100 lb (500 kg). It crushes clams and crabs in its powerful jaws.

Large head with powerful jaws

WHERE SEA TURTLES LIVE
Sea turtles are found in tropical and temperate waters throughout the world's oceans.

LEATHERBACK TURTLE

LEATHERY SHELL
The leatherback turtle is the largest sea turtle; it can grow to 6½ ft (2 m) long and weigh up to 1,500 lb (680 kg). Some have been found in Arctic waters.

IMMUNE TO POISON
Hawksbill turtles are found near coral reefs. They feed on invertebrates, such as sponges, many of which contain poisons. These do not affect the turtles but may kill animals that eat them.

NESTING TOGETHER
Ridley turtles come ashore in large numbers to nest together on certain beaches. Each female digs a hole in which she lays about 100 eggs. Olive ridleys live in the Atlantic, Indian, and parts of the Pacific Oceans.

CHELONIAN FEET

The limbs of marine turtles are very different from those of land and freshwater chelonians. Land tortoises have large, clawed feet. Freshwater turtles have webbing between the toes. The limbs of marine turtles have evolved into flippers.

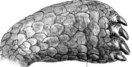

LAND TORTOISE — *Large claws for digging in soil*

MARINE TURTLE — *Flipper used for swimming*

FRESHWATER TURTLE

Turtles in danger

Sea turtles are among the world's most vulnerable animals. They are relatively slow moving and easy to catch, and their nest sites are mostly well known – for example, Kemp's ridley turtles only nest on one beach in Mexico. Turtle products are much in demand, and large numbers of turtles are killed. In addition, their overall rate of reproduction is slow; although a green turtle may lay 1,000 eggs in one season, only a few survive into adulthood.

TURTLE EXPLOITATION

Turtles are large, meaty animals and in many places are hunted for food; green turtles are especially prized, particularly for turtle soup. When polished, the shell of a green turtle is a popular tourist souvenir. Pieces of turtle shell are also used in furniture-making.

GREEN TURTLE EGGS

END OF THE LINE
Green turtle eggs are a popular food. The nests are easy to find since the females leave an obvious trail to the nest.

TURTLES FOR SALE
Trade in wild turtles is banned under international agreements, but illegal buying and selling still occurs. Some people think that breeding turtles in captivity could meet the demand for turtle products and help protect wild populations.

STUFFED TURTLES

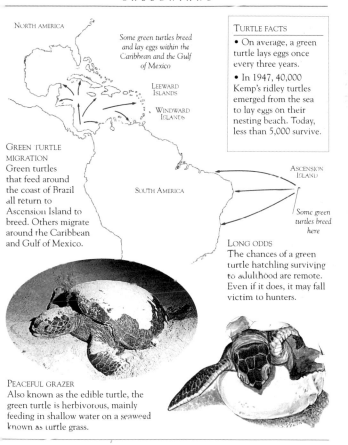

NORTH AMERICA

Some green turtles breed and lay eggs within the Caribbean and the Gulf of Mexico

LEEWARD ISLANDS

WINDWARD ISLANDS

TURTLE FACTS

• On average, a green turtle lays eggs once every three years.

• In 1947, 40,000 Kemp's ridley turtles emerged from the sea to lay eggs on their nesting beach. Today, less than 5,000 survive.

GREEN TURTLE MIGRATION
Green turtles that feed around the coast of Brazil all return to Ascension Island to breed. Others migrate around the Caribbean and Gulf of Mexico.

SOUTH AMERICA

ASCENSION ISLAND

Some green turtles breed here

LONG ODDS
The chances of a green turtle hatchling surviving to adulthood are remote. Even if it does, it may fall victim to hunters.

PEACEFUL GRAZER
Also known as the edible turtle, the green turtle is herbivorous, mainly feeding in shallow water on a seaweed known as turtle grass.

TURTLES AND TORTOISES

THE ORIGINS of the first chelonians are obscure because there is very little fossil evidence. However, it seems likely that their ancestors belonged to an early group of reptiles known as diadectomorphs that lived in swamplands. As some of them moved farther onto the land, they acquired protective shells. Some ancestors of modern chelonians remained on land; others returned to the water.

Soft shell

Snorkel-like nose for breathing when underwater

SOFT KILLER
The shell of a soft-shelled turtle is covered in leathery skin instead of horny plates. Soft-shelled turtles are found in southern Asia, Africa, and North America. They live in rivers where they feed on water creatures, striking with lightning speed.

Fish being sucked in

FISH SUCKER
Disguised as a rock, the matamata turtle of South America lurks on the river bed patiently waiting for a fish to swim close by. When its prey approaches, it expands its throat and sucks the fish into its gaping mouth.

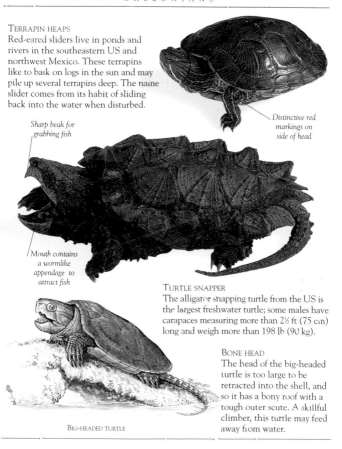

TERRAPIN HEAPS

Red-eared sliders live in ponds and
rivers in the southeastern US and
northwest Mexico. These terrapins
like to bask on logs in the sun and may
pile up several terrapins deep. The name
slider comes from its habit of sliding
back into the water when disturbed.

*Distinctive red
markings on
side of head*

*Sharp beak for
grabbing fish*

*Mouth contains
a wormlike
appendage to
attract fish*

TURTLE SNAPPER

The alligator snapping turtle from the US is
the largest freshwater turtle; some males have
carapaces measuring more than 2½ ft (75 cm)
long and weigh more than 198 lb (90 kg).

BIG-HEADED TURTLE

BONE HEAD

The head of the big-headed
turtle is too large to be
retracted into the shell, and
so it has a bony roof with a
tough outer scute. A skillful
climber, this turtle may feed
away from water.

More chelonians

Tortoises are among the most popular reptiles, being slow-moving, peaceful herbivores. Species of tortoise that have evolved in isolated places, where predators are few and competition for food is slight, may live to great ages and grow to vast sizes. Freshwater turtles are carnivorous and tend to be much more active.

RED-FOOTED TORTOISE

RED FEET
The red-footed tortoise is common in South America where it lives in rainforests. Large specimens can reach 19½ in (50 cm) in length.

PANCAKE TORTOISES
An African pancake tortoise's shell is light and flattened in shape, enabling it to move quickly and climb over rocks. It can also squeeze into small spaces when danger threatens.

PANCAKE TORTOISE

HINGE-BACK
The hinge-back tortoises of southern Africa have a hinge of cartilaginous tissue that allows the back of the shell to drop and protect the animal's rear. Hinge-backs sometimes share their burrow with lizards.

STARRED CAMOUFLAGE

The starred tortoise is found in India and Sri Lanka. It is well camouflaged; its shell blends in with dry grassland. Less than 9½ in (25 cm) long, it crawls slowly, at little over ⅛ mph (0.2 km/h).

STARRED
TORTOISE

Sturdy legs

Shell may be up to a foot (30 cm) long

SNAKE-NECK

The snake-necked turtles of Australia live in rivers, where they hunt freshwater animals. However, like all chelonians, they leave the water to lay eggs in a nest on dry land. When threatened, they fold the head back into the shell.

Neck is nearly as long as the shell

SNAKE-NECKED TURTLE

GALÁPAGOS GIANT

The lumbering giant tortoises of the Galápagos Islands weigh up to 198 lb (90 kg). They were originally present in large numbers, but predation by humans, dogs, and pigs, plus competition for food with goats, have brought about a severe decline in numbers.

GALÁPAGOS
TORTOISE

CROCODILE ANATOMY

CROCODILES AND ALLIGATORS are the only surviving reptiles from the archosaurs – the group to which the dinosaurs belonged. They are large animals with an armored skin that covers the whole body. They are usually found in freshwater rivers and lakes in warm regions of the world. Some species enter saltwater as well.

CROCODILE-
BONE
FIGURINE

CROCODILE BONE
Animal bones have often been used to make ornaments. This Egyptian figurine was carved from a crocodile bone.

NILE CROCODILE
The Nile crocodile is found in many parts of Africa, although its range has been much reduced due to hunting. It often swims out to sea, and so is also found in Madagascar.

Powerful tail

ANATOMY FACTS

• A crocodile's skin is composed of partly ossified (converted into bone) horny plates.

• Crocodilians propel themselves through the water with their powerful tail.

SKELETON
Like all crocodilians, a caiman has a long skull, with nostrils and eyes set high. The body is long with two pairs of short legs held out sideways from the body.

Hind feet with four toes

Tail vertebrae

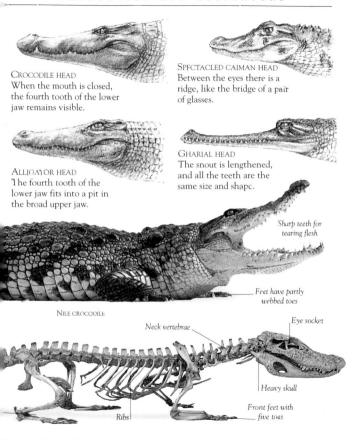

CROCODILE HEAD
When the mouth is closed, the fourth tooth of the lower jaw remains visible.

SPECTACLED CAIMAN HEAD
Between the eyes there is a ridge, like the bridge of a pair of glasses.

ALLIGATOR HEAD
The fourth tooth of the lower jaw fits into a pit in the broad upper jaw.

GHARIAL HEAD
The snout is lengthened, and all the teeth are the same size and shape.

Sharp teeth for tearing flesh

Feet have partly webbed toes

NILE CROCODILE

Neck vertebrae

Eye socket

Heavy skull

Ribs

Front feet with five toes

CROCODILES

CROCODILES ARE FOUND in many tropical parts of the world. Large species include the American crocodile and the Nile crocodile, which reach about 20 ft (6 m) in length, and the saltwater crocodile, which can exceed 23 ft (7 m). Smaller species include the mugger of Sri Lanka and India, and Johnston's crocodile of Australia.

Prominent tooth

SKULL
A crocodile's skull is almost solid bone. The jaws are long, for holding prey, but the teeth cannot slice or chew, only tear.

SALTWATER TRAVELER
The estuarine or saltwater crocodile can be found in coastal waters, in the brackish waters of estuaries, and some way inland up freshwater rivers. It is a strong swimmer, and sometimes travels long distances by sea.

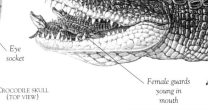

Eye socket

CROCODILE SKULL
(TOP VIEW)

Female guards young in mouth

SHARING A MEAL

In Africa, crocodiles feed mostly on antelopes, which are seized as they come near the water to drink. However, other animals are also taken, and crocodiles will feed on animals that have died, such as this zebra.

LYING IN WAIT

Even large animals, such as wildebeest, may fall victim to a crocodile attack. With a sudden rush, the crocodile grabs the prey in its jaws and drags it into the water to drown.

UNLIKELY PARTNERS

As a crocodile lies with its mouth open, to keep cool, a spur-winged plover picks food from between its teeth. This looks dangerous for the bird, but the crocodile may benefit from having its teeth cleaned and the plover's cry warns the crocodile of danger.

ESTUARINE CROCODILE

Crocodiles

An adult crocodile swallows stones, which accumulate in its stomach. The stones do not break up food, but scientists believe that they may act as ballast, allowing the animal to remain submerged under the water.

CROCODILE SKIN

NILE CROCODILE

CRACKING EGGS
When her eggs are about to hatch, the female uncovers them. She may gently crack them to help the young emerge.

SHOES AND HANDBAGS
Formerly many wild crocodiles and alligators were hunted for their skins, used for making shoes, handbags, and suitcases. Wild crocodiles are now protected, but are still illegally killed.

CROCODILE FACTS

• A saltwater crocodile arrived at the Cocos Islands in the Indian Ocean, having swum 684 miles (1,100 km).

• The ancient Egyptians worshiped a crocodile-headed god named Sebek.

ESTUARINE CROCODILE

CROCODILE TEARS
The estuarine crocodile gets rid of the excess salt it swallows with its food by excreting it via the tear glands in its eyes.

THE GHARIAL

The family Gavialidae contains just one species, the gharial, or Indian gavial. The Gavialidae is thought to have arisen during the Cretaceous period, some 100 million years ago. The modern gharial has rather weak limbs and spends nearly all its life in water, using its oar-like tail for swimming. It lives in India's Ganges, Mahanadi, Chambl, and Brahmaputra rivers, the Karnali River in Nepal, and the Koladan and Maingtha rivers in Southeast Asia.

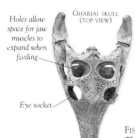

GHARIAL SKULL
(TOP VIEW)

Holes allow space for jaw muscles to expand when feeding

Eye socket

NO PROTECTION
For a long time, the gharial was protected from hunters because it was sacred to the Hindu god Vishnu. Today, however, it is illegally hunted for its skin.

FISH FEEDER
The gharial feeds entirely on fish. It lies in wait, moving its head from side to side to cover a large area, and catches its prey with a sudden jerk of its head.

LONG SNOUT
The main characteristic of the gharial is its long snout. At the tip it widens into an oval area that bears the nostrils; in males this region is bulbous. Each jaw contains more than 50 sharp teeth.

Nasal opening

ALLIGATORS AND CAIMANS

ALLIGATORS AND CAIMANS have shorter snouts than crocodiles, and they live solely in freshwater. There are two species of alligator, the American alligator and the rare Chinese alligator. The six species of caiman are all found in the Americas, ranging from Mexico down through much of South America.

SECURE FUTURE
American alligators were once killed in large numbers for their skins, but since they became a protected species in the 1960s, their populations have recovered. Today, they are the only crocodilians not endangered in the wild.

AMERICAN ALLIGATOR

Males bellow during breeding season to attract females

SKULL
An alligator's skull is shorter and broader than a crocodile's. The fearsome jaws can carry young with surprising delicacy.

HUNTED DOWN
American alligators are opportunist feeders, taking whatever they can, including fish, snakes, turtles, mammals, and waterbirds snatched from low branches.

CAIMAN ENEMIES

Adult spectacled caimans have few natural enemies, apart from anacondas, which can devour caimans up to 6½ ft (2 m) long, and egg-thieves such as tegu lizards, which raid their nests.

Caimans can move surprisingly quickly on land

The caiman may use its hind foot to scratch its body, rub its eyes, and tear its food

Caimans hiss when threatened

ALLIGATOR YOUNG

Alligators are 8 in (20 cm) long at hatching. They grow 1 ft (30 cm) each year, reaching maturity at six. The young are vulnerable to predators, including mammals, birds, and fish and, at any stage, may be eaten by other alligators.

YOUNG ALLIGATORS

Adults may catch raccoons and small deer

ALLIGATOR FACTS

• The English word "alligator" comes from the Spanish for lizard, "el largato".

• The Chinese alligator is nearly extinct in the wild due to hunting and the destruction of its habitat.

LIZARD ANATOMY

THE FIRST LIZARDS appeared 200 million years ago, in the Triassic period. They fed on insects and looked similar to modern lizards. Typically, a lizard has a broad head, a long, slender body with limbs held out sideways, and a long tail. However, there are more specialized forms, such as chameleons and legless lizards.

ANATOMY OF A
FEMALE LIZARD

Heart

Lungs

Ovary

Intestine

Opening
of cloaca

INTERNAL ANATOMY
A lizard's body is symmetrically arranged both externally and internally. As in nearly all reptiles, the heart has three chambers and the gut, oviduct, and ureter empty into a common chamber, the cloaca.

UNUSUAL LIZARD
A chameleon does not have the flexible spine of most lizards. In addition, its legs are proportionately longer, and it can raise its body higher than other lizards.

Spine is less
flexible than
other lizards'

Prehensile tail
for gripping
onto branches

CHAMELEON SKELETON

Broad body
with many ribs

Toes designed
for grasping

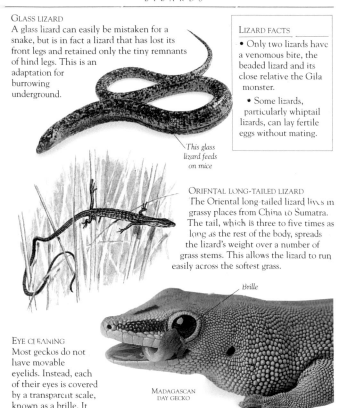

GLASS LIZARD

A glass lizard can easily be mistaken for a snake, but is in fact a lizard that has lost its front legs and retained only the tiny remnants of hind legs. This is an adaptation for burrowing underground.

This glass lizard feeds on mice

LIZARD FACTS

• Only two lizards have a venomous bite, the beaded lizard and its close relative the Gila monster.

• Some lizards, particularly whiptail lizards, can lay fertile eggs without mating.

ORIENTAL LONG-TAILED LIZARD

The Oriental long-tailed lizard lives in grassy places from China to Sumatra. The tail, which is three to five times as long as the rest of the body, spreads the lizard's weight over a number of grass stems. This allows the lizard to run easily across the softest grass.

Brille

EYE CLEANING

Most geckos do not have movable eyelids. Instead, each of their eyes is covered by a transparent scale, known as a brille. It keeps this clean by licking it.

MADAGASCAN
DAY GECKO

2 1 9

HOW LIZARDS FEED

SOME LIZARDS eat almost anything; others, such as the plant-eating Galápagos iguanas, have a specialized diet. Many lizards prey on insects, and some of them also eat vegetable matter. Some species prey on other animals, such as birds, small mammals, and other lizards.

VEGETARIAN
The Galápagos land iguana feeds only on plants, particularly the fleshy leaves and fruits of the prickly pear cactus. It deals with the spines by working the food around in its mouth until they break off.

GALÁPAGOS LAND IGUANA

CHAMELEON

Insect trapped in sticky mucus

Muscular tongue is as long as the lizard's body

STICKY TONGUE
A chameleon moves very slowly and deliberately toward its potential prey. When within range, it shoots out its long, muscular tongue at incredible speed. The insect is trapped on the end of the lizard's sticky tongue and drawn into its mouth.

EYED LIZARD

CATCHING INSECTS

The eyed lizard feeds on insects, small birds, rodents, other lizards, and some fruits. A large prey item is shaken rapidly to stun it and then passed to the back of the lizard's mouth. It is then crushed by the jaws in a series of rapid, powerful snaps.

The eyed lizard is native to southern Europe and North Africa

ANT EATER

Despite its fierce appearance, the Australian thorny devil, or moloch, lives solely on ants, which it eats in large quantities. It obtains much of its water from dew, which condenses on its spines and runs into its mouth.

THORNY DEVIL

KOMODO DRAGON

PREDATORY DRAGON

The huge Komodo dragon is a large monitor lizard found only on a few Indonesian islands. The lizard mostly eats carrion, but it is capable of catching and killing animals up to the size of a big deer.

FEEDING FACTS

• The caiman lizards of South America feed almost exclusively on marsh snails.

• The Galápagos marine iguana eats only seaweed, which it grazes from the seabed, sometimes diving for long periods to feed.

THE WORLD'S LIZARDS

BECAUSE THEY ARE COLD-BLOODED and use their
environment to maintain body temperature, lizards prefer
warm climates. Thus most species occur in
tropical and subtropical regions. There are
17–26 recognized families (different
experts have different opinions),
the largest being the skinks
(about 1,000 species), the
geckos (800 species), and
the agamids (300 species).

*Large toes with
hooked pads*

GECKO

MARINE IGUANA

OCEAN-LOVING LIZARD
The Galápagos marine
iguana uses its robust,
flattened tail to swim in
coastal waters. It has
glands in its nose for
excreting excess salt
taken in from seawater.

HOUSE GUEST
Pads on the
gecko's feet help it
cling to any surface.
Geckos can often be seen
hunting for insects on
walls in the tropics.

LIZARD FACTS

• Some lizards, such
as the common
lizard and slow worm
of Britain, do live in
temperate climates.

• On some West
Indian islands, there
can be more than
20,000 anole lizards
per hectare.

MADAGASCAN
DAY GECKO

FOREST
DWELLER
This gecko's
bright green coloration
is perfect camouflage for its
home – the forests of
Madagascar. Unlike most
geckos, it hunts during the day.

IN THE JUNGLE
Some rain forest iguanas are slender animals with long toes. Males are often larger and more brightly colored than females. In some species, the colors become more apparent during the breeding season.

PLUMED BASILISK
The most spectacular species of basilisk is the plumed basilisk of Central America, which has a sail-like crest along its head and back. The male displays its crest during the breeding season.

PLUMED BASILISK

Long hind legs

ON WATER
Basilisks are found in Central and South America, near streams and lakes. Their splayed feet and long tails enable them to run across the surface of the water.

WHIPLASH DEFENSE
The green iguana lives in Central and South America. It defends itself by lashing out with its claws and long, whiplike tail. There are about 30 species of iguana.

GREEN IGUANA

The Agamid family

Agamids, of which there are about 300 species, are found in central, south, and Southeast Asia, Australia, and Africa. The only species found in Europe is the starred lizard, or hardun, which lives on some Greek islands, in North Africa, and in southwest Asia. Many species spend their lives in the branches of trees, but agamids have adapted to a wide range of habitats. Some species live at high altitudes; *Laudakia tubercula* is found on Himalayan slopes at 11,000 ft (3,300 m).

GARDEN LIZARD

BLOODSUCKER
Like a chameleon, the garden lizard, or bloodsucker, can change color rapidly. It is found in India, Afghanistan, and China.

Large scales protect underside of jaw

BEARDED DRAGON
Some seven species of Australian lizard are known as bearded dragons because of the long, pointed scales on their throats.

BEARDED DRAGON

THORNY DEVIL

Spines provide excellent defense

HOT AND SPINY
The thorny devil, or moloch, is an Australian desert dweller. It allows its body to heat up to an almost lethal temperature so that it can spend as much time as possible feeding in the open.

SPINY TAIL
Spiny-tailed lizards tolerate very
high temperatures and are among
the hardiest lizards of the African
Sahara. They feed on plants
and insects and
survive on the
moisture they
obtain from their
food and from dew.

*Channels between
scales guide water
condensed from
the air toward
the mouth*

*"Eyebrows"
protect eyes
from twigs and
leaves*

*Spiny tail is
used for defense
and acts as a
fat store*

SPINY-TAILED
LIZARD

*Dorsal crest
of pointed
scales*

PRICKLY NECK
The pricklenape agama
lives high in the trees in
mountain forests from China
to Indonesia. Its name comes
from the long, sharp spines on
its neck. Its long toes have
fringed scales that help it
cling to branches.

PRICKLENAPE AGAMA

WATER DRAGON
The Thai water dragon lives mainly in trees
beside rivers and lakes. It usually basks on
a branch overhanging the water. When
threatened by a predator, it simply drops
from its branch into the water
and swims away.

THAI WATER
DRAGON

*Long rear legs for
rapid movement*

More lizards of the world

Many lizards are specially adapted for particular environments. A chameleon's body, for example, is greatly modified for living in trees. The body is flattened from side to side, a shape that helps the reptile avoid the heat of the sun during the hottest part of the day, but absorb heat in the early morning and late evening. It also helps to camouflage the body and makes it easier to balance on the branches of trees.

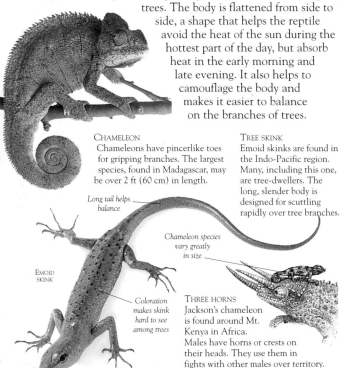

CHAMELEON
Chameleons have pincerlike toes for gripping branches. The largest species, found in Madagascar, may be over 2 ft (60 cm) in length.

TREE SKINK
Emoid skinks are found in the Indo-Pacific region. Many, including this one, are tree-dwellers. The long, slender body is designed for scuttling rapidly over tree branches.

Long tail helps balance

Chameleon species vary greatly in size

EMOID SKINK

Coloration makes skink hard to see among trees

THREE HORNS
Jackson's chameleon is found around Mt. Kenya in Africa. Males have horns or crests on their heads. They use them in fights with other males over territory.

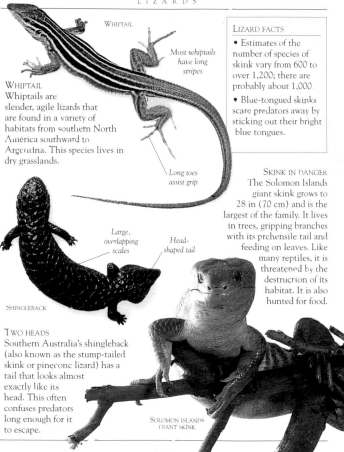

WHIPTAIL

Most whiptails have long stripes

WHIPTAIL
Whiptails are slender, agile lizards that are found in a variety of habitats from southern North America southward to Argentina. This species lives in dry grasslands.

Long toes assist grip

LIZARD FACTS
• Estimates of the number of species of skink vary from 600 to over 1,200; there are probably about 1,000.
• Blue-tongued skinks scare predators away by sticking out their bright blue tongues.

Large, overlapping scales

Head-shaped tail

SHINGLEBACK

SKINK IN DANGER
The Solomon Islands giant skink grows to 28 in (70 cm) and is the largest of the family. It lives in trees, gripping branches with its prehensile tail and feeding on leaves. Like many reptiles, it is threatened by the destruction of its habitat. It is also hunted for food.

TWO HEADS
Southern Australia's shingleback (also known as the stump-tailed skink or pinecone lizard) has a tail that looks almost exactly like its head. This often confuses predators long enough for it to escape.

SOLOMON ISLANDS GIANT SKINK

Lizard protection

For a small animal that lives in the open, a scaly skin affords only limited protection, and so some lizards have additional protective features. Girdle-tailed lizards and their relatives are well armored, and the armadillo lizard makes good defensive use of its spines. The beaded lizard and the Gila monster defend themselves with venom, while some monitor lizards find protection in their sheer size.

Hissing warns off an attacker

ON GUARD
Gould's monitor uses its tail as a third hind leg to threaten an attacker or simply raise itself up and survey its surroundings. Monitors include a number of large lizards, and 20 of the 30 known species are Australian.

GOULD'S MONITOR

Thick scales protect body

Male is brightly colored during the breeding season

Food consists mostly of insects, with some plant material

STUCK FAST
The girdled lizards of southern Africa live in rock crevices. When threatened, a girdled lizard inflates its body, jamming it into a crevice and making it impossible for a predator to pry out.

Female lays a few eggs in a communal nesting site

GIRDLED LIZARD
(ALSO CALLED ZONURE
OR FLAT LIZARD)

ARMOR PLATING
The plated lizards of Africa have an armored covering of large rectangular scales arranged in rows down the body. The body is thus fairly rigid, and to allow for expansion after a meal, there is a deep pleat of skin that runs from the angle of the jaw to the hind limbs.

Thick scales protect body

LIZARD FACTS
• The Gila monster feeds on birds' eggs, birds, and young mammals. It can eat a third of its body weight at one time

• The giant girdle-tailed lizard plugs its burrow with its tail.

Body is about 1 ft (30 cm) long but only ½ in (1 cm) thick

Inward fold of skin

Belly protected by spiky head and tail

BALL OF PRICKLES
The African armadillo lizard has an unusual method of defense, reminiscent of that of an armadillo. It curls itself up and grasps its tail in its mouth, presenting an attacker with a prickly problem.

GILA MONSTER
The Gila (pronounced "heela") monster of the southwestern US is one of only two venomous lizards. The venom glands are in the lower jaw; in snakes, they are in the upper jaw. The glands discharge venom into the mouth, and large, grooved teeth channel it into an opponent's wound when the lizard bites.

Pink and black coloration warns reptile is poisonous

TUATARAS

THE TWO SPECIES OF TUATARA look like lizards, but they have a different structure to their skeleton and skull. Tuataras are the sole survivors of the rhynchocephalians, a group of primitive reptiles that thrived between 100 and 200 million years ago, during the Jurassic and Triassic periods.

"Tuatara" is Maori for "peaks on the back"

LIVING FOSSIL
Tuataras are called living fossils because they have changed little in 200 million years. All their closest relatives died out; no one knows why tuataras alone survived.

FOSSILIZED RELATIVE
Homoeosaurus, an extinct relative of tuataras, lived about 140 million years ago. Rhynchocephalians were widespread and successful at the time.

LONG LIFE
Male tuataras grow to about 2 ft (61 cm) long; females are slightly shorter. Both sexes reach sexual maturity at the age of 20, and may live for another 100 years.

MALE TUATARA

Short, powerful legs for burrowing

A third, or pineal, eye under the skin may act as a thermostat or help to regulate the tuatara's "biological clock"

Crest runs down the back and tail

FEMALE TUATARA

A LONG WAIT
After mating, a female tuatara stores the male's sperm for 10–12 months before fertilization occurs. She then lays 5–15 eggs in a shallow burrow.

SKULL STRUCTURE
The tuatara skull is very different from that of a lizard. It resembles a crocodile's in having two bony arches at the back. Most lizards have just one arch, while in burrowing lizards and snakes the arches have disappeared.

Teeth are fused with the jaws

Two bony arches

Tuatara has large, wedge-shaped teeth at the front

TUATARA SKULL

ISLAND HOME
Tuataras are found on a few small islands off the coast of New Zealand. They live in burrows (which they often share with seabirds) and are active at night, when they come out to search for insects and earthworms. They grow very slowly.

TUATARA FACTS

• Eggs hatch 15 months after laying – the longest incubation period of any reptile.

• A tuatara breathes very slowly, about once every seven seconds, and can hold its breath for nearly an hour.

SNAKE ANATOMY

SNAKES ARE PROBABLY descended from burrowing
lizards that gradually lost their legs as they adapted to
an underground life. Today's snakes do not generally
live underground, but they
have retained their
ancestral form and
found new ways of
getting around.

RHINOCEROS VIPER

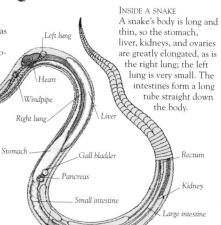

VENOMOUS RHINO
Like all snakes, the deadly
African rhinoceros viper has
a long, legless body. Its
name comes from the rhino-
like "horns" (actually long
scales) on its nose.

INSIDE A SNAKE
A snake's body is long and
thin, so the stomach,
liver, kidneys, and ovaries
are greatly elongated, as is
the right lung; the left
lung is very small. The
intestines form a long
tube straight down
the body.

Left lung

Heart

Windpipe

Right lung

Liver

Stomach

Gall bladder

Rectum

Pancreas

Kidney

Small intestine

Large intestine

Ovaries

ANATOMY OF A
FEMALE SNAKE

SNAKE FACTS

• The longest snakes
have skeletons with
some 400 vertebrae.

• King cobras may be
able to detect some
airborne sounds.

• Some snakes use part
of the windpipe as an
extra lung.

SNAKE SKELETON
A snake has a very long, flexible backbone, made up of at least 180 vertebrae. All the neck and trunk vertebrae have strong ribs, which are not attached at the front so that the snake is free to swallow large items of food.

Neck vertebrae

Trunk vertebrae

Skull

Tail vertebrae

Ribs

Backward-pointing teeth help move prey down the gullet

PYTHON SKELETON

SNAKE SKULL AND JAWS

Joints loosely held together by ligaments

Lower jaw bones are not joined

SNAKE SKULL
The upper jaw is loosely attached to the rest of the skull, and the two halves of the lower jaw are separated. This makes a wide opening possible for swallowing prey whole.

TEMPTATION
Because of their slithery nature, snakes have long been regarded as evil. In the Bible, a snake tempted Eve to eat from the Tree of Knowledge, destroying her innocence and causing her and Adam to be banished from the Garden of Eden.

THE SERPENT TEMPTS EVE

233

CONSTRICTORS

BOAS AND PYTHONS are constricting snakes – they kill by wrapping prey so tightly in their strong body coils that the animal suffocates. Their victims are usually mammals, but many constrictors kill birds as well, and some are known to prey on other reptiles.

The coils tighten each time the rat breathes out

BALL PYTHON

DEADLY SQUEEZE
This West African ball python is killing its prey, a rat, by coiling itself around the animal's chest and gradually tightening its grip. Soon, the rat will not be able to inhale, and it will die from suffocation.

BIRDS BEWARE
Tree boas hunt birds by creeping up on them as they roost in the branches of trees; mammals are also eaten. The emerald tree boa lives in the lush rain forests of the Amazon basin.

EMERALD TREE BOA

PRIMITIVE SNAKES

Scientists call pythons, boas, and some other species "primitive" because these snakes have tiny claws where the hind legs and hips of their lizard ancestors once were. The claws lie on either side of the cloaca. Males use them to stimulate females into mating.

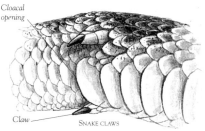

Cloacal opening

Claw

SNAKE CLAWS

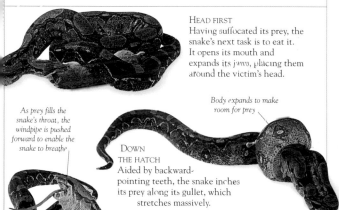

HOW A CONSTRICTOR CONSUMES ITS PREY

HEAD FIRST
Having suffocated its prey, the snake's next task is to eat it. It opens its mouth and expands its jaws, placing them around the victim's head.

As prey fills the snake's throat, the windpipe is pushed forward to enable the snake to breathe

Body expands to make room for prey

DOWN THE HATCH
Aided by backward-pointing teeth, the snake inches its prey along its gullet, which stretches massively.

TIME TO DIGEST
Eventually, the prey is completely swallowed. The snake may take several days to digest its meal.

Boas

Most species of boa are found in the Americas and the Caribbean, although boas can also be found in Africa, Madagascar, Europe, and the Pacific region. These constrictors have adapted to a wide variety of habitats. Many spend their lives in trees, while a number of others live on the ground or burrow into it.

RUSCHENBERGER'S TREE BOA

RAINBOW COLORS
The dazzlingly iridescent rainbow boa lives in the forests, woodlands, and grassy plains of northwestern South America. It feeds on small mammals and birds.

RAINBOW BOA

BOA CONSTRICTOR
The red-tailed boa is one of 10 subspecies of boa constrictor. It grows to an average of 10 ft (3 m) in length (although snakes over 13 ft [4 m] have been seen), and lives in the semidesert plains of northwestern Peru.

RED-TAILED BOA

RUSCHENBERGER'S TREE BOA
This snake is the largest of the four species of South American tree boa. The highly sensitive heat pits on the boa's lips enable it to hunt warm-blooded animals in total darkness, and even to catch bats in flight.

SOLOMON ISLANDS GROUND BOA

BOA FACTS

• When a rubber boa is threatened, it rolls itself into a ball, hides its head among its coils, and presents its tail toward the intruder.
• Boas do not hatch from eggs. Instead, females give birth to live young.

AMAZON TREE BOA

SOLOMON ISLANDS GROUND BOA
Found in the rainforests and plantations of islands in the southwestern Pacific, this nocturnal snake lives and hunts on the ground. It is relatively inactive, and spends most of the time hidden under logs or leaf litter waiting to ambush prey.

AGILE TREE DWELLER
This South American tree boa, or garden boa, uses its prehensile tail to cling to the branches of trees. Although the Amazon tree boa is not venomous, it can inflict a painful bite.

RUBBER ROBBER
The North American rubber boa lives in woodlands and meadows, where it hunts among fallen logs, in crevices, or down burrows. It also climbs trees to steal young birds from their nests. This snake looks and feels rubbery, hence its name.

RUBBER BOA

More constrictors

Pythons, from Australasia, Africa, and Asia, and anacondas (aquatic boas), from South America, are some of the world's biggest snakes. On very rare occasions, anacondas, rock pythons, and reticulated pythons have been known to attack people. But eating such a huge meal is risky, since the snake is defenseless for at least a week while it digests its food.

Distinctive "piano key" lip markings

D'ALBERTIS PYTHON

HUNTER IN THE TREES
D'Albertis python, which can reach 8 ft (2.4 m) long, hunts small mammals at night. It lives in New Guinea and on neighboring islands in a range of habitats, but prefers damp environments such as monsoon forests and rainforests.

LARGEST PYTHON
The reticulated python of Southeast Asia is well camouflaged for life on the forest floor. It may grow to 33 ft (10 m) in length, making it the longest snake in the world. It feeds on mammals, lizards and the occasional snake.

RETICULATED PYTHON

SHORT AND BLOODY
The blood python, or short-tailed python, gets its name from its colorful camouflage markings. It is also known as the short python because its tail is much shorter than those of other species. It lives in wet places on the central and southern Malay peninsula, and on the islands of Borneo and Sumatra.

BLOOD PYTHON

HUNTED FOR ITS SKIN
The Indian python lives in a wide range of habitats, feeding on mammals, birds, and reptiles. It is now an endangered species because people have slaughtered it for its skin and destroyed much of its natural habitat.

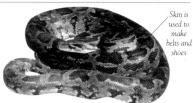

Skin is used to make belts and shoes

INDIAN PYTHON

ANACONDAS

YELLOW ANACONDA

SWAMP SNAKE
The yellow anaconda lives in swamps and marshes and on the banks of rivers and streams in Brazil, Bolivia, Paraguay, and Argentina. At 11½ ft (3.5 m) in length, it is about half the size of the common anaconda.

RECORD HOLDER
The common anaconda is probably the world's largest snake, being heavier than its rival for the title, the reticulated python. The average adult length is about 20 ft (6 m), although individuals of over 26 ft (8 m) have been seen. It is found in Trinidad and many parts of tropical South America.

COMMON
ANACONDA

COLUBRID SNAKES

ABOUT THREE-QUARTERS of the world's snakes – over 2,000 species – belong to the colubrid family. Some are venomous, but a large number are completely harmless. Among the harmless ones are kingsnakes, water snakes, ratsnakes, egg-eating snakes, and the grass snake.

CALIFORNIA KINGSNAKE

VARIABLE PATTERNS
The colors and patterns of California kingsnakes vary greatly – individuals may be cross-banded or have stripes running down the body. Kingsnakes eat a wide range of small animals, including venomous snakes.

Markings look similar to a coral snake's

CALIFORNIA MOUNTAIN KINGSNAKE

COLUBRID FACTS

• The Japanese ratsnake, or Aodaisho, is considered to be an earthly form of a fertility goddess called Benzai-ten.

• Scientists call colubrids "typical" snakes.

MOUNTAIN KINGS
California mountain kingsnakes prey on small animals, including rodents, lizards, and nestling birds. When not hunting, they often hide under stones, logs, or piles of leaves. They come from the west coast of the US.

MILK DRINKER?
The milksnake is a species of kingsnake; there are 25 subspecies. The name comes from the popular but totally incorrect belief that they take milk from cows. This subspecies occurs in Mexico, where it preys mostly on rodents, killing them by constriction.

SINALOAN MILKSNAKE

Colored bands mimic those of a poisonous coral snake

Markings resemble the patterns on an ear of corn

The shy corn snake uses logs and tree stumps for cover

CAPE FILESNAKE
This snake is widespread in east and southern and east Africa, but rarely seen. An inhabitant of savanna grassland and coastal woodland, the Cape filesnake is a deadly predator of other snakes, including venomous species. It is harmless to humans.

Triangular body shape

CORN SNAKE

CAPE FILESNAKE

CITY SLICKER
The natural suroundings of corn snakes, also called red ratsnakes, are woodlands in the southeastern US, where they prey on rodents and lizards. But these snakes are also sometimes found in towns and cities. They are popular as pets, and if they escape they often manage to survive on a diet of urban mice.

More colubrid snakes

Nonvenomous colubrid snakes kill either by constriction or by overpowering and swallowing the victim. For defense, they usually rely on camouflage and the ability to escape quickly. Many will try to scare off attackers by vibrating their tails against leaves. Bullsnakes inflate their bodies to make a prolonged aggressive hiss, while red-tailed racers puff themselves up to appear more formidable.

Flowerlike patterns give this snake its Chinese name

MOELLENDORFF'S RATSNAKE

FLOWERY SNAKE
Moellendorff's ratsnake, known poetically as the "hundred flower snake" in Chinese, comes from southeastern China, where it feeds on rodents and birds.

VIPERINE WATERSNAKE

Markings look like an adder's

COLUBRID FACTS

• When threatened ratsnakes vibrate their tails, they are often mistaken for rattlesnakes.

• In the US, farmers sometimes use bullsnakes to catch rats and mice in barns.

HARMLESS VIPER
The viperine watersnake from Spain has warning markings that resemble those of a venomous adder. It is actually completely harmless, like all other watersnakes, although it may launch mock strikes with its mouth closed. A good swimmer, the viperine watersnake feeds on fish and frogs.

BAT CATCHER
The fast-moving red-tailed racer lives in the rainforests of Southeast Asia. It preys on birds and small mammals, including bats, which it catches as they fly out to feed. If threatened, it inflates its body to look larger than normal.

RED-TAILED RACER

SPECIAL SPIKES
The egg-eating snake's backbone has about 30 ventral spikes, which are used for breaking up eggs inside the snake's body.

EGG-EATER'S SPINE

Ventral spikes

EGG-EATER
Egg-eating snakes are virtually toothless and have unusually elastic skins. This enables them to swallow a whole egg, which is crushed inside the body. About 15 minutes later, the snake ejects the shell remains from its mouth.

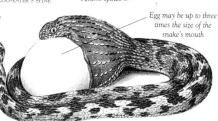

Egg may be up to three times the size of the snake's mouth

AFRICAN EGG-EATING SNAKE

VENOMOUS SNAKES

VENOM – a poisonous fluid produced by an animal – is widely used for killing or incapacitating prey. Snake venom, which is a very complex substance, serves two main purposes. First, the poison quickly subdues a prey animal, thus reducing the risk to the snake of injury from retaliation. At the same time, chemicals within the venom start to break down the prey's tissues, making digestion easier.

KING COBRA

FIXED FANGS
Cobras have fixed fangs at the front of the mouth, as do kraits, sea snakes, coral snakes, the taipan, and the tiger snake.

WARNING RATTLE
A rattlesnake is a typical front-fanged snake. As it opens its mouth the snake rotates its fangs forwards, ready to inject venom. The snake's first line of defense is to vibrate its rattle. If that does not deter the attacker, it delivers a deadly bite.

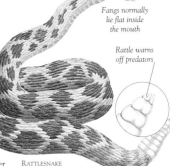

Fangs are in forward position, ready to strike

Fangs normally lie flat inside the mouth

Rattle warns off predators

RATTLESNAKE

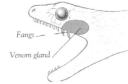

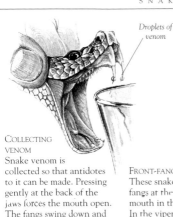

REAR-FANGED SNAKES
In snakes with fixed fangs at the back of the mouth, venom drains from glands down grooves in the front of each fang.

COLLECTING VENOM
Snake venom is collected so that antidotes to it can be made. Pressing gently at the back of the jaws forces the mouth open. The fangs swing down and produce drops of venom.

Droplets of venom

FRONT-FANGED SNAKES
These snakes have a pair of fangs at the front of the mouth in the upper jaw. In the viper and cobra families, the fangs are hollow tubes through which venom is pumped.

VENOMOUS FACTS
• The king cobra is the only snake that builds a nest in which to place its eggs.

• The eastern diamondback is the largest rattlesnake. It can grow to about 8 ft (2.5 m).

VARIABLE VIPERS
The bush vipers of Central Africa are found in rainforests, open woodland, and swamps. Their coloration is extremely variable and may be anything from pale green to reddish brown.

REAR-FANGED SNAKES

SNAKES WITH FANGS in the back of their mouth are found in both the Old and New Worlds, and, as with other groups of snakes, they vary greatly in color, size, and habitat. They are not as efficient as front-fanged snakes at injecting venom, and so most species are harmless to humans. Large rear-fanged snakes, however, can be dangerous.

Large, light-gray eyes with vertical pupils resemble those of cats

FOREST DWELLER
The false coral snake preys on lizards, small mammals, and other small snakes. It is found in the forests of Central America, from Venezuela to Costa Rica.

FALSE CORAL SNAKE

Colors are similar to those of the more dangerous coral snakes

MANGROVE SNAKE
In the mangrove swamps of the Malay Peninsula, this long snake – adults grow to over 6½ ft (2 m) – preys on a wide variety of small animals. Its large head and mouth enable it to swallow birds' eggs and even squirrels.

BLUNT-HEADED TREESNAKE

LIZARD HUNTER
The blunt-headed tree snake is found
in trees and shrubs from southern
Mexico to Bolivia and Paraguay. It is
active by night and feeds mostly on
lizards such as anoles and geckos.

PARROT
SNAKE

*Gaping mouth
is a warning
to enemies*

BOLD BITER
When threatened, a parrot
snake raises its head and opens its
mouth. This is no idle threat, since
parrot snakes are very aggressive and
will bite readily. They hunt lizards
and amphibians in
the dense foliage of
the rainforests
of Central and
South America.

TREETOP KILLER
The green catsnake lives
in the forests of Southeast
Asia. It hunts at night for
lizards, other snakes, and
small mammals, which it
easily subdues with a
combination of
venom and
constriction.

*Slender and camouflaged
for life in the treetops*

GREEN
CATSNAKE

More rear-fanged snakes

Many rear-fanged snakes use weak venom to kill small animals such as lizards or frogs. Sometimes the venom is specific to a particular prey – the venom of a snake that usually eats frogs may be more toxic to frogs than to other animals, such as mice. Some rear-fanged species have stronger venom. The boomslang and the African twigsnake, for example, occasionally kill people.

HOG-NOSED BURROWER
The Madagascan giant hognose snake eats birds and small mammals. It shelters in rock crevices, beneath debris, or in burrows that it digs. It lives in grassland and grows to about 5 ft (1.5 m) in length.

When threatened, this snake flattens its neck like a cobra and hisses loudly

MADAGASCAN
GIANT HOGNOSE
SNAKE

SONORAN LYRE
SNAKE

REAR-FANGED FACTS
• The mussurana first constricts its prey, and then injects venom into it.

• The Australasian brown tree snake, introduced into Guam, has caused the decline of many native birds.

LYRE HEAD
Lyre snakes get their name from the lyre-shaped marking on the head. They live in rocky places in California, Arizona, and Mexico, feeding on lizards, small birds, and mammals. They are nocturnal.

FROG-EATER

The American cat-eyed snake spends most of its time in trees and hunts at night for frogs and lizards. It often feeds on eggs laid on leaves by frogs. Cat-eyed snakes are found from the US down into northern South America.

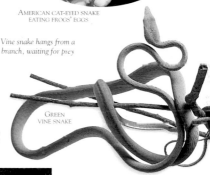

AMERICAN CAT-EYED SNAKE
EATING FROGS' EGGS

Vine snake hangs from a branch, waiting for prey

VINE CREEPER

The green vine snake's camouflage allows it to creep unseen among vines and branches. Ranging from southern Mexico to Argentina, it eats frogs, mice, and lizards, and is particularly skilled at catching birds. In some areas, it waits by flowers for hummingbirds to arrive to feed.

GREEN
VINE SNAKE

BOOMSLANG

The agile African boomslang moves with speed and grace through woodland, scrub, savanna, and swamp. It uses its quick-acting venom to kill chameleons and birds. The name boomslang is Afrikaans for "tree snake."

FRONT FANGS

FRONT-FANGED SNAKES, such as cobras, can inject venom into almost any animal, making them among the most dangerous of all reptiles. As with all venomous snakes, their venom is normally used for killing or disabling prey, but it is equally effective as a defense. However, most snakes usually prefer to escape rather than attack a predator.

HORUS
The Egyptian sky god, Horus, demonstrates his dominion over reptiles by grasping snakes and standing on a crocodile.

COBRA FACTS
• Every year, thousands of Asian cobras are killed for their skins.
• The king cobra is the world's largest venomous snake – individuals exceeding 16 ft (5 m) in length have been recorded.

RED SPITTING COBRA

Cobra rears up before spitting

VENOM SPITTER
A spitting cobra has a very effective method of defense. When threatened, and with no means of escape, it rears up and squirts a jet of poison into the attacker's eyes, causing severe pain and even permanent blindness.

FALSE-EYE MARKING
Some cobras have an eye-like marking on the back of their hood that warns off aggressors. In Chinese and monocled cobras it resembles a monocle; in the Indian cobra it looks more like glasses.

CHINESE COBRA

"Eye" is meant to deter attackers

Cobras are active at dawn and dusk

Some snake charmers remove the cobra's fangs

Cobras follow the instrument's movements

SNAKE CHARMER AND COBRAS

HOODED MENACE
All cobras have a hood, created by spreading the neck ribs as the front of the body is raised off the ground. This characteristic is particularly well developed in Asian species, such as the monocled, or Thai, cobra. The snake raises the hood to scare off enemies.

A cobra can move forward while keeping its front raised

CHARMED SNAKES
Snake charmers in Asia and North Africa have long induced cobras to "dance" to their tunes. The snakes, however, are deaf and are probably reacting to the swaying movements of the instrument, not to the music.

The hood is spread as the body is raised

MONOCLED, OR THAI, COBRA

Vipers

With their long, hollow fangs, vipers and their close relatives, the pit vipers, are among the most dangerous snakes in the world. When one of these snakes opens its mouth to bite, it swings its fangs downward and forward, ready to stab the victim. The snake has absolute control over the movement of its fangs – it can even choose to erect them one at a time.

RECORD RANGE
The adder has the greatest range of any land snake. It is found throughout Europe and Asia, as far north as the Arctic circle and eastwards through northern China to the Pacific coast.

This viper's venom is very toxic

Blunt nose gives the snake its alternative name

Depending on the climatic conditions, this viper lays eggs or gives birth to live young

LEVANT VIPER

SAND VIPER
This snake from northern Africa wriggles down into the desert sand until only its eyes are visible. From this hidden position it strikes out with lightning speed to ambush lizard prey.

SAHARAN SAND VIPER

LEVANT VIPER
Levant, or blunt-nosed, vipers, of which there are seven subspecies, are found in dry, rocky places from Georgia southward to northern Israel, Iraq, Iran, and a few of the Greek islands.

YELLOW PERIL
The eyelash viper has spiny scales above its eyes that resemble eyelashes. This tree-dwelling pit viper is found in rain forests from southern Mexico southward to Ecuador and western Venezuela. It varies in color from brown or green to lemon yellow.

EYELASH VIPER

LOOKS LIKE A VIPER...
The death, or deaf, adder looks and behaves like a viper, but is related to the cobras, coral snakes, and kraits. It lives in grassland, forest, and mountain valleys in Australia and New Guinea.

DEATH ADDER

ALL PUFFED UP
A good swimmer, the puff adder occurs in sub-Saharan Africa and Morocco, where it is found in all habitats except desert. It preys on a wide variety of animals and, like all vipers, it prefers to lie in wait for its victims. The puff adder's venom is highly toxic.

Gray and brown coloring for camouflage in dry grass

PUFF ADDER

Rattlesnakes

The distinctive features of these well-known, front-fanged snakes are the warning rattle at the end of the tail and the heat-sensitive pits on their heads (they are pit vipers). Rattlesnakes, all of which are found in the Americas, are under threat, mainly from excessive slaughter by hunters, together with the continued spread of agriculture and urban development. All rattlesnakes give birth to live young.

SOUTHERN PACIFIC
RATTLESNAKE

NEOTROPICAL
RATTLESNAKE

ADAPTABLE
The southern Pacific rattlesnake is found in rocky and sandy environments. An adaptable species, it can also survive in urban and agricultural areas. It preys mainly on rodents.

RATTLESNAKE FACTS
• Organized hunts called "rattlesnake roundups" in the US have wiped out many local populations.

• Western diamondbacks always return to the same den to hibernate.

NEOTROPICAL RATTLESNAKE
This snake lives in savanna grasslands and woodlands from Mexico down into South America. Like all rattlesnakes it gives birth to live young, producing up to 47 offspring. It does not always rattle a warning before it strikes.

RODENT CATCHER
Black-tailed rattlesnakes are found in
Mexico, Arizona, and Texas, usually
in rocky places and sometimes in
woodland and open grassland. They
may be active at any time of the day,
and they prey on small rodents.

BLACK-TAILED RATTLESNAKE

WIDE-RANGING RATTLER
The western rattlesnake has
the widest range of any
rattlesnake in North
America, being found
from southeastern
Canada to northeastern
Mexico. There are nine
subspecies – the one
shown here is the prairie
rattlesnake. It hibernates in
the winter, gathering in large
numbers in suitable den sites
such as rocky crevices or
disused animal burrows.

WESTERN
(PRAIRIE)
RATTLESNAKE

*On the prairies,
western rattlesnakes
prey mainly on
rabbits and ground
squirrels*

PYGMY RATTLER
The dusky pygmy rattlesnake lives in
dry, sandy places near water. It is active
at any time of the day or night, and it
preys on small animals, including
snakes, lizards, and large insects. It grows
to only about 20 in (50 cm) in length.

DUSKY PYGMY RATTLESNAKE

Other front-fanged snakes

Front-fanged snakes that have fixed fangs include tiger snakes, taipans, kraits, and seasnakes. Unlike true vipers and pit vipers, these snakes cannot stab their prey with their fangs and must actually bite. The cottonmouth and its close relatives, the moccasin and the copperhead, are pit vipers and are thus members of the Crotalinae, the viper subfamily that includes the rattlesnakes.

COMMON SEA KRAIT

SEA SERPENT
The sea krait is found on mangrove-fringed coasts and coral reefs in southern Asia. Highly venomous, it poses no threat to people, since it does not bite. It lays its eggs on land; true seasnakes give birth to live young at sea.

TIGER SNAKE

TOXIC TIGER
The venom of southern Australia's tiger snake is highly toxic – just 3 mg is enough to kill a human. It feeds mainly on frogs, but also kills small mammals and lizards. The tiger snake is quick to attack if disturbed.

NEVER FATAL
The American copperhead is found in open woodland, where it feeds on mice, birds, frogs, and insects. Contrary to popular belief, its bite is never fatal, although this has not stopped the widespread killing of these snakes.

Copperheads hibernate in communal dens

COPPERHEAD

WETLAND PREDATOR

The cottonmouth, also called the water moccasin, is an impressive-looking, heavy-bodied snake that lives in swamps and marshes in Alabama, Georgia, and Virginia. Its prey includes small turtles and young alligators.

COTTONMOUTH

Taipans shelter in mammal burrows, rock crevices, or under piles of forest litter

TAIPAN

DO NOT DISTURB

The taipan is a large, slender snake found in northern Australia and southern New Guinea. It shelters when not hunting, and, whenever possible, will retreat when disturbed. If cornered, however, it becomes fearsomely aggressive.

Prey consists of small mammals

Taipan is one of Australia's most dangerous snakes

COMMON KRAIT

The common, or blue, krait is a highly venomous snake found in the dry woodland plains and meadows of Bangladesh, India, and Sri Lanka. It hides during the day and at night hunts rodents, lizards, and other snakes.

FRONT-FANGED FACTS

• Young cottonmouths use the bright tip of their tail to lure prey.

• A bite from a krait is fatal in over 75 percent of cases.

• Some species of sea snake are considered to be a delicacy in the Far East.

BIRDS

WHAT IS A BIRD?

BIRDS ARE DIFFERENT from all other animals because they have feathers – usually over a thousand of them. They also have two wings, a strong bill, no teeth, scaly legs and feet, and three or four toes with claws on the end. Most birds can fly, and they are the largest, fastest, and most powerful flying animals. Like us, birds breathe air, have a skeleton inside their bodies, and are warm-blooded. Unlike us, birds lay eggs.

JUVENILE STARLING FEATHER

ADULT STARLING FEATHER

FEATHERS
Birds' feathers are light, yet strong and flexible. The feathers of young birds are often a different color from those of the adults.

Secondary flight feathers

Primary flight feathers

Rump

Upper tail coverts

Wing coverts

Under tail coverts

Ankle

Tail

STARLING

STARLING EGGS

EGGS
A bird's egg is a survival capsule that protects and nourishes a baby bird while it develops inside. When it is ready to hatch, the baby bird has to force its way out.

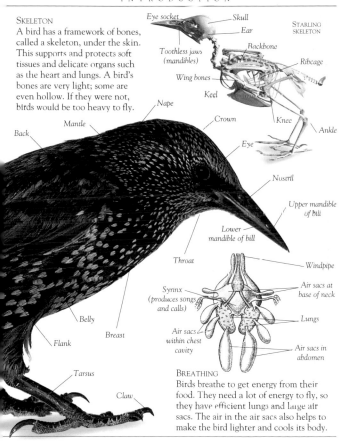

SKELETON

A bird has a framework of bones, called a skeleton, under the skin. This supports and protects soft tissues and delicate organs such as the heart and lungs. A bird's bones are very light; some are even hollow. If they were not, birds would be too heavy to fly.

STARLING SKELETON

Eye socket

Skull

Ear

Toothless jaws (mandibles)

Backbone

Wing bones

Ribcage

Keel

Knee

Ankle

Nape

Crown

Mantle

Eye

Back

Nostril

Upper mandible of bill

Lower mandible of bill

Throat

Windpipe

Syrinx (produces songs and calls)

Air sacs at base of neck

Lungs

Air sacs within chest cavity

Air sacs in abdomen

Belly

Flank

Breast

Tarsus

Claw

BREATHING

Birds breathe to get energy from their food. They need a lot of energy to fly, so they have efficient lungs and large air sacs. The air in the air sacs also helps to make the bird lighter and cools its body.

Types of birds

The huge variety of birds alive today – over 9,500 species – evolved from reptilelike creatures that climbed trees about 150 million years ago. Reptile scales developed into bird feathers, although there are still scales on a bird's legs. Now, there are birds of all shapes and sizes, from huge ostriches to tiny wrens. Some of the main types of birds are shown here.

PIGEON

PIGEONS

Most pigeons and doves have rather small heads, plump bodies, dense, soft feathers, and a powerful straight flight. They live all over the world.

ARCHAEOPTERYX

The earliest known bird was *Archaeopteryx*, which means "ancient wing." It may not have been able to fly well, but it had feathers similar to those of modern birds.

ANCIENT BIRD FACTS

• Birds are thought to be living descendants of the dinosaurs, some of which are now known to have been feathered.

• Unlike modern birds, *Archaeopteryx* had teeth.

• *Dromornis stirtoni*, the heaviest bird, was about four times heavier than an ostrich.

ZEBRA FINCHES

PERCHING BIRDS

Over half of the birds alive today are perching landbirds. Many are strong fliers and most have well-developed songs.

PARROTS
Colorful, noisy, tree-
living birds of the
tropics, parrots
have powerful,
hooked bills.

RED-AND-
GREEN
MACAW

DUCKS
These are broad-bodied
waterbirds with a wide, flat
bill, webbed feet, and
short legs set well
back on the body.

WOOD
DUCK

KING
PENGUIN

GOLDEN
EAGLE

PENGUINS
The wings of these
flightless seabirds
are modified
into flippers.

EAGLES
These
birds of prey
have a hooked
bill, strong,
sharp claws
(talons), and
long,
broad
wings.

JUVENILE
BLACK-
HEADED
GULL

GULLS
Stocky seabirds, gulls have a
strong bill, long, pointed
wings, and webbed feet.

Bird senses

Birds rely mainly on their eyes and ears to find food or a mate, to fly, and to escape from danger. Their eyes are so large that there is not much room for them to move in the skull. Instead, birds have a flexible neck and move their whole head to see things. Most birds have a poor sense of smell.

Large eyes to spot danger coming

SIGHT
A bird's huge eyes are often as big as its brain. Much of the brain deals with the information picked up by the eyes. Like us, birds see in color, but they may have better eyesight than we have.

PIED AVOCET

The avocet uses its sense of touch to catch small water creatures.

TOUCH
Some birds, such as the avocet, have a well-developed sense of touch in the tongue and bill tip. Nightjars have bristles around their broad bills to help them funnel moths into their mouths as they fly at night.

WOODCOCK EYES

To watch for danger, woodcocks have their eyes set high on the side of their head. This helps them to see all around, but there are two blind spots immediately behind and in front of the head.

Binocular vision

Blind spot

Monocular vision (can see with one eye)

Binocular vision (can see with both eyes)

HEARING

Birds hear a higher frequency of sound – more sounds per second – than we can. Good hearing is very important to birds that hunt in the dark, but all birds need to hear other birds singing so that they can communicate.

A bird breathes and smells through two openings in its bill.

BROWN KIWI

SMELL

Most birds seem to have a poor sense of smell, but there are a few exceptions. The kiwi smells food with nostrils at the tip of its long bill. The turkey vultures of the Americas can detect the smell of rotting dead animals from some distance. Some seabirds can pick up scents carried by the wind.

265

FEATHERS

A BIRD'S BODY is almost completely covered with feathers, although many birds have bare legs. Feathers keep the bird warm, give it shape, color and pattern, and help most birds to fly. Some birds have special display feathers. Feathers carry out many important jobs, so they need to be kept in good condition.

What is a feather?

There are three main types of feather – flight, body, and down. Feathers grow out of pits or follicles in a bird's skin, like the hairs all over our bodies. They can be easily smoothed because of the way the parts of the feather hook together.

Web or vane

Smooth, curved shape for flight

Shaft or rachis

MACAW FLIGHT FEATHER

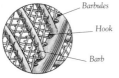

Barbules

Hook

Barb

BARBS AND BARBULES
Each side of a feather consists of parallel barbs, held in place by tiny hooks on side branches called barbules. There are many thousands of barbules on a flight feather.

FEATHER STRUCTURE
Feathers have a central shaft with a web or vane on either side. They are made of a strong, flexible material called keratin, which also forms our hair and nails.

FLIGHT FEATHERS

Found in the wings, flight feathers provide a large surface area over which air can flow. The wings' special airfoil shape (see p.273) lifts the bird into the air, and controls the way it twists and turns in flight.

PEACOCK DOWN FEATHER

Short shaft

REGENT PARROT FLIGHT FEATHERS

Long shaft

AFRICAN GRAY PARROT BODY FEATHER

Inner fluffy part to keep bird warm

Quill

DOWN FEATHERS

The soft down feathers trap warm air next to the body and are very important in young birds. The barbs are long and soft and the barbules do not hook together so the feather stays fluffy.

BODY FEATHERS

Overlapping like tiles on a roof, body feathers act as a weatherproof jacket. The inner part has softer barbs and the barbules have no hooks.

FEATHER FACTS

• Swans have 25,000 feathers, sparrows 3,500, and hummingbirds fewer than 1,000.

• The male crested argus pheasant has the longest and largest tail feathers of any wild bird at 5.7 ft (173 cm) long, 5.1 in (13 cm) wide.

• Grebes eat their own feathers, which form a soft lining in the gut and prevent damage from sharp fish bones.

Feather color

The colors of feathers are produced in two main ways.
One is by chemical pigments laid down in the feather as
it grows. The other is by the feathers' microscopic
structure affecting the way they reflect the light. Colors
help birds of the same species to recognize each other,
attract mates, threaten rivals, or camouflage themselves.

SHINING COLORS
The feathers forming the "eyes" of a male
peacock's fan are iridescent – they change
color as they move. Their barbules split
the light falling on them into different
colors. The colors you see depend
on the angle from which you
view the feathers.

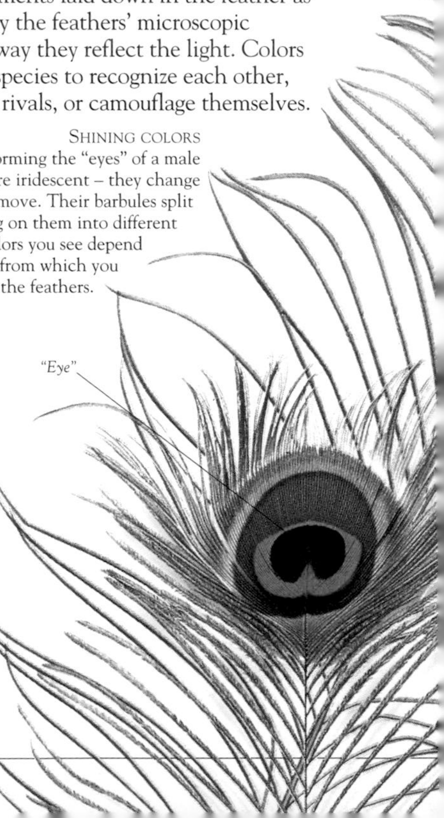

"Eye"

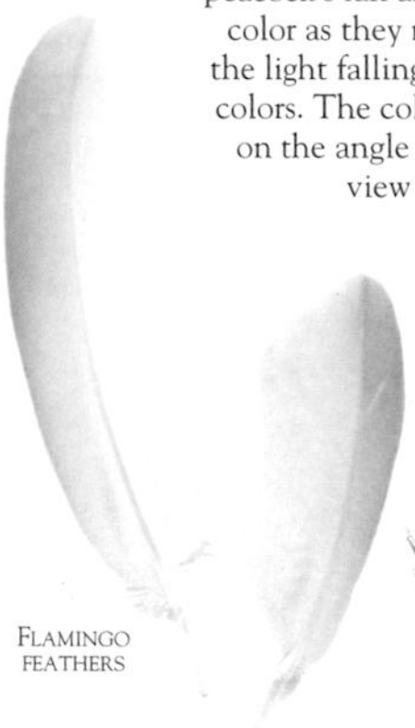

FLAMINGO
FEATHERS

FOOD COLOR
The color of flamingo
feathers comes from a
pink pigment in the
shrimps and other small
water creatures which the
birds sieve from the water.

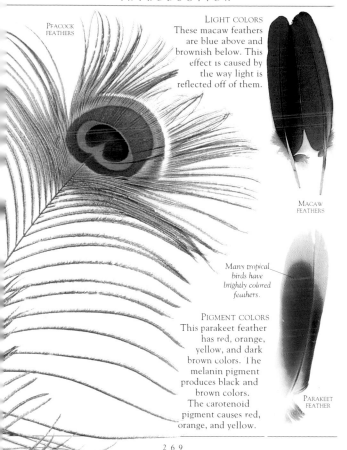

PEACOCK
FEATHERS

LIGHT COLORS
These macaw feathers are blue above and brownish below. This effect is caused by the way light is reflected off of them.

MACAW
FEATHERS

Many tropical birds have brightly colored feathers.

PIGMENT COLORS
This parakeet feather has red, orange, yellow, and dark brown colors. The melanin pigment produces black and brown colors. The carotenoid pigment causes red, orange, and yellow.

PARAKEET
FEATHER

Looking after feathers

Birds must take great care of their feathers
and spend a few hours each day preening
(cleaning and tidying
their plumage). They
use the bill to pull
ruffled feathers
into shape, and
may also take
water or dust
baths. Many
birds spread
a special oil
over their
feathers to
keep them
waterproof.

YELLOW
CANARY
PREENING

PREENING

To preen its feathers, a bird draws
each one carefully through its bill.
This fits the barbs and barbules back
into place – like pulling up a zipper –
and cleans and smooths the feathers.
Preening also removes parasites, such
as feather lice, which live on feathers
and eat them.

*Most birds use
their feet to
preen their head
feathers.*

*The oil used for preening
comes from a special
preen gland at the base of
the tail, on the rump.*

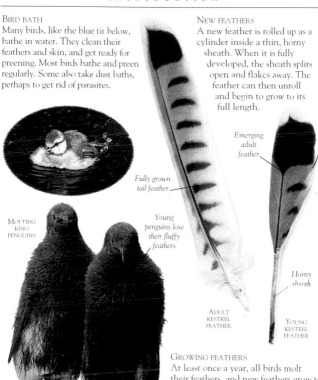

BIRD BATH
Many birds, like the blue tit below, bathe in water. They clean their feathers and skin, and get ready for preening. Most birds bathe and preen regularly. Some also take dust baths, perhaps to get rid of parasites.

NEW FEATHERS
A new feather is rolled up as a cylinder inside a thin, horny sheath. When it is fully developed, the sheath splits open and flakes away. The feather can then unroll and begin to grow to its full length.

Emerging adult feather

Fully grown tail feather

MOLTING KING PENGUINS

Young penguins lose their fluffy feathers

Horny sheath

ADULT KESTREL FEATHER

YOUNG KESTREL FEATHER

GROWING FEATHERS
At least once a year, all birds molt their feathers, and new feathers grow to replace old ones. Molting allows birds to replace worn or damaged feathers, and to change color as they grow up or the seasons change.

HOW BIRDS MOVE

TO FIND FOOD and escape danger, birds walk, run, hop, wade, swim, and dive. Most birds can also fly. They have light bones, powerful flight muscles, and an efficient respiratory system. A few birds cannot fly. Some of these flightless birds run very fast indeed.

Flight

Birds flap their wings up and forward, then down and backward. The wings' downstroke pushes the air back, and the bird moves forward. Air flowing over and under the wings creates the lifting force.

LIFT
Birds have curved wings covered with feathers to push and steer them through the air. The inner part of a bird's wing can stay still to provide lift.

TAKEOFF
A heavy bird, such as a swan, has to run while flapping its wings to get enough lift for takeoff. Smaller birds take off by jumping into the air and then flapping their wings to create lift.

TAWNY OWL

COMING IN TO LAND

To land, birds slow down in midair, then drop gently to the ground, onto a perch, or the surface of the water, spreading out their wings and tail like brakes. Heavy birds land into the wind to help slow themselves down.

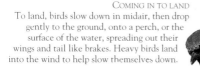

Strong legs to absorb impact of landing

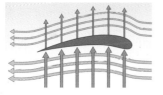

Wings and tail spread to increase air resistance and drag

BLUE-AND-WHITE FLYCATCHER

CURVED WINGS

A bird's wing is an airfoil shape – curved on top and slightly hollow underneath. The air flows faster over the top, creating low air pressure, while air pressure underneath stays much the same. The difference in pressure produces lift.

Fingerlike feathers to push and steer through the air

MUTE SWAN

Neck stretched out and feet tucked up to streamline bird's body

FLIGHT FACTS

• Common swifts may stay in the air for up to four years without landing.

• Some hummingbirds beat their wings up to 200 times a second.

• A Rüppel's griffon vulture was recorded flying at a record height of 37,000 ft (11,277 m).

• Diving peregrine falcons can reach speeds of 112 mph (180 km/h).

Flight patterns

Different types of bird have differently shaped wings. The way wings are used in flight depends on a bird's lifestyle. To save energy, some birds like gulls and vultures soar on rising air, while smaller birds glide between flaps of the wings. Ducks and other heavy birds flap their wings all the time they are in the air. Some, such as hummingbirds and kestrels, can hover in one spot.

Feathers spread apart on upstroke for air to slip through wing

UP AND DOWN FLIGHT
Small birds, like this minla, have a bounding, undulating flight. Bigger birds such as cranes, ducks, and geese tend to fly in straight lines.

RED-TAILED MINLA

Eagles thermaling

Hot air rising

Seabirds have powerful flight muscles.

GLIDING IN A THERMAL

GLIDING AND SOARING
Seabirds glide upward on air currents rising from waves or over cliffs. Some large birds, such as eagles, vultures, and storks, also use natural currents of rising hot air to lift them higher into the air. These currents are called thermals.

HOVERING
Hummingbirds can hover, move straight up or down, and even fly backward. They do this by turning each wing in a circle, and using up and down wingbeats for extra power.

HUMMINGBIRD

Unlike other birds, hummingbirds have rigid wings with a swivel joint at the shoulder.

Between flaps, wings fold against body so bird can glide and save energy

Feathers closed together on downstroke to push against the air

Tail used for steering and changing direction

GLIDING
HERRING GULL

Long, narrow wings for gliding

Feathers hug the body, creating a streamlined, aerodynamic shape that enables air to flow past more easily

WING SHAPE
The size and shape of wings give clues to how a bird lives and help with identification, especially if the bird is high in the sky.

Long and wide for soaring – vultures and some hawks

Long and narrow for gliding – fulmars and albatrosses

Wide and rounded for short, fast flight – pheasants

Narrow and pointed for fast flight – swallows and swifts

Flightless birds

A few birds do not fly at all. Some of them swim or run so well that they do not need to fly. Many flightless birds, such as ostriches, rheas, or emus, are very large birds that can run faster than their enemies, or can defend themselves so well that they do not need to fly away. Other flightless birds live on remote islands where there are few enemies from which they need to escape.

CASSOWARY AND CHICK

DEFENSE
With powerful legs and daggerlike claws, birds such as cassowaries do not need to fly away. Cassowaries even attack people, lashing out with strong feet and sharp nails.

GALAPAGOS CORMORANT

FLIGHTLESS FACTS
• The heaviest bird ever was the flightless *Dromornis stirtoni*. It died out 25,000 years ago.

• Ostriches are nearly seven times too heavy to fly. They have the biggest legs of any bird, over 4 ft (1.2 m) long.

• The Inaccessible Island rail, the world's smallest flightless bird, is the size of a newly hatched farm chick.

WINGS
Flightless birds usually have small, weak wings which are not strong enough for flight. The Galapagos cormorant uses its wings to help it balance on land.

BIRDS IN DANGER
The kakapo is the heaviest of the parrots. Like many flightless birds, kakapos are threatened by cats and rats that people have introduced to their island homes.

KAKAPO

GREATER RHEA

FAST RUNNERS

Running away from danger can be just as effective as flying. Rheas can sprint faster than a horse, reaching speeds of 31 mph (50 km/h), and are also good swimmers. Rheas are related to ostriches and emus and follow a similar lifestyle, but they live on the South American grasslands, rather than on the grasslands of Africa or Australia.

Fluffy wings used for display, not flight

Long neck to see over tall grasses

HUMBOLDT PENGUIN

FAST SWIMMERS

Penguins are so well suited to their life in the sea that they look more like fish when they swim. They use their wings as flippers for swimming, while their feet and tail steer like a rudder.

Large leg muscles provide power for running

Three strong toes on each foot for defense and for running fast

LEGS AND FEET

BIRDS USE their legs and feet for moving around and, in some bird groups, for holding food. The size and shape of their feet depends on where they live and how they feed.

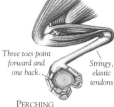

Three toes point forward and one back.

Stringy, elastic tendons

PERCHING
Birds that perch can sleep without falling off a branch. They bend their legs, pulling the tendons tight and drawing in the toes. This locks their feet tightly around the perch.

TAWNY OWL TALON

TALONS
Birds of prey, such as owls and eagles, have strong, sharp, curved claws called talons. They use these to catch, carry, and often kill prey.

Long toes are spread wide

WATTLED JACANA

Lobe of skin along each toe

WIDE TOES
Some water birds, such as coots, have lobes

COOT TOES

of skin on each toe. When spread, the lobes push aside the water for faster swimming and help stop the coot from sinking into mud.

LONG TOES
Jacanas, or lily trotters, have very long, thin toes. These spread the weight of the bird over a bigger area so it can "trot" across lily pads on the ponds and lakes where it lives.

SPEED
Ostriches have long legs and strong toes to run at speeds of up to 45 mph (72 km/h). They have only two toes on each foot; most birds have three or four.

WEBBED FEET
Waterbirds, such as ducks, gulls, and flamingos, have webs of skin between their toes. The webs work like paddles when the bird is in water. They also spread its weight when the bird walks on soft, marshy ground.

GRIPPING TOES
The two outer toes of a parrot's foot point backward, and the two inner toes point forward. This gives parrots a very powerful grip for climbing through the trees. It also allows them to hold food up to the bill.

BLUE-FRONTED PARROT

Two toes forward, two toes back

FLAMINGO

FOOD AND FEEDING

COLLARED
SUNBIRD SIPPING
NECTAR

BIRDS SPEND MUCH of their time finding food, whether pecking at berries and nuts, or snapping up fish or small mammals. They rely mainly on their eyes and ears to find food, and their bill or claws to catch it. A few birds steal their food from other birds. Some birds eat plants; others eat animals (alive or dead) or have a mixed diet.

Hunting and fishing

Meat-eating birds often target young, weak, or unfit prey. They may lie in wait to ambush their quarry, or chase after it through air or water. Most of these birds hunt by day; a few, such as most owls, hunt at night.

GREAT WHITE
PELICAN

GOLDEN
EAGLE

BIRDS OF PREY
Many birds of prey, such as this golden eagle, soar high in the sky to search for food, then swoop down to seize and crush their prey with their sharp talons. However, nine out of ten attacks are unsuccessful and the prey manages to escape.

Prey is either seized with the bill-tip, or trapped in the pouch, and then swallowed.

UMBRELLA FISHING
Some birds have developed their own special techniques for catching food. The black heron shades the water with its wings. This cuts out reflections and makes it easier for the bird to see fish.

Great white pelicans eat about 2½ lb (1.2 kg) of fish a day

SNAKE HUNTERS
Secretary-birds are unusual because they search for their prey mainly on foot. They have tough scales on their legs for protection from snakebites. They pin prey to the ground with sharp claws.

SECRETARY-BIRDS

Sharp, hooked bill to pull and tear at food

EGYPTIAN VULTURE

Bare skin on face to avoid soiling feathers

FISHING IN GROUPS
Great white pelicans usually fish in groups. The birds gather in a circle on the water, lifting their wings and plunging their bills into the water to drive the fish into the middle of the circle. Then they scoop up the fish.

USING TOOLS
A few birds use tools to find and obtain their food. Egyptian vultures throw or drop stones onto ostrich eggs to break open the thick shells.

What birds eat

Birds have healthy appetites. They need to eat large amounts of food to give them enough energy to fly, keep warm, build nests, and lay eggs. Some birds eat only one kind of food, while others, such as starlings, crows, and jays, eat almost anything. Vultures eat carcasses, the dead bodies of animals.

HELMET BIRD

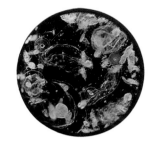

MICROSCOPIC SEAFOOD
A drop of seawater teems with tiny organisms such as diatoms, plankton, and crab larvae. This plankton floats about the oceans and is a vital part of the diet of many seabirds.

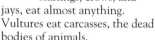

ACORN

SEEDS

RASPBERRY

HIBISCUS FLOWER

FLOWERS, FRUITS, AND SEEDS
For hummingbirds, the sweet liquid called nectar produced by flowers is a high-energy food. Many birds eat the fruits and seeds that develop when the flowers are pollinated.

CABBAGE LEAF

CONIFER

GRASS AND LEAVES
A few birds, such as geese and grouse, eat grass and leaves. These can be hard to digest and poor in nutrients, so the birds have to eat a lot of this sort of food to get the energy they need.

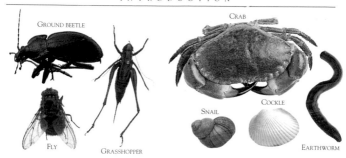

GROUND BEETLE

FLY

GRASSHOPPER

CRAB

SNAIL

COCKLE

EARTHWORM

INSECTS
Adult insects are more abundant in warmer weather, but caterpillars and grubs survive colder periods buried in soil or under bark. Insects are a body-building food, vital for young birds.

INVERTEBRATES
Invertebrates such as crabs and shellfish are an important source of food on the seashore, where there are few insects. Garden and woodland birds, such as thrushes, eat juicy earthworms.

COMMON FROG

VOLE

GRASS CARP

NEST AND YOUNG

VERTEBRATES
Birds that feed on vertebrates (animals with backbones) have to work hard for meals. The animals they hunt can run, swim, or slither away, and often succeed in escaping.

EGGS AND YOUNG
Some birds eat the eggs and helpless young of other birds. For example, skuas pounce on puffin and penguin chicks, while magpies may steal eggs and young birds from the nest.

Bird bills

A bird uses its bill like a hand to carry out all sorts of tasks, from catching and holding food to preening its feathers and building a nest. Parrots also use their bills to help them climb. The size and shape of a bird's bill depends mainly on what it eats and where it finds its food.

YELLOW-HEADED PARROT

FRUIT-AND-NUT EATERS
A parrot uses its muscular tongue to hold a nut, seed, or fruit in its bill so that it can split the hard skin or inedible husk with the chisel-like edge of its lower mandible. It also uses its feet to hold food.

FLAMINGO

A flamingo dips its bill in the shallow water upside-down

FILTER-FEEDER
The upper mandible of the flamingo's bill filters out tiny seeds, algae, shrimp, and other invertebrates from the water. The lower mandible and the pistonlike tongue move up and down to pump water through comblike fringes on the inside and edges of the bill.

Bee-eaters beat stinging insects against a branch to get rid of the stings.

WHITE THROATED BEE-EATER

INSECT EATERS
Birds that feed on insects have thin, pointed bills to probe under bark and stones. Birds that eat flying insects have wide, gaping bills to scoop them up as they fly.

BLACK-CROWNED
NIGHT-HERON

*Bill used to
seize fish*

GOULDIAN
FINCH

*Powerful bill that is
broad at the base and
pointed at the tip.*

FISH EATERS
Some fish-eating birds, such as herons, have
a long, narrow bill that can rapidly snap shut
around prey. Others, including cormorants,
have a hooked bill to grip slippery fish firmly.

SEED EATERS
To crack open seeds, seed-eating birds
such as finches have cone-shaped bills.
The hawfinch's bill is so strong it can
even crush cherry stones.

SCARLET-CHESTED
SUNBIRD

*Flaps over
nostrils keep out
flower pollen*

NECTAR EATERS
Various kinds of smaller bird
feed on nectar. Sunbirds and
hummingbirds push their
needlelike bills into flowers and
lick up the sweet nectar.

*Powerful
hooked bill to
tear up food*

GOLDEN
EAGLE

MEAT EATERS
Often called birds of prey, these include
eagles, owls, and falcons. They use their
bills to pull apart animals they kill into
bite-sized chunks. Owls swallow small
animals, such as voles and mice, whole.

COURTSHIP

BEFORE MATING, male birds usually court the
females. Some males grow more colorful or
elaborate feathers for the breeding
season. They may give singing or
dancing displays. Some show off
nest-building or
hunting skills.

YELLOW-
THROATED
LAUGHING-
THRUSH

TERRITORY
Many birds nest in an area, or
territory, which has enough food for
their young when they hatch out. Male
birds sing in their territory to attract a
mate and keep away other males.

*Laughing-thrushes
make loud,
cackling sounds*

MALE
PIN-TAILED
WHYDAH

MALES AND FEMALES
Male and female birds of
the same species often
look different. The
male is usually more
colorful, but the
dull colors of the
female help
camouflage
her on the
nest.

*Female bird
duller, with
short tail*

*Long tail
feathers used in
display flight to
impress females*

FEMALE
PIN-TAILED
WHYDAH

MALE
PEACOCK

Male's tail is small;
it is the feathers
overlying it that
form the fan

DISPLAY
The male
peacock erects his
long, colorful feathers
in a shimmering fan to
impress a female. After the
breeding season, the long fan
feathers fall out.

RED-CROWNED
CRANES

The "eyes"
attract female
peacocks.

DANCING
Some birds dance together
before they mate. Cranes jump
up and down in the air with
their partners. Great crested
grebes perform a series of
dances, including head-shaking.

NESTS AND EGGS

ALL BIRDS LAY EGGS and most build nests
to keep eggs and young safe and warm.
Birds know instinctively how to
build a nest, and female birds
usually do most of the work. Nests
vary from a shallow scrape in the
ground and simple cup shapes, to
more elaborate constructions.

NEST BOX

Building a nest

Birds use a wide range of
nesting materials and may
make hundreds of trips to
collect material. Nest materials must both
support the nest and keep the young warm.
Nest boxes encourage birds to nest in
gardens or woods with few
natural tree holes.

WAGTAIL
NEST

PEBBLE NEST
Oystercatchers lay their
eggs in a shallow dip, or
scrape, on the shoreline.
Their eggs are difficult to
see among the pebbles.

TWIGS
Most hedgerow and
woodland birds use twigs
and sticks to support
their nests since these
are readily available.

FEATHERS
Birds may use feathers –
3,000 or more in the case
of long-tailed tits – to
make a warm nest lining.

To make the cup shape, birds turn around and around.

MOSS
Moss traps warm air in the nest and stops heat loss. It helps to keep both eggs and young birds warm

STRING
Birds often collect household materials when nest-building. Pieces of string have been found in many nests.

MUD
Some nests are lined with wet mud mixed with saliva and droppings. When it dries, it forms a hard and strong lining.

Woodpeckers have chisellike bills.

TREE NEST
Woodpeckers dig nest holes in rotten trees with their strong beaks. Many other birds use existing tree holes. The nests inside the holes are usually lined with grass or feathers.

GRASS
Grass is a flexible nest material. It is used by many birds because it is easy to weave into differently shaped nests.

MUD NEST
Swallows and martins collect hundreds of little pellets of wet mud with their bills and stick them together to form a nest.

HOUSE MARTIN NEST

Unusual nests

From woven purses and saliva cups to mud ovens and compost heaps, some birds' nests are quite unusual, while others are very elaborate. They may be a strange shape, such as the trumpetlike weaverbird nests, or made with unusual materials, such as the bird's own saliva.

PENDULINE-TIT NEST

False entrance

Strong and lightweight basket

WOVEN NEST
A male West African weaver knotted grasses to weave this nest. The entrance tunnel stops snakes and other enemies from getting inside.

PURSE NEST
The penduline-tit weaves a hanging nest from grasses, leaves, and moss. A false entrance leads to an empty chamber and dead end.

THATCHED COTTAGE
Each colony of the social weaverbirds of South Africa builds a huge "haystack" that is up to 13 ft (4 m) deep and 24 ft (7.2 m) across. Up to 300 pairs then build their nests under the protection of this thatched roof.

WEAVER NEST

NEST FACTS

- The biggest tree nest ever found belonged to a bald eagle. It was 9.5 ft (2.9 m) wide and 20 ft (6.1 m) deep.

- A bee hummingbird's nest is no bigger than a thimble.

- A malleefowl's nest is a "compost heap" of rotting vegetation.

- A hamerkop nest may consist of over 10,000 sticks.

BASKET NEST

Reed warblers join their nest to several reed stems. This helps to hold the nest steady as the wind blows. The nest is made from grass, reed fibers, and feathers.

Nest is joined to reeds

TAILORBIRD NEST

REED WARBLER NEST

SEWING BIRD

The tailorbird sews a pocket of leaves to support its nest. Its sharp bill makes holes along the edges of the leaves. Then the bird pulls spider or insect silk or plant material through the holes to "stitch" the leaves together.

NORTHERN ORIOLE NEST

HUNG UP

Many birds suspend nests from branches, to make it difficult for predators to reach them. The Baltimore orioles that built this nest used string to hang it up, and also in the construction of the nest.

All kinds of eggs

Like dinosaurs and other reptiles, birds lay eggs in which the embryos grow and are nourished. Some birds lay one large clutch (set of eggs) in a season, while others lay several smaller clutches. Some birds, such as snowy owls, lay extra clutches if there is plenty of food. No two eggs have exactly the same markings. The color and shape depend on where the eggs are laid and how much camouflage they need.

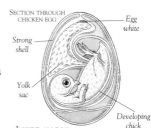

SECTION THROUGH CHICKEN EGG

Egg white

Strong shell

Yolk sac

Developing chick

INSIDE AN EGG
A bird's egg contains a developing bird – an embryo – plus a store of food and a supply of air. Pores in the shell allow air to pass through from outside. The egg white supplies proteins, water, and vitamins.

EGG FACTS

• An average-sized ostrich egg has the same volume as 24 hen's eggs.

• Cuckoos can lay eggs in a few seconds; some birds take 1–3 minutes.

• About 80 species of bird lay eggs in the nests of other species.

• Gray partridges lay the biggest clutches among wild birds, up to 17 eggs.

• Many small eggs take under an hour to hatch.

BARN OWL EGG

CURLEW EGG

WHITE EGGS
Birds that nest in holes or burrows, such as owls or kingfishers, usually lay white eggs. They do not need to be camouflaged because they are hidden.

SPECKLED EGGS
Birds that nest in the open, where there is little cover, usually lay patterned eggs. The camouflage colors hide the eggs from predators.

PALE EGG

SPECKLED EGG

DARK EGG

DISGUISE
Female cuckoos lay their eggs in the nests of other birds such as catbirds, robins, wrens, or meadow pipits. The foster parents raise the cuckoo chick as their own. The cuckoo's egg often looks similar to those of the foster parents.

COLORS IN A CLUTCH
The three eggs above were laid by a single snipe but come from different clutches. In one clutch, the eggs usually look similar.

CUCKOO EGG

COMMON MURRE EGG

Pear shape to roll in a circle

EURASIAN ROBIN EGGS

BIG AND SMALL
Ostriches lay the largest eggs of any living bird. Each weighs up to 3.9 lb (1.8 kg) and is the size of an adult human's hand. The smallest hummingbird eggs, however, are only as big as peas.

PATTERNS
Common murre eggs show a variety of patterns and colors, possibly to help parent birds recognize them. The pear shape stops it from rolling off cliff ledges.

HUMMINGBIRD EGGS

OSTRICH EGG

HATCHING AND GROWTH

MOST PARENT BIRDS SIT on their eggs to keep them warm so that the chicks inside can develop properly. This is called incubation. After the chicks hatch, the parents work hard feeding the chicks, keeping them warm and clean, and protecting them from enemies.

Egg to chick

SWAN INCUBATING EGGS IN NEST

In order to incubate, most birds develop patches of bare skin, brood patches, to let body warmth through to the eggs. Small birds incubate eggs for about two weeks, eagles for six or seven weeks, and albatrosses and kiwis for up to 12 weeks.

First the chick pecks at shell to make a hole

Then chick cuts a circle

Chick pushes to widen crack

HATCHING

To break out of its shell, a baby bird chips away with a pointed "egg tooth" on top of its bill. This egg tooth disappears soon after hatching. Some clutches hatch together; others hatch at intervals of a few days.

Helpless young
are usually born
in a nest

BLUE TIT
NEST

HELPLESS CHICKS
Birds born naked,
blind, and feeble are
called altricial. They
grow at a very fast
rate, often eating
their own weight
each day. Songbirds,
such as thrushes and
chaffinches, are
born like this.

INDEPENDENT CHICKS
Some chicks are born
with feathers, and are
able to see and run soon after
hatching. They are called
precocial. Ducks, geese, and
terns are born like this.

Dry and
fluffy
feathers

Wet and
bedraggled chick
struggles free

SCALED QUAIL
CHICK

Growing up

Baby birds take a few weeks or a few months to grow up. Almost all rely on their parents to keep them warm and out of danger, and most chicks are fed by their parents as well. Small birds may make hundreds of feeding trips in a day; larger birds only two or three. Chicks that are born helpless grow faster than chicks that hatch fluffy and alert.

RED KITE
AND CHICKS

HEN AND
CHICKS

BIRDS OF PREY
Kites, eagles, and other birds of prey tear up food for their chicks at first. As the chicks grow bigger, they learn to tear it up for themselves.

INDEPENDENT FEEDERS
Some baby birds, such as chicks, ducklings, and goslings, can feed themselves soon after hatching. At first, they peck at anything; then they watch their parents to find out what to eat.

PECKING SPOT
A herring gull chick pecks at a red spot on its parent's bill to make the parent cough up food. Herring gulls feed out at sea, so they swallow food rather than carry it long distances.

HERRING
GULL

CRECHE OF YOUNG
KING PENGUINS

SAFETY IN NUMBERS
Young penguins cannot join their
parents in the water until they
have grown waterproof adult
feathers. The parent birds leave
them behind when they go to
sea to feed. When they
return, the adults regurgitate
partly digested fish for the
chicks, but there may be a
wait of days or even
weeks between meals.

*Young penguins huddle
together for warmth and
protection while their
parents are away.*

JUVENILE
STARLING

*A young starling
takes off unsteadily
for its first flight*

FIRST FLIGHT
Baby birds have to learn how to fly
as quickly as possible to avoid
predators and other dangers. They
flap their wings while they are in the
nest to exercise their muscles and make
them strong. Taking off and landing is
not easy – many young birds crash-land.

MIGRATION

NEARLY HALF the world's birds migrate
to find food and water, to nest, or to
avoid bad weather. They navigate by
instinct, but use familiar landmarks, the
Sun, Moon, and stars, and
the Earth's magnetic field to
find their way. Migration
journeys are often dangerous
for birds and use up a
lot of energy. Some
small birds double
their weight to
provide enough
fuel for traveling.

RED-BREASTED
GOOSE

NESTING
This goose is one of many
birds that migrate to arctic
tundra to nest in the brief
summer when there is plenty
of food available.

MIGRATION ROUTES

ARCTIC TERN
This is the champion bird migrant,
flying from the Arctic to Antarctica
and back each year. It spends
summer in both polar regions.

AMERICAN GOLDEN-PLOVER
This plover has the longest
migration of any land bird. It breeds
in northern Canada and flies to the
Argentinian pampas for the winter.

V-FORMATION

Flying in a V-shaped formation helps birds to save energy on a long journey. The birds following the leader fly in the slipstream of the bird in front. When the leader tires, another bird takes over.

SNOW GEESE
MIGRATING

Snow geese breed in the arctic tundra and migrate to the Gulf of Mexico for the winter.

MIGRATION FACTS

• Some American golden plovers cover 2,050 miles (3,300 km) in 35 hours.

• The ruby-throated hummingbird travels 2,000 miles (3,200 km) across the Americas

• Most migrating birds fly below altitude of 5,000 ft (1,500 m).

MOUNTAIN MIGRATION

Some birds migrate short distances. The Himalayan monal, a pheasant, migrates up and down the mountains with the seasons, moving to warmer, lower slopes in winter.

HIMALAYAN
MONAL
PHEASANTS

SHORT-TAILED SHEARWATER

Between breeding seasons off southern Australia, this bird flies in a figure-eight route from Australia to the North Pacific and back again.

GREATER WHITETHROAT

This small warbler breeds in Europe in spring and summer, and then migrates to Africa just south of the Sahara Desert for the winter.

WHERE BIRDS LIVE

FROM BUSY CITIES to frozen polar regions, birds
have adapted to a range of habitats on every
continent. Where birds live depends on the food they
eat and their nesting requirements, as well as their
competitors and predators. In many parts of
the world, people have had a
destructive influence on the
distribution of birds.

NORTH
AMERICA

SOUTH
AMERICA

SEAS, CLIFFS, AND SHORES
Marine habitats are a huge
feeding ground for many
birds. They nest on islands
and continental shores.

DESERTS, SCRUB, AND
GRASSLANDS
These dry, mainly hot
habitats provide little
shelter for birds. Food and
water may be hard to find.

POLAR AND TUNDRA REGIONS
In the Antarctic, Arctic, and
tundra, it is cold and windy.
Birds breed there in summer.

RIVERS, LAKES, AND SWAMPS
Lakes and rivers are freshwater,
while marshes and
swamps are fresh-
or saltwater.

FORESTS AND WOODLANDS
Conifers and broad-leaved
trees grow in temperate
climates where there is
usually rain all year.

TOWNS, CITIES, AND FARMLAND
Birds that have adapted to
live near people can take
advantage of the extra food
and the less severe climate.

RAINFORESTS
These are mostly hot, wet
habitats near the Equator in
the Americas, Africa, southeast
Asia, and northeast Australia.

MOUNTAINS AND MOORLANDS
Moorlands occur in cool, wet
uplands. Mountains have a
variety of habitats.

TOWNS, CITIES, AND FARMLAND

BIRDS HAVE LEARNED to live close to people, and eat the food we give them, as well as insects, plants, and crops around our homes. Birds that used to nest on cliffs or in caves, nest in buildings or under bridges. Woodland birds nest in hedgerows.

EURASIAN KESTREL

HUNTING BIRDS
Most birds of prey do not like living near people, but kestrels hunt along roadsides and sparrowhawks in parks.

HABITAT FACTS

• At night, a city is as much as 9°F (5°C) warmer than the surrounding countryside.

• Some starling roosts in cities have contained over one million birds.

• As few as one in ten captured wild birds may reach the pet shop alive.

• The African red-billed quelea is the world's worst agricultural bird pest.

BLUE BUDGERIGAR

CITY BIRDS
Birds such as geese fly over cities on migration routes, or land to feed and roost in city parks. Starlings roost in city centers at night because it is warmer than the countryside.

CAGED BIRDS
Many people keep birds such as budgerigars, canaries, and parrots in cages. They like their colors, their company, and their songs. People breed birds to create colors never seen in the wild.

BARN
SWALLOW
FEEDING
YOUNG

NESTS IN BUILDINGS

Window ledges, attics, barns, and even chimney pots make ideal nesting places for birds used to nesting on cliffs, rocky hillsides, or trees. Barn swallows used to nest in caves, but now almost all nest inside buildings

NESTS IN HEDGEROWS

Hedgerows are strips of trees and shrubs where birds such as the song thrush can nest safely. Birds roost and feed in hedgerows, which are an important refuge in open areas of crops and grass.

SONG THRUSH

SONG THRUSH NEST

HOMES AND STREETS

MANY BIRDS HAVE LOST their natural fear of people and live near our homes and in our cities, despite all the noise and pollution. These urban birds change their diet or the places they nest to take advantage of our leftover food scraps, the artificial habitats we build, and the warm climates we create.

HOUSE SPARROW
By following people from country to country, the fearless house sparrow has spread from Europe and Asia over two-thirds of the world's land surface. It nests in buildings close to people.

This is a male with a gray crown and black bib.

CAGED BIRDS
Every year, people take thousands of birds from the wild, often illegally. This has critically reduced the numbers of some wild birds, especially parrots.

The house sparrow is bold and adaptable.

WHITE STORKS
In many parts of Europe, white storks are believed to bring good luck. They often nest on roofs, and people may put up platforms to encourage them.

Red streak below eye and upright black crest

HOUSE CROW
The aggressive house crow is always ready to grasp a tasty morsel of food. It lives near busy towns and small villages in India, as well as in other parts of Asia, often swarming in large, busy groups.

Likes to perch on a high branch to sing

Pigeons are tame enough to be fed by hand.

RED-WHISKERED BULBUL
The inquisitive red-whiskered bulbul is not frightened of people and is a common species around the villages of Asia. It has a pleasant and varied song and is often kept as a pet.

PIGEON
The city pigeons of today are descended from the wild rock doves that people originally kept for food and, later, for racing. Pigeons are the only bird group to feed their young with a secretion called pigeon's milk.

City pigeons have been known to travel on subway trains.

PARKS AND GARDENS

FROM TREES AND FLOWERBEDS to grassy lawns and garden ponds, parks and gardens contain a great variety of habitats for birds. People put up feeding tables, birdbaths, and nesting boxes to encourage birds to live near houses. Unfortunately, pets, especially cats, often catch and kill garden birds.

BLACK-BILLED MAGPIE
This adaptable magpie visits surburban gardens. It eats a range of food, especially insects and plant matter, but also steals eggs and young from the nests of other birds.

Pale gray border

Red breast and face used in threat displays by adult robins

EUROPEAN ROBIN
These birds are aggressive. Males often set up territories in gardens and sing loudly to keep away other male robins. In winter, both males and females defend feeding territories.

BLUE TITS

These bold, lively birds often visit gardens in winter to feed on nuts, seeds, and leftover food scraps put out by people. They can easily land on nut feeders and often use the nest boxes that people build and put up for them.

Blue tits are agile, acrobatic birds.

Cone-shaped bill typical of a seed eater

WATERFOWL IN PARKS

The artificial lakes in parks make a welcome feeding, resting, and nesting area for geese, ducks, and coots. Islands in the middle of lakes provide safe nesting places.

NORTHERN CARDINAL

These cardinals are frequent visitors to feeders in the backyards of North America. They often move around in pairs or family groups to feed on seeds that people leave out for them.

SUPERB STARLING

A common visitor to campsites and hotels in East Africa, the superb starling is a tame bird, not frightened of people. It feeds mainly on the ground, pecking up seeds, fruit, and insects.

FIELDS AND HEDGEROWS

FARMLAND HAS TAKEN the place of woodlands, grasslands, and wetlands, but some birds have adapted to this habitat. They feed on the crops and nest in the animal pastures, hedges, orchards, and farm buildings. However, their numbers have been reduced by intensive farming, including the removal of hedges and the use of poisonous pesticides.

EUROPEAN GOLDFINCH
Flocks of goldfinches feed on weeds along the edges of fields. They are light enough to perch on thistle heads and eat the seeds.

FOLLOWING THE PLOW
Large flocks of birds, such as black-headed gulls, often follow a tractor plowing a field. The birds feed on the insects and other invertebrates, such as worms, exposed by the plow.

Gulls feed on newly plowed land.

HOOPOE
In the Mediterranean the weeds and grasses under the olive groves teem with invertebrates. Hoopoes probe the ground with long curved bills for worms and insects.

DUNNOCK
Sometimes called the hedge sparrow, the dunnock is not related to sparrows. It has a slim, insect-eating bill, rather than a seed-eating one. It nests in hedges, where it builds cup-shaped nests.

RING-NECKED PHEASANT
The female pheasant may nest in hedgerows, making a shallow scrape in the ground in which she lays her eggs. Pheasants wander over farmland, feeding mainly on grains, seeds, berries, and insects.

The chicks are well camouflaged, like their mother.

The gray head and underparts help to tell the dunnock from a sparrow

FOREST AND WOODLAND

WITH PLENTY OF FOOD and safe nesting places, forests and woodlands provide a rich habitat for birds, from the treetops right down to the forest floor. A greater variety of birds live in the deciduous and eucalyptus woodlands than in the dark coniferous forests, because of the more favorable climates.

EURASIAN JAY

Jays store acorns in fall

FOOD AND FEEDING

Woodland birds feed on buds, berries, and seeds from the trees and shrubs. Some eat insects and small animals. Diets may vary with changes in season.

BIRDSONG

Most woodland birds, such as the nightingale, have loud songs and calls to attract mates, and establish breeding territories in the thick undergrowth or in the trees.

RING-NECKED PHEASANT WING

WINGS

Many woodland birds have short, broad, rounded wings to help them rise quickly into the air and avoid twigs and branches. Pheasants can fly quickly for short distances.

NIGHTINGALE

NESTS IN HOLES
Holes in trees are safe and warm places for birds such as redstarts to raise a family. In the nesting season, the adults frequently fly in and out with food for the growing young.

MALE REDSTART

CAMOUFLAGED WOODCOCK

FOREST FACTS

• The northern forest called the taiga is the largest in the world.

• There are over 600 species of eucalyptus in Australia.

• Up to half of all woodland birds nest in tree holes.

• The woodpecker family may have existed for 50 million years.

CAMOUFLAGE
Many woodland and forest birds are well camouflaged to protect them from predators. The dull, mottled colors of this woodcock hide it against the decaying leaf litter of the woodland floor.

DECIDUOUS WOODLAND

IN THESE WARM, moist woodlands, a great variety of birds can live together by feeding at different levels, sharing the available food. In warm weather, the birds nest, raise young, and eat as much as they can. In cold weather, leaves fall off the trees and some birds migrate to warmer places.

Thick skull

Long, curved claws to cling to tree trunks

WOODPECKER SKULL

YELLOW-FRONTED WOODPECKER
This small woodpecker of Eastern Brazil hammers into decaying tree trunks to find insect larvae and make nesting holes. It licks up insects with its long, sticky, barbed tongue.

Strong, stiff tail feathers for support

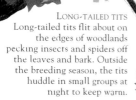

LONG-TAILED TITS
Long-tailed tits flit about on the edges of woodlands pecking insects and spiders off the leaves and bark. Outside the breeding season, the tits huddle in small groups at night to keep warm.

GREEN WOODHOOPOE
These birds probe tree trunks with their long, curved bills searching for food. They live in noisy family groups in African woodlands.

Long bill is used to find insect grubs or eggs and spiders

The bill is broad at the base to catch insects

SPOTTED FLYCATCHER
Perching on exposed branches, spotted flycatchers dart out to snap up passing insects. In cold weather, they migrate to Africa, south of the Sahara, to find food.

Green woodhoopoes have high, cackling calls

WHIP-POOR-WILL
By day, this camouflaged nightjar sleeps on the woodland floor. At night, it flies near the ground catching insects.

CONIFEROUS FOREST

DARK CONIFEROUS FORESTS – the taiga – stretch across the top of the Northern Hemisphere, bordered by the tundra in the north and the more open deciduous woodlands farther south. The leaves stay on the trees all year round, but winters are bitterly cold and most birds leave for warmer places. In the short summer, they feed on berries, seeds, or insects.

CAPERCAILLIE
The capercaillie is able to eat pine needles to help it survive through the winter. Comblike fringes on its toes keep it from sinking into snow.

EURASIAN SISKIN
The restless and acrobatic siskin often hangs upside-down to pull the seeds out of pine and larch cones. Siskins are social birds and build nests high in conifer trees, where predators cannot easily reach the young birds.

The siskin feeds on the seeds of pine, larch, alder, and birch trees.

RED CROSSBILL
Crossbills use their scissor-like bill to lever apart the scales on the cones of pine, spruce, larch, and other conifers to reach the seeds. Parent crossbills cough up partly digested pine seeds to feed to their young.

PINE
CONES

Scales levered apart by a crossbill

BOHEMIAN WAXWING
These birds are named after the red, waxlike tips on some of their flight feathers. Waxwings eat berries or fruit in winter, and insects during summer. They migrate south in the autumn in large numbers.

Waxwings have soft, silky plumage

Male and female birds are similar in color

JUVENILE BALD EAGLE
Bald eagles breed in forests near water, where they hunt for fish and waterbirds. They do not grow the white feathers on the head and tail until they are four years old.

EUCALYPTUS WOODLAND

IN THE EVERGREEN eucalyptus woodlands of
Australia, there is food and shelter for a variety
of unique birds all year. The birds
help to pollinate the trees and
shrubs and spread their seeds.
In the rainy season, waterbirds
gather in marshy areas on the
border of these woodlands.

*Strong, hooked
beak characteristic
of parrot family*

MALLEEFOWL
These birds build a huge mound
of rotting vegetation covered
with sand to keep their eggs
warm. The male checks the
temperature with his bill.

*Plumage
varies, but
most have a
yellow collar*

RAINBOW LORIKEETS
Noisy flocks of rainbow lorikeets feed
high in the trees. They crush the flowers
of eucalyptus and other flowering trees to
soak up the sticky mixture of nectar and
pollen with their fringe-tipped tongues.

Large, broad-based bill to catch and swallow prey

Large head and bill with brown ear patch

LAUGHING KOOKABURRA
Named for its very noisy, chuckling calls, the laughing kookaburra is a giant kingfisher that rarely eats fish. Instead, it pounces on reptiles such as snakes, small mammals, birds, and invertebrates.

OWLS

MOST OWLS SLEEP by day and hunt by night. Their sharp hearing and keen eyesight help them catch prey such as mice and small birds. Many owls roost in trees and have brown feathers for camouflage.

Feathers are fanned out to make owl look frightening.

SCOPS-OWL
Almost impossible to spot because of its superb camouflage, the scops-owl eats large insects. It raises its feathers to scare off its enemies.

In a complete pellet, animal fur and bones are all stuck together.

Owl mucus binds pellet together

OWL FACTS
- Order *Strigiformes*
- About 174 species
- Mainly nocturnal
- Birds of prey
- Eat birds, insects, and small mammals
- Habitat: mainly woodland
- Nest in tree holes or other bird's nests
- Eggs: white

OWL PELLETS
Once or twice a day, owls cough up pellets containing indigestible bits of their last meal, such as fur or bones. Pulling a pellet apart reveals what an owl has eaten.

SOUTHERN BOOBOOK
This small Australian owl gets its name from its double hoot. It feeds mainly on insects.

Large feet with hooked talons

BARN OWL
A heart-shaped face is the trademark of the barn owl, a bird so different from other owls that it is in a separate family. The disk of feathers on the face collects sounds like a radar dish. Barn owls make a haunting shrieking sound.

Owls catch and kill prey with their sharp talons.

"Ears" are only tufts of feathers...

EURASIAN EAGLE-OWL
The largest of all owls, eagle owls are powerful hunters, strong enough to attack young foxes and other owls. They have very loud hoots: male eagle owls can be heard hooting over ½ mile (1 km) away.

BARN OWL FEATHER

TAWNY OWL FEATHER

OWL FEATHERS
Soft, velvety feathers with fringes on the flight feathers muffle the sound made by the wings in flight.

Thick covering of soft feathers

RAINFORESTS

TROPICAL RAINFORESTS are the richest bird habitats. They provide a wealth of food and safe nesting places, and a warm, wet climate throughout the year. Rainforest birds usually have short, broad wings to twist and turn easily when flying through the trees. This unique habitat is under threat from forestry, mining, dams, and farming.

CANOPY

UNDERSTORY

FOREST FLOOR

BIRDS-OF-PARADISE
Male birds-of-paradise have ornate and colorful feathers to attract females. They live only in the dense rainforests of northeastern Australia and Papua New Guinea.

LAYERS OF LIFE
The birds live at different levels in the trees. In this way, they share the available food and nesting places, so a huge variety of birds live close together.

SPREADING SEEDS
Fruit-eating birds such as aracaris (small toucans) and parrots help to spread the seeds of rainforest trees. They feed on fruits and pass the seeds in their droppings.

Wide tail helps the aracari to balance on branches

CHESTNUT-EARED ARACARI

Long bill with serrated edge

Groups of crested oropendolas hang their woven nests from tree branches.

NESTING
To keep their nests out of sight and out of reach of predators, rainforest birds nest high in the trees or in dense thickets above the ground. Some, such as parrots and hornbills, nest in tree holes.

COLOR
The bright colors of rainforest birds like these macaws are surprisingly hard to see among the leafy trees. These birds are feeding on mineral-rich clay soil.

HABITAT FACTS
• Since 1945, over half the rainforests have been destroyed; an area the size of a soccer field is cut down every second.

• Rainforests contain over 50 percent of all plant and animal species.

• One-fifth of all the world's bird species live in South America's Amazon rainforest.

UNDER THE CANOPY

BENEATH THE GREEN ROOF of the forest is the dark, cool understory of smaller trees, shrubs, and climbing plants, and below this, the leafy forest floor. There is less food and warmth at these lower levels than up in the canopy, so there are fewer birds. Large birds such as trumpeters and cassowaries stalk across the forest floor. In the understory, hummingbirds and jacamars flit through the branches.

HOATZIN CHICK

HOATZIN
Groups of hoatzins live along riverbanks in the rainforests of South America. They are poor fliers and make short, noisy flights through the trees.

Chick has claws on its wings for climbing

DOUBLE-WATTLED CASSOWARY
This huge cassowary melts into the forest if it senses danger. Males make loud, booming calls during courtship. The horny casque on its head is probably a badge of rank and dominance.

SUNBITTERN
This bird is named for the sunset colors on its wings, visible during its courtship display. At other times, it is well camouflaged by the mottled gray and brown colors of its feathers.

Male not displaying

Courtship display of male

BLUE BIRDS-OF-PARADISE
The male blue bird-of-paradise performs a dramatic upside-down display to show off his iridescent feathers to a female. He also utters a weird buzzing noise that sounds something like an electric motor.

These birds live in the middle or upper levels of the rainforest, rarely coming down to the ground.

ASIAN FAIRY-BLUEBIRDS
Noisy fairy-bluebirds move busily through the trees searching for fruit, such as figs. The metallic blue of the male is not easy to see in the shade of the trees.

Fairy-bluebirds often make sharp, whistling calls.

IN THE TREETOPS

HIGH UP IN THE RAINFOREST CANOPY it is light and warm and there is plenty of food, especially fruits, seeds, and insect life. Bird life includes large bird predators such as eagles which patrol the treetops looking for prey. Canopy birds, such as parrots and toucans, climb well and have strong feet for grasping branches.

Bare, orange-yellow face and bill

HARPY EAGLE
The huge harpy eagle is one of the most powerful birds of prey. It swoops into the canopy to seize monkeys (like this capuchin), birds, sloths, and reptiles. It can fly very fast through the branches.

LADY ROSS'S TURACO
This African turaco lives in small, noisy groups, usually high in the canopy. Although clumsy fliers, turacos are good at running along tree branches. They make a great variety of cackling and croaking calls.

TOCO TOUCAN
This is the largest toucan, with a bill up to 7½ in (19 cm) long. The bill is hollow with supporting struts, so it is not as heavy as it looks. The colors help it to recognize other toucans and find a mate.

ORANGE-BELLIED LEAFBIRD
This Asian leafbird helps to pollinate the forest trees as it feeds on nectar. It also spreads the seeds of plants in the mistletoe family by eating the berries.

This leafbird is good at mimicking other birds' songs

The casque is a thin layer of skin and bone over a honeycomb structure.

GREAT HORNBILL
The hornbills of Southeast Asia and Africa look like the toucans of South America because they live and feed in a similar way. They are named for the horny casques on their bills. No-one knows how these bony growths are used.

PARROTS

MOST PARROTS are brightly colored and live in tropical forests. They mainly fly around in flocks, making harsh, screeching calls. Many species are threatened by habitat destruction. There are three main groups: the lories, the cockatoos, and the parrots.

Narrow, tapering wings to fly fast through the trees

CANARY-WINGED PARAKEET
This small parrot's long tail helps it balance as it flies. Larger parrots usually have broad, rounded wings and fly more slowly. One parrot, the kakapo, cannot fly at all.

CHATTERING LORY
The chattering lory spends most of its time high in the trees feeding mainly on pollen and nectar. Lories have a long tongue with a brushlike tip which picks up pollen as they drink.

YELLOW-CRESTED COCKATOO
Cockatoos raise and lower their head crests when they are excited, frightened, or angry. They also do this when landing on a perch.

PARROT FACTS
• Family: *Psittacidae*
• About 330 species
• Diurnal
• Tropical land birds
• Eat fruits, seeds, nuts, and other plant parts; also some invertebrates
• Habitat: forest, scrub, grassland, and mountains
• Nest: usually tree hole, hole in bank or among rocks

ECLECTUS PARROTS
These parrots are unusual because the bright red female is such a different color from the green male. Males and females mostly look alike. Eclectus parrots feed on fruits, nuts, and leaf buds.

Nutcracker bill to crush seeds and nuts

SKULL AND BILL
Parrots have large, broad skulls with a fairly big space for the brain – they are intelligent birds. The top bill curves sharply down, fitting neatly over the broad bottom bill, which curves upward.

Many parrots have green feathers to camouflage them in the leaves of the trees.

Two toes point forward and two backward, giving a good grip when climbing.

RIVERS, LAKES, AND SWAMPS

WATERY HABITATS are home to a rich variety of birds. There are plenty of plants, invertebrates, and fish for birds to eat, and safe nesting places in reeds and on riverbanks. Many birds rest and feed on lakes, marshes, and swamps during migration. But drainage schemes, dams, acid rain, and pollution from farms and factories threaten these habitats.

KINGFISHER DIVING

WEBBED FEET

Many waterbirds, such as Canada geese, have webbed feet to push the water aside as they swim. Long legs to wade in deep water and long toes to walk over soft mud are other common features of waterbirds.

CANADA GOOSE FOOT

HUNTING FOR FISH

To catch fish, birds like this kingfisher dive into the water to seize their prey. Others, such as herons, stand still and catch fish that swim past. The pelican's technique is to scoop up fish from the surface.

CATCHING FISH

Birds need strong bills and feet to hold slippery prey. Merganser ducks have serrated edges to their bill to help them keep a grip on fish they catch.

HOODED MERGANSER SKULL

NORTHERN
SHOVELER

FILTER FEEDING
Ducks like the shoveler
filter tiny floating plants
and animals from water.
The shoveler has "combs"
on its bill to trap food.

CAMOUFLAGE
The dark, mottled colors of some
birds, such as the buff-banded
rail, help to
camouflage them
as they skulk
noiselessly through the reed
beds of marshes and swamps.

BUFF-
BANDED
RAIL

NESTING
Hiding a nest from predators is a relatively easy
task in these habitats. Nesting materials such as
dried reeds are also easy to find. Some birds
even build floating
platforms of
vegetation for
extra security.

> **HABITAT FACTS**
>
> • Siberia's Lake Baikal
> is the oldest freshwater
> lake – at least 25
> million years old.
>
> • About six percent of
> the Earth's surface is
> covered by marshes,
> bogs, and swamps.
>
> • One-fifth of all the
> freshwater on Earth
> flows through the
> Amazon River daily.

COOT
NESTING IN
REEDS

RIVERS AND LAKES

THESE FRESHWATER habitats are important for birds, especially in undisturbed areas free of pollution. Some birds prefer the still waters of ponds and lakes while others, such as dippers, are adapted to move in fast-flowing waters. Around the edge of the water are many places to nest and a variety of food for the young, including water insects.

GRAY WAGTAIL

The busy gray wagtail patrols upland streams, darting out to snap up flying insects in its long bill. It has sharp claws to grip slippery rocks and wet branches.

CLARK'S GREBES

The courtship dance, like that of the Western grebe, is elaborate. In it, a pair of grebes stands up tall and races fast across the water with heads tilted forward.

Long legs to wade through deep water while feeding

Flamingoes hold their bills upside down as they filter food from the water

At the last moment, the feet swing forward to grasp the fish.

OSPREY

The osprey is a powerful hunter, plunging feet first into water to snatch fish from near the surface. It sometimes goes right under before pulling up into the air again. Stong claws and spines under the toes help it hold slippery fish.

All flamingos have some black feathers in their wings.

WHITE-CROWNED FORKTAIL

These Asian birds live by rocky streams, perching on boulders wagging their long tails. They have a loud, high-pitched whistle to communicate above the noise of the water.

Lesser flamingos are the smallest of the six species of flamingo.

Crop

LESSER FLAMINGOS

Flamingos live in noisy colonies, sometimes containing thousands of birds. They nest on mounds of mud, and both parents feed the young on a rich "milk" produced in the crop.

SWAMPS AND MARSHES

Permanently waterlogged swamps and seasonal marshes are often referred to as "wetlands." They can be freshwater or saltwater habitats. Fish-eating birds, such as egrets and pelicans, are common in wetlands, but a wide variety of birds manage to feed together by eating different kinds of food at different levels in the water.

SCARLET IBIS
Spectacular flocks of scarlet ibis feed, roost, and nest together in the tropical swamps of South America. Scarlet ibises feel in soft mud or under plants for insects, crabs, shellfish, frogs, and fish. Young scarlet ibises have gray-brown upperparts for a year while they mature into adults.

Long, thin, down-curved bill to probe for food

Slim body to slide easily through dense vegetation

BLACK CRAKES
These East African birds have long, widely-spaced toes to keep them from sinking into the mud and help them walk over floating water plants. Their thick bills are too short to probe in mud, so they peck small invertebrates and seeds off the surface.

WHOOPING CRANES
Among the world's rarest birds, the whooping crane breeds only in one Canadian national park, and winters only on a few coastal marshes in Texas, US.

BEARDED PARROTBILL
Active and acrobatic bearded parrotbills fly low over reed beds on their rounded wings. They feed on insects in warm weather, and seeds in cold weather. Both parents build the nest in the reeds and share the care of their young.

Male has black mustaches

A bird's "knee" is really its ankle, so it bends backward, just like a person's ankle.

DUCKS

WEBBED FEET and broad, flat bills are distinctive features of ducks. These birds are good swimmers and strong fliers. There are two main types of duck – dabbling ducks, such as the mallard, that feed on the surface, and diving ducks, such as the pochard. Many ducks migrate to avoid cold weather.

DOWN FEATHERS
Female ducks pluck down feathers from their breasts and use them to line their nests and cover the eggs to keep them warm.

FEMALE

MALE

Short legs set well back on body

MANDARIN DUCKS
These ducks live near ponds and lakes surrounded by woods, and nest in tree holes. The male is more colorful than the female, except when he molts his feathers once a year.

WOOD DUCK
Found in North America, wood ducks are related to Asian mandarin ducks. The females look after the nest, eggs, and ducklings on their own.

The ducklings swim soon after hatching

DIVING DUCKS
These ducks have shorter, rounder bodies than ducks that feed on the surface. Pochards can stay submerged for up to 30 seconds. Some species can dive for even longer.

DUCK FACTS
• Family: *Anatidae* includes ducks, swans, and geese
• About 150 species
• Diurnal
• Waterfowl
• Eat water plants and water animals
• Habitat: wetlands, ponds, lakes, rivers, sea.
• Nest: near water, or in tree holes
• Eggs: white or pale

PLUMED WHISTLING-DUCK
Whistling-ducks live in the tropics and look more like geese than ducks. They feed mainly on the surface.

MALE MALLARD

Webbed feet used like paddles for swimming

MALLARD
These dabblers feed on the surface of the water or upend themselves to reach plant and animal food a little way below the surface. Mallards are the ancestors of most domestic ducks.

Wide, flat bill with comblike fringes to sift food from water

SEAS, CLIFFS, AND SHORES

SOME SPECIALLY adapted birds spend most of their lives gliding over the open oceans. But they nest on shores and in the safety of cliff ledges, usually in large colonies. The rich feeding grounds of estuaries attract huge numbers of waders and wildfowl, especially on migration.

FLIGHT
Tubenoses such as fulmars have long, narrow wings to glide fast over the waves for long distances. However, they are not very good at walking, and are clumsy and ungainly on land.

FULMAR IN FLIGHT

Fulmars have tube-shaped nostrils above the bill. Albatrosses and petrels are also tube-nosed birds.

Fulmars have a stiff-winged flight, hardly bending their wings at all.

| CURLEW | REDSHANK | LITTLE STINT | RINGED PLOVER |

FEEDING
Finding food out at sea is not always easy, and seabirds spend most of their time looking for the next meal. Terns dive to take fish at or near the surface. Other seabirds, such as puffins, dive underwater.

PUFFIN WITH CATCH

SHARING FEEDING PLACES
Waders avoid competion because their bills are different lengths, enabling them to feed at different levels in the mud. The curlew's long bill reaches worms in deep burrows, while the ringed plover picks insects off the surface.

HERRING
GULL EGGS

Most seabird eggs are more pointed at one end than the other.

CAMOUFLAGED EGGS

Birds such as gulls or terns that nest in the open on beaches or dunes have camouflaged eggs. The spots and other markings help the eggs to blend into the background so predators find it hard to see them.

HABITAT FACTS

• Oceans cover about 70 percent of the Earth's surface.

• The sea cools more slowly than the land, keeping coastal areas warmer in winter.

• The tidal range in open oceans is only about 20 in (50 cm).

• In 10 sq ft (1 sq m) of estuary there may be 50,000 crustaceans.

GANNET
ON NEST

NESTING

Many seabirds nest in tightly-packed colonies of thousands or even millions of birds. The vast numbers stimulate them to breed at the same time. Gannets nest close together in noisy, smelly colonies.

ESTUARIES AND SHORES

APART FROM CLIFFS, other areas
along the shoreline, such as dunes
and beaches, provide nesting areas
for seabirds. Where rivers meet
the sea, the shallow, muddy waters
of estuaries teem with a wealth of
food such as fish, worms,
and shellfish. Estuaries
are particularly important
in cold weather, when
inland feeding areas
are frozen.

PURPLE SANDPIPER
Stocky purple sandpipers
migrate south in colder
weather to feed on rocky
shores. They search the
shoreline for food, finding
their prey by sight rather
than by touch.

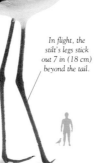

BLACK-NECKED STILT
This stilt has
extremely long legs
that allow it to feed in
deeper water than
other shorebirds.
However, it prefers to
feed in shallow water
and on muddy shores,
using its long bill to
catch insects and small
aquatic creatures.

*In flight, the
stilt's legs stick
out 7 in (18 cm)
beyond the tail.*

SLEEPING
On an estuary, shorebirds
such as this dunlin feed when
they can, and sleep when the
tide comes in and covers
their feeding grounds. They
flock to the safety of high-
tide roosts, like small islands.

INCA TERN
This South American tern often gathers in flocks of many thousands, and roosts on sandy beaches. Inca terns are graceful fliers, hovering over the sea and dipping down to snatch food from the surface.

Inca terns may follow whales and seals to seize scraps of food.

GREAT BLACK-BACKED GULL
This huge gull is a fierce predator of coastal seabird colonies. It has a hooked bill and long, powerful wings.

RINGED PLOVER
As soon as the ringed plover stops moving, its colors make it hard to see among the pebbles on the beach. Parents may pretend to be injured to draw predators away from eggs and young.

SEA AND CLIFFS

OVER THE OPEN OCEAN, seabirds search for food, also
landing on the surface to rest and preen. Seabirds
have waterproofed feathers, webbed feet for
swimming, and sharp bills to catch slippery prey.
Many nest on cliffs where eggs
and young are safe
from predators.

NESTING SPACE
To share the nesting sites on a
cliff, the birds nest at different
levels. Gannets and kittiwakes
nest near the top, and razorbills
and murres in the middle.
Shags and cormorants
nest lower down.

*After fishing,
cormorants hold
their wings open
to dry.*

GANNET SKULL
To catch fish, gannets plunge into
the sea like torpedos from heights
of up to 100 ft (30 m). They have
a strong skull to withstand the
impact when they hit the water
with such a great force.

GREAT CORMORANT
With feathers that trap very little air and
heavy bones, the great cormorant
sinks in water more easily than other seabirds,
and can feed on bottom-dwelling creatures.

A frigatebird robs a tropicbird of its fishy meal.

PIRACY AT SEA
Frigatebirds steal much of their food from other birds such as pelicans and gulls. They are speedy fliers and can swoop, dart, soar, and hover better than most other seabirds.

Nests of grass, seaweeds, and mud sit snugly on narrow ledges

KITTIWAKES
These small gulls nest close together in colonies consisting of hundreds of birds. They are named after their call. Unlike many other gulls, they are rarely found inland.

DESERTS, SCRUB, AND GRASSLANDS

IN THESE MAINLY HOT, dry habitats, birds may have to travel long distances to find food and water, or migrate to avoid dry seasons. Seeds and insects are the main sources of food, but some larger birds also feed on reptiles, small mammals, and dead animals.

Bee-eaters often feed on flying insects, especially honey bees.

INSECT EATERS
Birds such as bee-eaters and warblers feed on the insects that are most abundant during a rainy season. In the dry season, insect eaters often have to migrate to find enough to eat.

White-throated bee-eaters fly to wetter grasslands in the dry season.

ROADRUNNER

VARIED DIET
Food is often hard to find, so birds survive by eating any food they come across. Reptiles are a common source of food. This roadrunner has caught a lizard.

WHITE-THROATED BEE-EATER

These birds have been endangered by the caged bird trade.

SEED EATERS

Grass seeds are a vital source of food for many birds, such as these Australian Gouldian finches. When the grasses die back in the dry season, the finches migrate toward wetter areas on the coast.

GOULDIAN FINCHES

GARBAGE CLEAN-UP

The carcasses of large grazing animals and human dumps provide food for birds such as marabou storks. Despite the harsh habitat, there is plenty to eat.

BURROWING OWLS

UNDERGROUND SHELTERS

To keep out of the heat of the Sun, burrowing owls rest and nest safe from enemies inside burrows dug by small mammals like prairie dogs.

MARABOU STORK

HABITAT FACTS

• More than a quarter of all the land on Earth is covered in grass.

• Deserts have less than 10 in (25 mm) rain a year.

• In Death Valley, in the Southwest, temperatures reach 131°F (55°C).

• The African ostrich is the heaviest, tallest, and fastest-running bird in the world.

DESERTS

BIRDS THAT LIVE in deserts have to get most of their water either from their food or by flying long distances. By day, they may rest in the shade of rocks, or inside cacti or underground burrows. Some come out to feed at night, when it is cooler. Many birds of prey survive in deserts on a diet of reptiles and small mammals.

SANDGROUSE
These birds are strong fliers and travel many miles to find water. The males carry water back to their chicks in their belly feathers.

Hooked beak typical of bird of prey

ELF OWL
The sparrow-sized elf owl nests in holes dug out by woodpeckers inside giant saguaro cacti. The spines of the cactus protect the eggs and young from predators. Elf owls hunt for insects in the cool of the night.

It is much cooler inside the cactus.

BAY-WINGED HAWK
A fearless hunter of birds, lizards, and small mammals, this species sometimes hunts cooperatively in pairs, or even in groups. It is often found near roadsides in the desert regions of the Americas.

The female does not have orange cheek patches and her bill is a duller red.

The male has zebralike stripes on the chest.

ZEBRA FINCHES

These lively little birds are common in the Australian outback. They nest after the rains when there are plenty of seeds and insects to feed to their young. They live in flocks of up to 100 birds, and several may nest together.

SCRUB AND BUSH

THE BIRDS OF these warm, dry, dusty habitats may roam widely in search of food, or follow the rains. The thorny bushes and shrubs often form dense thickets and these make safe nesting places. The berries that grow on the shrubs can be a useful source of food in colder weather for many species.

Males have brighter markings on the face than the females.

COCKATIELS
These small cockatoos wander over the Australian bush country looking for fruits and grass seeds. They usually nest after rainfall at any time of year.

BLUE-CAPPED CORDONBLEU
Small groups of cordonbleus search the ground for grass seeds and insects in the thorn scrub of East Africa. They feed their young mainly on a protein-rich diet of insects.

Short, stubby bill to crush seeds

GRAY FRANCOLIN
These birds are common in southern
Asia because they are able to survive
in dry conditions. They usually live in
small family groups, and feed
on weed seeds and grain
crops. In warm weather,
they also eat
insects.

*Francolins try to
escape danger by
running.*

SCRUBLAND
The scrubland habitats of small trees and
thorny shrubs are halfway between
grassland and woodland. They include
the Mediterranean scrublands, the
Californian chaparral, and the bush, or
outback, of Australia.

EMU
Small flocks of flightless
emus roam widely through the
Australian bush in search of
seeds, berries, and insects.
The male looks after
the chicks for
up to 18 months.

WHITE HELMETSHRIKE
Tame and active white
helmetshrikes live in small
flocks of two to 20 birds. They
hop through the African bush
snapping up insects and spiders
with their strong, hooked bills.

GRASSLANDS

A VARIETY OF seed- and insect-eating birds live in grasslands, especially those birds that can adapt to living near people. Some birds follow herds of grazing animals to snap up the insects disturbed by their feet. Other birds feed on the animals when they die. Long legs enable birds such as ostriches and rheas to see over tall grasses and watch for danger.

Oxpeckers and giraffe

OXPECKERS
Using their sharp claws to cling to the skin of large mammals such as giraffes and zebras, oxpeckers pick off ticks and insects living in their fur.

In breeding plumage, male is bright chestnut, with black head and throat

This weaver is a shy bird with a fast, dashing flight.

CHESNUT WEAVER
These weavers nest in dense colonies in the African grasslands. Out of the breeding season, both male and female are dull brown.

OSTRICH
Able to survive in very dry conditions, ostriches stride over the African savannah on their long legs, searching for leaves, seeds, and insects. They are threatened by hunting and habitat destruction.

Bare head
and neck

HOODED VULTURE
The bare head
and neck of the
hooded vulture allow it to reach
right inside an animal carcass to
feed without getting its feathers
dirty. Vultures fly high, using
their sharp eyesight to spot
carrion.

*It is sometimes called
the "ovenbird"
because its nest looks
like an old-fashioned
baker's oven*

RUFOUS HORNERO
There are few trees on the South
American pampas grasslands, so the
rufous hornero builds a huge nest of mud
and straw. The nest dries, forming a hard
"birdhouse" to protect the eggs and young.

349

MOUNTAINS AND MOORLANDS

MOORLANDS TEND TO BE wet, boggy places while mountains can be very cold and windy. Only a few hardy birds live on mountains and moorland year-round because of the harsh climate and lack of food, especially in the cold seasons. However, these habitats are important breeding areas for some birds.

This shy, secretive bird rarely emerges from the bamboo thickets and dense forest where it lives.

SEASONAL MIGRATION
Hardy pheasants such as this Lady Amherst's pheasant live in the mountain forests of Asia. They move up and down the mountains with the seasons. Many pheasants are threatened by hunting.

Feathered feet to insulate against the cold

Neck ruff

CAMOUFLAGE
In fall, ptarmigans grow white feathers for camouflage amid the winter snow, in which they bury themselves to escape cold, biting winds. Their mottled, gray-brown summer plumage hides them among lichen-covered rocks.

LADY AMHERST'S PHEASANT

NESTING
CURLEW

MOUNTAIN FORESTS

The warmer forests on the lower slopes of mountains provide many birds with plenty of food and nesting places. In colder weather, birds may move down to these forests from the upper slopes.

RUFOUS-BELLIED NILTAVA

These Asian flycatchers live in mountain forest above 3,000 ft (1,000 m).

NESTING PLACES

Shorebirds such as this curlew nest on windswept moorlands in summer. They hide their nests among grasses and bushes. Their young feed on insects, worms, frogs, and snails. In winter, they move to the coast.

GROUSE
EGG

MOORLAND EGGS

Heavy blotches of color help to camouflage the eggs of moorland nesters such as grouse and shorebirds among the heather and bracken. The eggs are laid in a shallow scrape on the ground.

CURLEW
EGG

Male has long tail for display

HABITAT FACTS

• The Appalachians were formed over 250 million years ago; the Himalayas formed only 40 million years ago.

• The world's longest mountain chain is the Andes at 4,500 miles (7,250 km) long.

• Some moorlands are created by a change to a wetter climate; others by people clearing trees for farmland.

MOUNTAINS

IN COLD WEATHER food is scarce on mountains, but these areas are undisturbed breeding areas for birds. Birds' feathers keep them warm when it is freezing cold, and efficient lungs enable them to get enough oxygen from the thin air. Many mountain birds are large and powerful fliers.

RAVEN
The largest of all perching birds, this member of the crow family patrols the mountain slopes, searching for prey or carrion with its sharp eyes.

WALLCREEPER
This nimble bird clings onto rock faces with its sharp claws, probing for insects with its slender bill. In cold weather, it moves to lower slopes where there are more insects for it to eat.

SWORD-BILLED HUMMINGBIRD
This hummingbird lives high in the Andes. It has a very long bill, which it uses to sip nectar from flowers.

SNOW, ICE AND ROCK

GRASSY MEADOWS

CONIFEROUS FOREST

TEMPERATE FOREST

HABITAT ZONES
Mountains have a variety of habitats. There are warm, deciduous forests on the lower slopes, cooler coniferous forests higher up, and, just below the snow covered peaks, grasslands and scrub.

The lammergeier is also called the bearded vulture

LAMMERGEIER

Soaring over the mountain slopes on rising warm air currents, the lammergeier searches the steep slopes for animals killed by the harsh climate. It drops the skeleton bones on rocks to smash them open, then scoops out the marrow with its long beak.

Lammergeiers fly to great heights and drop bones onto rocks to break them apart.

ANDEAN CONDOR

The Andean condor, the world's heaviest bird of prey, has sharp vision and long, broad wings. As it soars over the Andes, it scans the slopes below for dead animals to feed on. This bird has been heavily persecuted and also suffers from pesticide poisoning.

MOORLANDS

THIS WATERLOGGED, tundralike habitat is found
in cool, upland areas with lots of rain. It is an
important breeding ground for shorebirds and
grouse. Predators such as harriers and golden eagles
find many small birds and mammals to eat here,
and there are plenty
of insects
breeding in the
peaty bogs.

*Golden-plovers
feed on
insects, worms,
and seeds.*

*The upperparts
of this species
have golden
color all year.*

EURASIAN GOLDEN-PLOVER
In late spring, golden-
plovers migrate to
moorlands to breed. They
lay their well-camouflaged
eggs in a shallow scrape
in the ground.

STONECHAT
The restless stonechat
perches on bushes and posts
to watch for insects, worms,
and spiders. It builds a nest of
moss, grass, and hair, well
hidden in bushes or thick grass.

PEREGRINE FALCON
These falcons stoop at an
incredible speed to kill prey
such as golden-plovers or
pigeons with their talons.
They pluck the feathers from
prey before eating the flesh.

RED GROUSE
This bird is a distinctive British
and Irish subspecies of the willow
grouse or willow ptarmigan. Many
moorlands are carefully managed to keep a
lot of these birds for
shooting in the fall
grouse season.

*Birds such as red
grouse shelter, hide,
and nest in heather.*

*Many stonechats
do not migrate
but stay in their
breeding range
all year.*

EAGLES

WITH THEIR SHARP eyes, huge wings, and strong legs and feet, eagles are the most powerful of the birds of prey. Females are larger than males. Many species of eagle are threatened by people hunting them, poisoning them, and destroying their habitat.

Light-colored crown and neck feathers

Strong talons to grip and crush prey

COURTSHIP

During courtship, many eagles show off their amazing flying skills. A pair of bald eagles may tumble and spin through the sky, while trying to touch or grip one another's talons.

Courtship display of bald eagles

IMPERIAL EAGLE

The imperial eagle belongs to a group called the booted eagles, which all have feathered legs. Imperial eagles are widespread in parts of Asia, but rare in Europe.

GOLDEN EAGLE

This booted eagle is a strong flier, soaring high on outstretched wings to search for prey. It is named for the golden feathers on the top of its head and the back of its neck.

Large primaries for power and steering

BATELEUR

This eagle's name comes from the French word for "juggler" because of its aerial courtship display. It has long wings and a short tail. When it is excited or angry, it raises its crest.

Raised crest

A bald eagle's eyrie

EYRIE

Eagle nests are called eyries and bald eagles have made some of the biggest eyries in the world. They use the same nest year after year, adding more and more twigs and sticks each time they nest.

EAGLE FACTS

- Family: *Accipitridae* – diverse family of about 70 species, including snake eagles, booted eagles, and others

- Diurnal

- Eat a variety of animals, alive and dead

- Habitat: wide range

- Nest: mass of sticks in tree or on cliff ledge

- Eggs: white or marked with brown

POLAR AND TUNDRA REGIONS

THE FROZEN POLAR REGIONS are the coldest and windiest places on Earth. Few birds can survive there all year around. Most migrate there to breed in the short summer months, when the Sun shines 24 hours a day and there is plenty of food. These unique habitats are threatened by mining, tourism, and pollution.

TUNDRA LANDSCAPES
Around the edge of the Arctic Ocean lie the flat tundra lands, which have a frozen layer called permafrost under the ground. In summer, the soil above the permafrost thaws out, and lakes and marshes form on the surface.

Tundra means "barren land" in Finnish

Ice floating on water

Shoreline

Tundra with permafrost under the ground

Marshy tundra landscape in summer

MIGRATION
In summer, millions of ducks, swans, and geese, such as the barnacle goose, migrate to the tundra lands to feed and nest there. They eat new vegetation sprouting from the warm, moist ground.

DOVEKIE

ADAPTATIONS
The Arctic alcids, such as dovekies look like the Antarctic penguins. They have flipperlike wings for swimming, but can fly.

KEEPING WARM

Birds such as the eider duck cover their eggs with soft down which the female plucks from her own breast. This helps to keep the eggs warm until they are ready to hatch.

PENGUIN FLIPPER

SWIMMING

Many birds of these habitats are good swimmers. Penguins have stiff, densely packed scalelike feathers on their wings to reduce the drag of the water against them when swimming.

EIDER NEST

LAPLAND LONGSPUR

FACTS

• Antarctica has 90 percent of all the ice on Earth and 70 percent of all the water.

• Permafrost under the tundra can be up to 4,760 ft (1,450 m) thick.

• The Arctic is an ice-covered ocean surrounded by land – Antarctica is frozen land surrounded by ocean.

FOOD

The tundra summer is brief, but thousands of insects swarm over marshy pools. So birds like the Lapland longspur have plenty of food to collect for their young.

ARCTIC AND TUNDRA

AROUND THE NORTH POLE is a huge ice-covered ocean surrounded by tundra landscape. This region is called the Arctic. In summer months, gulls, auks, and terns feed on the fish at sea, and nest on the coast. The insects and seeds on the tundra are food for shorebirds, ducks, geese, and small songbirds. Before winter, the birds fly south to warmer regions.

Male giving his mate a fishy gift during courtship

ARCTIC TERNS
After courtship, terns raise their young in the Arctic summer, then fly all the way to Antarctica for the summer there. They do an incredible round trip of 22,000 miles (35,400 km).

SNOWY OWL FEET

SNOWY OWL
The plumage of the snowy owl camouflages it against the Arctic landscape, as it glides over the ground looking for prey. Feathers on its legs and feet help it to keep warm.

COMMON REDPOLL
This little bird can survive low
temperatures. It eats a lot of seeds,
and some small insects and their
larvae in summer. Some redpolls
nest in dwarf birches near the
ground in tundra habitats.

*Redpolls are named
after their red
forehead, or "poll."*

EMPEROR GOOSE
This handsome goose breeds
on the tundra in extreme
eastern Russia and in
Alaska. It winters
farther south.

*Adults have
orange legs.*

*In winter, the male
snow bunting turns
browner and looks more
like the female*

SNOW BUNTING
Hardy snow buntings breed in
the Arctic – farther north than
any other perching bird.
They usually hide their
nest from predators
in crannies
in the rocks.

*Snow buntings
may burrow in
the snow to
escape intense
cold.*

ANTARCTICA

THIS VAST AREA of frozen land surrounded by ocean has little rain or snow, so the birds have little fresh water to drink, apart from melted snow. The only land birds are two species of sheathbill. The rest are seabirds, including albatrosses, petrels, and penguins, millions of which nest around the Antarctic coast in summer. They have dense feathers or layers of fat to keep warm, and are strong swimmers or fliers.

BROWN SKUA
With their hooked bills and strong claws, skuas are fierce predators of penguin eggs and chicks. In summer, they regularly invade penguin colonies in Antarctica.

ADELIE PENGUINS
Adelies are one of the two species of penguin that nest on the rocky coasts of Antarctica itself. In spring, they march inland from the sea to nest on the ground in huge rookeries.

BLACK-BROWED ALBATROSSES
Albatrosses mate for life and reinforce the pair bond each year when they return to the nest. This pair are bill-touching and preening each other.

The only bird found in Antarctica that does not have webbed feet

SNOWY SHEATHBILL
Relatives of plovers and other shorebirds, sheathbills scavenge around seal and penguin colonies for all sorts of food scraps, including penguin chicks, seal afterbirths, and even feces.

IMPERIAL SHAGS
These cormorants nest in large colonies on coastal ledges or among rocks. They have strong, hooked bills to grasp slippery fish. In the breeding season, they grow wispy crests.

BLACK-BROWED ALBATROSSES

Nest is a big heap of mud and grass about 24 in (60 cm) high

PENGUINS

WITH THEIR SMOOTH, streamlined shape, and stiff, strong wings, penguins are expert swimmers. They dive to catch fish and squid with their spiky tongues. Dense, oily feathers and thick fat under the skin keep them warm in the cold southern oceans.

Penguins only come out of the water to molt and breed, some in colonies of 500,000.

EMPEROR PENGUINS
These are the biggest penguins. They never come on land, but breed on the ice that floats around Antarctica in winter. Males incubate the single egg for about nine weeks.

KING PENGUINS
The striking golden orange ear patches of these birds are used for display during courtship. The markings also help them to recognize other king penguins. These large penguins can dive as deep as 1,056 ft (322 m).

Powerful, narrow wings for swimming

Stiff tail feathers used to support body on land

Male king penguin incubates egg against bare patch of warm skin

*Porpoising
Adelie penguins*

*In the water,
penguins look dark
from above and
pale from below
– this helps to
camouflage them*

*Feet well
back on
body to act
as rudder*

SWIMMING AND DIVING

In order to breathe while swimming fast, penguins leap in and out of the water. This technique is called porpoising. By porpoising, penguins are thought to be able to swim at up to 17 mph (27 km/h), using their stiff wings to push themselves along.

MACARONI PENGUIN

During their courtship displays, these birds shake their bright yellow head crests. The crests also help them to recognize other macaronis.

*Spread
flippers
cool bird
down*

CHINSTRAP PENGUIN

These penguins are named because of the black line under their chin. They are noisy and quarrelsome birds.

PENGUIN FACTS

- Family: *Spheniscidae*
- About 17 species
- Diurnal and nocturnal
- Flightless seabirds
- Eat fish, squid, and small sea creatures
- Habitat: southern oceans, cool temperate islands, tropical shores
- Nest: stones, grass, mud, caves, or burrows
- Eggs: whitish

MAMMALS

WHAT IS A MAMMAL?

ALL MAMMALS HAVE FUR or hair and a backbone for support, and they are all warm-blooded. Females give birth to live young and feed them with milk from their mammary glands – from which the word *mammal* derives. The most intelligent and adaptable of all animals, they have come to dominate the animal world. There are over 4,600 different kinds of mammals, from enormous whales to tiny bats and shrews.

It takes just less than a year for a foal to grow inside its mother.

Foal, or baby horse, drinks milk from teats between its mother's hind legs

HORSE AND FOAL

YOUNG MAMMALS
Female mammals feed their young by producing milk in mammary glands. For a long time, as their young grow and develop, parents take care of them, passing on survival skills.

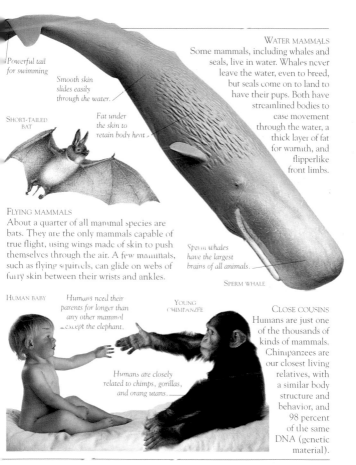

WATER MAMMALS
Some mammals, including whales and seals, live in water. Whales never leave the water, even to breed, but seals come on to land to have their pups. Both have streamlined bodies to ease movement through the water, a thick layer of fat for warmth, and flipperlike front limbs.

Powerful tail for swimming

Smooth skin slides easily through the water.

SHORT-TAILED BAT

Fat under the skin to retain body heat

Sperm whales have the largest brains of all animals.

SPERM WHALE

FLYING MAMMALS
About a quarter of all mammal species are bats. They are the only mammals capable of true flight, using wings made of skin to push themselves through the air. A few mammals, such as flying squirrels, can glide on webs of furry skin between their wrists and ankles.

HUMAN BABY

Humans need their parents for longer than any other mammal except the elephant.

YOUNG CHIMPANZEE

Humans are closely related to chimps, gorillas, and orang utans.

CLOSE COUSINS
Humans are just one of the thousands of kinds of mammals. Chimpanzees are our closest living relatives, with a similar body structure and behavior, and 98 percent of the same DNA (genetic material).

REPRODUCTION

MAMMALS FALL INTO THREE categories of reproduction. Most, including humans, are placental: through an organ called a placenta, mothers nourish their unborn young inside the womb. Marsupial mammals begin developing in the womb but, when still tiny, crawl out to finish growing in their mother's pouch, called a marsupium. The rarest kind are monotremes, the only mammals to lay eggs. Though these three types of mammals reproduce differently, they all feed their young on milk.

PREGNANT WOMAN

Baby develops in mother's uterus.

Baby, or fetus, facing head-down, ready to be born.

Placenta

Blood reaches placenta through umbilical cord.

Muscles of uterus will contract to push baby out.

PLACENTAL MAMMALS
The placenta is a disk-shaped organ that forms in the lining of the uterus after fertilization. The umbilical cord is attached to the placenta. This allows the baby to receive food, oxygen, and antibodies from its mother, and to pass waste products back into her blood.

Amniotic sac is filled with fluid to cushion the baby.

Mucous plug blocks cervix during pregnancy.

FETUS AT 28 WEEKS

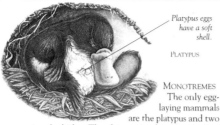

*Platypus eggs
have a soft
shell.*

PLATYPUS

AMAZING FACTS

• At birth, a baby
kangaroo would fit
into a teaspoon.

• While a baby squirrel
takes just 22–45 days to
develop in its mother's
womb, a young elephant
takes as long as two
years to be born!

• Female Norway
lemmings can breed
at just 15 days old.

MONOTREMES

The only egg-
laying mammals
are the platypus and two
species of echidna. The platypus incubates its eggs in a
nest for about three weeks. During incubation, the egg
yolk nourishes the embryo. When they hatch from the
eggs, young monotremes suck milk from their mother.

*Mother's teat swells in
the baby's mouth,
keeping it attached
for 1–2 months.*

*Baby kangaroo,
or joey, stays in
the pouch for
more than
six months*

KANGAROO
AND JOEY

MARSUPIALS

Young marsupials, such as
kangaroos, spend only 12–30 days in
the mother's uterus, and are born in an
immature stage of development. They
then crawl into the pouch to reach
the mother's teats, and feed on her
milk, staying there until fully
developed.

BIRTH AND GROWTH

MOST MAMMALS are born live. Seals, whales, and monkeys and apes have one or two young at a time. On the other hand, some mammals bear 10 or 15 babies in a single pregnancy. Mice can have a litter of 18! Most tropical mammals are born at various times of the year; in temperate and cold climates, however, births usually take place in spring and summer. Mammals tend to spend a lot of time caring for and teaching their young.

HAIRLESS BABIES
Baby mice are born without hair or fur. Unable to see or hear, they are totally dependent on their mother. Fur starts to appear when they are one week old; and after ten days, their eyes open. The young are ready to leave the nest after two or three weeks.

Nesting material helps keep mice warm

NEWBORN MICE

HAIRY BABIES
Kittens are born with all their fur. The mother licks the fur, making it dry and fluffy, so it traps body heat and keeps the kitten warm. Though newborn kittens are active, their eyes and ears are sealed, leaving them temporarily blind and deaf. But they're ready to leave their mother in eight weeks.

Mother cuts through umbilical cord with her teeth

Young hang upside down while their mothers go out to feed.

Each female can recognize the cry of her own young.

BAT ROOST

AMAZING FACTS

• Female rats may have up to 100 babies a year.

• A mother chimpanzee spends six years looking after her young chimp.

• Baby giraffes can run a day after they are born.

• Whales and dolphins give birth in the water.

BAT NURSERY
Young bats are blind and hairless when born. They cling together in a nursery roost, clustered for warmth, while their mothers go off to feed. Newborn in small species fly in about 20 days, but larger species, like flying foxes, take three months to fly.

PARENTAL CARE
Some mammals, including primates such as gorillas, spend many years raising their young – teaching them how to find food and communicate. Mothers provide most of the care; but, as in other social species, like bats, elephants, and lions, infant care may be shared among members of the group.

Gorillas teach their young life skills.

GORILLA AND BABY

SKIN AND HAIR

A MAMMAL'S SKIN forms a protective outer layer that, aided by hair, regulates body temperature. Among all animals, only mammals have hair, which grows as fur, whiskers, wool, prickles, and spines. It retains body heat and keeps out cold, heat, wind, and rain. Some mammals, like chinchillas, have thick, dense fur coats. Others, like whales, have very little hair.

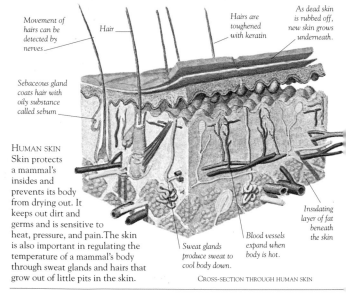

Movement of hairs can be detected by nerves.

Hair

Hairs are toughened with keratin

As dead skin is rubbed off, new skin grows underneath.

Sebaceous gland coats hair with oily substance called sebum

HUMAN SKIN
Skin protects a mammal's insides and prevents its body from drying out. It keeps out dirt and germs and is sensitive to heat, pressure, and pain. The skin is also important in regulating the temperature of a mammal's body through sweat glands and hairs that grow out of little pits in the skin.

Insulating layer of fat beneath the skin

Blood vessels expand when body is hot.

Sweat glands produce sweat to cool body down.

CROSS-SECTION THROUGH HUMAN SKIN

BOTTLENOSE
DOLPHIN

Fatty blubber under the hairless skin smoothes out body contours.

WATERPROOF SKIN
Members of the whale group, which includes dolphins, have smooth, rubbery skin with few hairs. Along with their streamlined bodies, this helps water flow over them. Many seals have heavy, oily fur, which traps air bubbles and keeps them warm and dry. Whales rely on blubber for warmth.

Since they live in hot deserts, camels don't need insulating layers of fat.

MOLTING
Many mammals molt, or shed, their fur coats with the changing seasons. This process is triggered by changes in temperature or light and enables mammals to grow thin summer coats and thicker winter ones. Some mammals, such as Arctic foxes, also change the color of their coat with the seasons.

Fur looks ragged when camel molts its thick winter coat.

MOLTING CAMEL

Teeth and limbs are used to comb and brush the fur.

KEEPING CLEAN
To keep their skin and fur clean and free from parasites, mammals groom by licking, picking, and nibbling at their coats. Some, like elephants, bathe every day. Social mammals groom each other, which reinforces the bonds between individuals.

RAT GROOMING

SENSES

TO PICK UP INFORMATION about their surroundings,
and to communicate with each other, mammals
use their senses of sight, hearing, smell, taste,
and touch. They are the only animals that have
external ear flaps.
Most mammals
see the world in
black and white.

*Some dogs are trained to sniff
out drugs and explosives.*

SMELL

Vital for identifying individuals
and food, along with possible
predators or mates, the sense of smell is
highly developed in some insectivores,
carnivores, (such as dogs) and rodents. In
whales and higher primates, such as
humans, it is much less developed.

BLACK LEOPARD,
OR PANTHER

BEAGLE

*A dog's sense
of smell is a
million times
more sensitive
than our own.*

*Wet nose helps
pick up scents*

CATS WHISKERS

Whiskers are long hairs that usually grow on the
face. Some mammals, however, have whiskers on
their legs, feet, or back. Whiskers respond when
they are touched, helping mammals to feel objects
in the dark and gauge the width of narrow spaces.

*Long,
sensitive whiskers*

Horseshoe bat

Large ears to pick up sound echoes

Sound echoes bouncing off prey

Insect prey

Bats can detect insects as small as midges from a distance of 65.5 ft (20 m)

HOW A BAT USES ECHOLOCATION

ECHOLOCATION
Some bats and dolphins use echolocation to find food. They make high-pitched sounds that bounce off objects in their environment and return as echoes, which can reveal the location of the objects.

BUSHBABY

Large ear flaps funnel sound.

Large eyes to spot prey.

NIGHT SENSES
Many mammals are nocturnal and have sensitive eyes and ears to navigate and locate food in the dark. Bushbabies have huge eyes with pupils that open wide to let in as much light as possible. Their large ears swivel to track small flying insects.

FEEDING AND DIET

MAMMALS MUST EAT regularly to maintain a constant body temperature, particularly small mammals, which need to eat more often than large ones. Most are plant eaters; however, some eat meat, and others have a diet that combines both. Most mammals have three kinds of teeth: incisors and canines for biting and tearing, and molars for grinding. These develop from two sets of teeth – milk teeth in young, and adult teeth that grow as the jaws become larger.

PLANT EATERS
Herbivores, such as cows, horses, camels, sheep, goats, and deer eat only plants. They have long jaws to hold rows of molar teeth, which grind and crush tough plant material. Many have a hard pad instead of top front teeth.

Deep lower jaw to anchor large chewing muscles

Horny pad

Jaws move sideways, as well as up and down.

Gap for tongue to curl around bulky plant food

GOAT SKULL

Carnassial teeth work together like shears

MEAT EATERS
Carnivores, like lions, tigers, and wolves eat meat. Their jaws are shorter and more powerful than those of herbivores. Carnivores have special cheek teeth called carnassials, which have pointed edges that can slice meat or crack bones.

JACKAL SKULL

Powerful canine teeth

BEAVER

Back part of tooth wears away more easily than the front, forming a sloping, chisel-like edge

AMAZING FACTS

• Shrews eat their own weight in food each day and can starve to death in just three hours.

• An adult elephant tooth weighs 10 lb (4.5 kg) – heavier than a brick!

• Vampire bats lap up two teaspoons of blood a day.

EVERGROWING TEETH

Rodents, such as beavers, have four strong front teeth called incisors, which keep growing. Continually worn down, they are kept sharp by constant use. The teeth of pet rodents can grow too long if they lack hard materials to gnaw on.

Curved upper jaw to hold long lengths of baleen

Section cut away to show baleen plates with fringes facing inside the mouth

FOOD STRAINER

Some whales, like the humpback, the gray, and the blue whale, have no teeth. Instead, they have long, fringed plates hanging from their jaws. They draw sea water into their mouths and spit it back out through the baleen fringes, which trap food like a sieve.

BALEEN WHALE

BONES AND MUSCLES

ALL MAMMALS HAVE a skeleton, an internal framework of bones that supports the body and protects its delicate internal organs. Bones cannot move on their own. They are pulled into different positions by firmly attached groups of powerful muscles, enabling mammals to move. Some mammals have especially strong bones and muscles, and can run and swim faster than other animals.

INSIDE A GORILLA
This model of a female gorilla's internal structure shows the position of the bones and muscles. The gorilla is pregnant – the baby inside its womb is almost ready to be born.

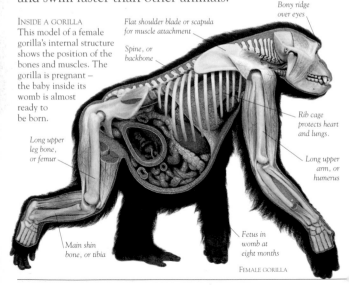

Bony ridge over eyes

Flat shoulder blade or scapula for muscle attachment

Spine, or backbone

Rib cage protects heart and lungs

Long upper arm, or humerus

Long upper leg bone, or femur

Main shin bone, or tibia

Fetus in womb at eight months

FEMALE GORILLA

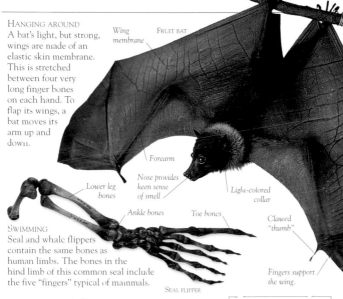

HANGING AROUND
A bat's light, but strong, wings are made of an elastic skin membrane. This is stretched between four very long finger bones on each hand. To flap its wings, a bat moves its arm up and down.

Wing membrane

FRUIT BAT

Forearm

Nose provides keen sense of smell

Light-colored collar

Clawed "thumb"

Fingers support the wing.

SWIMMING
Seal and whale flippers contain the same bones as human limbs. The bones in the hind limb of this common seal include the five "fingers" typical of mammals.

Lower leg bones

Ankle bones

Toe bones

SEAL FLIPPER

BIG FOOT
Although it seems to have flat feet, an elephant walks on the tips of its toes. Its enormous weight rests on the toes and a fibrous cushion under each heel. This heel cushion acts as a shock absorber, and the sole spreads out to cushion the impact of each step.

Heel cushion

Toe bone

INSIDE AN ELEPHANT'S FOOT

AMAZING FACTS
• Nearly all mammals, even giraffes, have seven neck bones.
• Almost half a human's bones are in the feet and hands – 26 in each foot and 27 in each hand.
• The average mammal has about 200 bones in its skeleton.

DEFENSE

PLANT-EATING MAMMALS, especially small ones, have many enemies. Among these predators are meat-eating mammals, snakes, and birds. To avoid detection, some herbivores are camouflaged. Others bear weapons – from claws and spiky coats to horns, armor, and terrible smells.

Horns are not shed each year, like a deer's antlers.

Pointed tips of horns could injure a predator.

Curved (annulated) horn

ANTELOPE SKULL

Joints between bones

Unlike antlers, horns are never branched but are curved and twisted.

PORCUPINE

SPIKE ATTACK
If threatened, a porcupine will turn its back, rattle its quills, grunt, and stamp its feet. If the enemy won't retreat, the porcupine charges it in reverse, sticking quills into its skin.

HORNS, ANTLERS, AND TUSKS
Used mainly to fight other males in competition for a mate or territory, horns, antlers, and tusks are also useful in defense. The horns of antelope, cattle, and sheep are hollow structures made of bone that has a slightly softer covering.

ODOR POWER

The striking color of the skunk alerts enemies to stay away. If they don't, the skunk will turn its back, stamp its feet, and raise its tail. Then it squirts its enemy with foul-smelling liquid, which takes a long time to wear off.

Skunk can spray smelly liquid 12 ft (3.6 m)

Body armor is impossible to penetrate.

ARMADILLO

ARMOR-PLATING

The body of an armadillo is encased in bony plates, or scutes. Some of the 20 armadillo species roll up into a ball when attacked, to protect their soft underparts.

Handstand warns enemy to watch out!

SPOTTED SKUNK

OKAPI

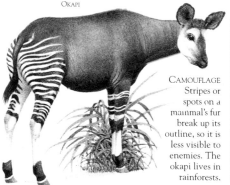

CAMOUFLAGE

Stripes or spots on a mammal's fur break up its outline, so it is less visible to enemies. The okapi lives in rainforests.

DEFENSE FACTS

- Opossums play dead if attacked – predators prefer live animals.

- Zebra stallions kick lions, sometimes smashing their teeth.

- Only two mammals are poisonous: the male platypus has poison spurs on its back legs, and the water shrew has poisonous saliva.

MAMMAL HOMES

BUILT IN TREES, under the soil, in riverbanks and lakes, or even in people's houses, mammal homes provide a safe, warm shelter that protects them and their young from the weather and from enemies. To construct their dwellings, mammals use natural materials, such as grass, leaves, sticks, and fur and use their teeth and limbs to shape them. Many of these homes, such as badger setts, are permanent, while others are built daily or seasonally.

Outer layer of twigs and leaves

Cozy lining of grass, moss, leaves, bark, feathers, and sheep's wool

GRAY SQUIRREL IN NEST

TREE HOUSES
As trees are exposed, they are battered by wind and rain. For protection, squirrels build round tree-nests, in which they rest, sleep, and raise their young. Most nests are built in a new tree each year. Winter nests are stronger than summer ones, and special nurseries are built for the young.

Gerbil carries straw for lining its nest.

GERBIL

Vent at the top lets fresh air in and stale air out.

Beavers live in a chamber in the middle of the lodge.

GRASSY HOMES
Mammals use grass and straw for lining burrows and nests and weave it into the walls of their homes. Gerbils line their homes with shredded plant matter.

BEAVER LODGE

STICK HOMES
Beavers use sticks and mud to build a dome-shaped lodge in the middle of a pond. They weave the sticks into place with their front feet. Sticks are also used by pack rats or wood rats in North America.

BURROWS
Underground burrows protect mammals from extremes of temperature and from predators. Moles spend a lot of time underground.

Fortress – large molehill above nest

Breeding nest is lined with grass, leaves, and other soft material

INSIDE A MOLE BURROW

Tunnels are about 2 in (5 cm) wide

Moles use front feet to dig tunnels in the soil.

Moles patrol their tunnels, repairing them and eating worms and insects that fall in through the walls.

Fresh worms in a "larder"

WHERE MAMMALS LIVE

MAMMALS LIVE all over the world, from mountaintops and the icy poles to baking hot deserts. They can do this because they are warm-blooded, which enables them to keep a constant body temperature – even when their surroundings are extremely hot or very cold.

WOODLANDS AND FORESTS
There is plenty of food and shelter in these habitats, but mammals have to cope with seasonal changes that bring cold weather and less food.

NORTH AMERICA

ATLANTIC OCEAN

PACIFIC OCEAN

SOUTH AMERICA

AFRICA

Woodlands and forests

Rainforests

Grasslands

Deserts

Mountains and polar

Oceans and seas

Freshwater bodies

RAINFORESTS
The year-round warm, wet climate encourages a variety of mammals that live in the trees and on the forest floor.

FRESHWATER BODIES
Mammals in rivers, lakes, and swamps are often strong swimmers with waterproof fur and webbed feet.

OCEANS AND SEAS
These habitats form 70 percent of the earth's surface. Some mammals breed on land; others never leave the water.

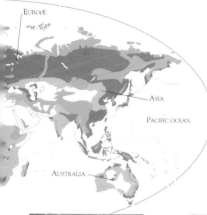

EUROPE

ASIA

PACIFIC OCEAN

AUSTRALIA

MOUNTAINS AND POLAR
With cold temperatures, strong winds, and little moisture, these habitats are home to some of the hardiest mammals.

GRASSLANDS
Small burrowers and herds of grazers live in both hot and cool grasslands, which occur where it is too dry for trees.

DESERTS
Desert mammals are specially adapted to survive dry conditions and extreme temperatures. Many store food and rarely drink.

WOODLANDS AND FORESTS

PLENTY OF FOOD, shelter, and nesting places are to be found in woodlands and forests. The main large herbivores are deer. Many small herbivores, such as mice and voles, live in the undergrowth away from predators such as stoats and wolverines. Much of this habitat is protected, but some is still threatened by logging and pollution.

Powerful legs help pine martens climb

Long, bushy tail helps provide balance.

FOOD AND FEEDING
From nuts and berries to leaves and bark, food for plant eaters like chipmunks is abundant here and varies with the seasons. Small mammals scurrying through fallen leaves are a major source of food for predators.

NIGHT HUNTERS
Many woodland mammals rest during the day and become active at night, especially at dusk or dawn. The pine marten is a swift and agile hunter of birds and rodents in trees and on the ground.

Chipmunks crack nuts with their strong front teeth.

CHIPMUN[K]

MOVING THROUGH THE FOREST
Some woodland mammals climb trees, or glide or fly between them, to find food or places to shelter and nest. Climbers, such as squirrels and koalas, have sharp claws for gripping, while gliding mammals can parachute from tree to tree. Only bats fly freely though the branches.

SUGAR GLIDER

Flaps of skin are spread along sides of body to glide between trees.

WINTER SURVIVAL
Mammals survive the winter in many ways. Some, such as the sable, have a thick fur coat to keep warm, while others build up food stores for the hard times ahead. Certain mammals hibernate, or rest, during cold periods.

Sable is up to 18 in (45 cm) long

Thick fur coat

Even the soles of the feet are furry.

Hedgehogs have up to 5,000 sharp, stiff spines.

HEDGEHOG

HIBERNATING HEDGEHOGS
When a mammal such as a hedgehog or a dormouse hibernates, its body processes slow down, keeping it barely alive. In this deep sleep, there is no need to waste energy finding food or keeping warm. A hibernating mammal relies on stores of food or body fat and a protected den to help it survive.

No spines underneath body

DECIDUOUS WOODLANDS

IN TEMPERATE WOODLANDS, mammal lifestyles change with the seasons. Young are born in spring, so they can grow strong by the time winter comes. In summer and autumn, mammals feed as much as possible to gain stores of fat for winter's lean months. While larger mammals spend the winter resting in their burrows, many small ones stay active to keep warm.

Meadow vole is hard to see among dead leaves.

UNDER COVER

Hidden in vegetation and leaf litter, small mammals, such as voles, depend on camouflage for survival. As they must feed frequently, many climb trees to collect nuts and other food for storage in underground chambers.

SKILLED CLIMBERS

Leaping nimbly from branch to branch, gray squirrels are masters of life in the trees. They can balance on the thinnest twigs and run up and down tree trunks by climbing with their sharp claws. Food is kept in their twiggy tree nests, called drays, or buried in the ground.

Squirrels eat nuts and seeds.

Bushy tail used for balance

Badgers have keen senses of smell and hearing but poor eyesight.

Black-and-white face markings break up the outline of the badger, so it is hard to see in twilight.

Long, strong claws for digging underground homes

Whiskers brush against surroundings to help the weasel navigate in the dark.

BURROWING BADGERS

A family of badgers lives in a system of underground burrows which may be hundreds of years old. Signs of occupied burrows include well-marked paths, piles of old bedding material, and dung pits.

AMAZING FACTS

• The largest system of badger burrows had 50 underground chambers and 178 entrances.

• Gray squirrels carry acorns up to 100 ft (30 m) from an oak tree before burying them.

• Dormice in some countries hibernate for as long as nine months.

WOODLAND PREDATOR

Ferocious hunters of small animals, weasels are slim enough to chase mice or voles right into their burrows. During the winter months in cold, snowy climates, weasels may grow a white coat, making it hard for both prey and predators to see them.

Sharp claws

Weasels often stand up on their hind legs to look for signs of food and danger.

CONIFEROUS FORESTS

STRETCHING ACROSS northern Europe, Asia, and North
America, coniferous forests provide year-round shelter
for mammals. In the bitter winters, some mammals
hibernate and others turn white for camouflage. To
conserve heat, mammals that live here have thick
fur coats and are larger than their southern relatives.

*Powerful
muscles give
bears great
strength.*

SLEEPY BEAR
In autumn, brown
bears eat as much as
possible to build up fat
stores that keep them
alive during the winter.
In winter, females give
birth to cubs, while
males have periods of
inactivity. Bears are not
true hibernators – if it
turns warm, they wake
up and begin feeding.

*Powerful jaws and
teeth allow the bear to
eat a variety of foods.*

*Thick fur coat
protects the bear
against freezing
temperatures.*

*Strong claws for
killing prey or digging
for plant food*

Fur is molted in summer

Long ears pick up sounds clearly

AMAZING FACTS

• A hibernating bat may breathe only once every 45 minutes.

• Red squirrels can smell and find pinecones buried 12 in (30 cm) underground.

• A wolverine can drag prey carcasses several times its own weight for several miles.

BIG EARS!
Long-eared bats hover in the trees where they catch insects. They feed at night, navigating by making high-pitched sounds and picking up the echoes as they bounce back off nearby objects.

Powerful jaws give a crushing bite.

Thick fur keeps in heat.

PERSISTENT PREDATOR
As the largest member of the weasel family, the fierce wolverine can catch animals as large as caribou (reindeer), pursuing them for up to 40 miles (65 km). Inuit peoples once prized wolverine fur for making coats because it can shed ice crystals.

Widespread toes help the wolverine to travel over snow without sinking

Young have more distinct stripes than adults.

WILD THING
The striped coat of the wildcat provides good camouflage for stalking the forest. Wildcats live a solitary life, hunting at night. They are closely related to domestic cats.

EUCALYPTUS WOODLANDS

AUSTRALIA'S HOT, DRY woodlands provide food
and shelter all year round. Most mammals here are
marsupials (pouched mammals) that come out at
night, using their sharp senses of smell and hearing
to find their way around. Some, such as koalas,
live in the trees, while others,
including bandicoots,
live on the forest floor.

POUCHED JUMPER

During the day, groups, or mobs, of gray
kangaroos rest under the trees, but at
night they search for plants to eat. Young
kangaroos stay in the pouch for up to 11
months, longer than any other marsupial,
and suckle until they are 18 months old.

*Large ears and
eyes and keen
sense of smell
to detect signs
of danger.*

AMAZING FACTS

• A baby kangaroo,
or joey, is the fastest-
growing animal. When
born, it is thimble-sized,
but it grows by 30,000
times in its lifetime.

• The common wombat
is the largest burrowing
marsupial. It burrows
at 10 ft (3 m) an hour.

*Front
limbs
have five
clawed
digits.*

*Kangaroos
graze with
all four feet
on the ground*

*Powerful back legs for
bounding away from
enemies*

*Tail helps
keep balance.*

FUSSY EATERS

The tree-dwelling koala seldom comes to the ground, clinging to branches with its strong limbs and sharp claws. Koalas spend about 18 hours a day snoozing in the trees. When awake, they feed only on the leaves of 12 out of the 100 species of eucalyptus tree, eating about 3 lb (1.5 kg) of leaves each day.

A baby koala lives in its mother's pouch for six months, then spends another six months carried on her back.

Koalas have a long intestine to help digest tough leaves.

Tail can grow 8 in (20 cm) long

Numbats have about 50 teeth.

TERMITE HUNGRY

One of the few mammals in these woodlands to be active during the day, numbats eat thousands of termites, which they collect with their long, narrow tongue.

Striped coat camouflages numbat from predators such as eagles.

NUMBAT

The name "devil" comes from its black color and eerie call.

LETHAL PREDATOR

The huge head and strong jaws of the Tasmanian devil allow it to crush and eat its prey, bones and all. Tasmanian devils live in dens under rocks or tree stumps and are mainly nocturnal. Their young stay in the pouch for about 15 weeks and then are left in the nest or carried around on the mother's back until 20 weeks of age, when they are weaned.

Sensitive nose to sniff out prey

Deer

Woods and forests, home to many kinds of deer, provide ample food and shelter. In this habitat, deer are hard to spot, with their camouflaged coat and shy nature. They use their sharp senses to detect danger, and long legs to nimbly leap away.

Upper canines form tusks

MALE MUNTJAC SKULL

Grinding teeth
The narrow snout of the deer allows it to reach into small spaces to find food. Molar teeth grind and mash tough plant matter.

Long legs and broad hooves to move through swamps or deep snow

Males have broad, flat antlers, which they use to joust with each other in competition for a mate.

Overhanging top lip tears off leaves and branches.

Flap of skin is known as the bell.

Strong neck and shoulder muscles support heavy head and antlers.

Largest deer
Moose, or elk, are the largest deer, weighing up to 1,000 lb (450 kg) and standing 6.5 ft (2 m) tall at the shoulder. Unlike most deer, moose do not live in groups and, excluding the autumn breeding season, are usually alone or with their young. In winter, moose eat woody plants, but in summer, they wade into water for more tender vegetation.

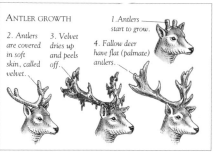

ANTLER GROWTH

2. Antlers are covered in soft skin, called velvet.

3. Velvet dries up and peels off.

1. Antlers start to grow.

4. Fallow deer have flat (palmate) antlers.

RED DEER AND FAWN

DEER ANTLERS

All male deer, apart from Chinese water deer, have, on their head, a set of bony antlers which serve as a sign of strength and dominance. They shed and grow a new set of antlers each year. In the autumn rutting (mating) season, male deer use their antlers in pushing contests to win females.

ROE DEER

The reddish brown coat of the roe deer blends in well with the summer colors of woods and forests. In winter, it grows a thick, gray-brown coat for warmth and camouflage.

Antlers no more than 12 in (30 cm) long

MALE ROE DEER

AMAZING DEER FACTS

• Deer are the only animals in the world to have antlers.

• The American wapiti and the caribou have the longest antlers, at about 5 ft (1.5 m) in length!

• The South American pudu is the smallest deer, at 15 in (38 cm) tall!

• Red deer are likely to live for over 30 years.

RAINFORESTS

THE WORLD'S RICHEST habitat, rainforests provide a year-round warm, wet climate and a variety of food and resting places. Most mammals here are agile climbers that live in trees, but large predators stalk the forest floor. Rainforests are being destroyed at an alarming rate.

Thin "wings" of skin run along the sides of the body.

COLUGO, ALSO CALLED FLYING LEMUR

GLIDING IN THE TREES
Gripping with long toes, claws, or tails; gliding on skin flaps; or flying with wings, mammals move easily from branch to branch in search of food or mates or to escape danger.

Canopy: monkeys, fruit bats, sloths, gliders

Understory: jungle cats, tree kangaroos, lorises

Forest floor: peccaries, tapirs, okapis, elephants

LAYERS OF THE RAINFOREST
Mammals share the rich resources of the rainforest by living at various levels. In the trees, there are leaves, flowers, insects, fruits, and nuts on which to feed. The forest floor provides a feast of millions more insects, spiders, worms, and other invertebrates, as well as plant roots, shoots, and fungi.

FOREST ECHOES
Visual communication is difficult among thick tangles of vegetation, so many mammals, especially monkeys and apes, rely on sound or scent signals instead. They mark territorial boundaries by scent or shrill cries, sounding alarms and remaining in contact with one another by calling.

Tail can be 3 ft (90 cm) long

HOWLER MONKEY

A tiger's stripes help it stalk its prey without being seen.

Every tiger has a different pattern of black stripes on its face.

Calls of the howler monkey can be heard up to 2 miles (3 km) away.

Tigers live in the forests of Southeast Asia and mark their territories with scent and droppings.

WELL CAMOUFLAGED
Spots, stripes, and other markings on rainforest mammals help to camouflage them in the dappled forest light. They break up the animal's outline and blend it in with the background. Both predators, such as tigers, and their prey, such as deer, use camouflage. Young mammals are often better camouflaged than their parents.

TIGER

IN THE TREES

HIGH UP IN the rainforest, tangled tree branches form tricky walkways. Mammals living here may be swift-moving climbers or flyers, or slow movers that can grasp branches well. Many tree-dwelling mammals come out at night to avoid predators such as cats, hawks, eagles, and snakes.

SPIDER MONKEY

Gripping tail

Long fingers to catch onto branches

JUNGLE ACROBAT
The strong tail of the spider monkey supports its weight, allowing it to reach fruits and leaves that would otherwise be out of reach. Spider monkeys can make acrobatic leaps of 33 ft (10 m) through the branches.

LAZING IN THE TREES
Hanging upside down from branches in the rainforests of Central and South America, sloths spend 20 hours a day snoozing in the canopy. Their fur grows toward the spine so that rain runs straight off their backs. Green algae grow in the hair, camouflaging the sloth.

The sloth hooks its claws around branches and moves only one limb at a time

Nine neck vertebrae allow the sloth to turn its head farther than other mammals

SLOTH

FRUIT BAT

Bats roost in trees, folding their wings around their body and gripping tightly with their strong claws

Figs and mangoes are easily crushed with strong teeth and tongues.

Fruit bats have excellent eyesight and a fine sense of smell for detecting ripe fruit.

Because their faces look like those of foxes, fruit bats are sometimes called flying foxes.

NECTAR SPREADER
The flowering and fruiting trees of the rainforest make ideal homes for bats that eat pollen, nectar, or fruit. These bats are useful in spreading the pollen and seeds of rainforest plants. Long, bristly tongues help pollen- and nectar-eaters to scoop up food.

TREE KANGAROO

Sharp claws for climbing

Feet are strong and wide, with rough pads for gripping branches.

The tree kangaroo lives in the cooler forests of New Guinea and has a warm fur coat.

KEEPING A BALANCE
Living in northeast Australia and New Guinea, tree kangaroos have long tails that help them to balance on branches. They do not hop like other kangaroos. Small groups of tree kangaroos live and sleep together in the same tree, but they usually come down to feed.

IN THE TREES FACTS

• Three-toed sloths are slow movers, with an average ground speed of just 6–8 ft (1.83–2.44 m) a minute.

• The tail of a spider monkey can grow to 3 ft (90 cm)   a third longer than its body length!

• Fruit bats are the largest of all bats, with wing spans as great as 7 ft (2 m)!

ON THE FOREST FLOOR

THE RAINFOREST FLOOR is home to larger mammals. Herbivores, such as elephants, and gorillas feed on leaves, while anteaters, pangolins, and armadillos eat termites and other invertebrates. Peccaries dig out roots, keeping a lookout for predators, such as jaguars and ocelots.

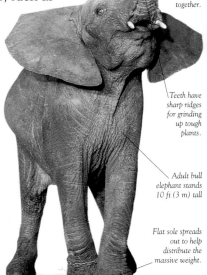

Long trunk reaches up to pick fruit or tear down branches.

Trunk is a long nose and top lip joined together.

STURDY HERBIVORE
Consuming around 375 lb (170 kg) of fibrous plant matter a day, elephants need to have tough stomachs. Their trunks are vital for reaching understory vegetation.

Teeth have sharp ridges for grinding up tough plants.

FOREST FLOOR FACTS

• The armadillo's front claws, used for digging up prey, are larger than any other animal's.

• You can tell an Asian elephant from an African one by its smaller ears and shorter tusks. Its dome-shaped forehead also contrasts with the African elephant's rounded one.

Adult bull elephant stands 10 ft (3 m) tall

Flat sole spreads out to help distribute the massive weight.

AFRICAN ELEPHANT

SHY ANTELOPE

Rabbit-sized royal antelope, which live in African rainforests, are one of the smallest hoofed mammals. They are timid, coming out at night to feed on leaves. Royal antelope can slip away silently or leap as high as 10 ft (3 m) into the air to escape predators such as birds and snakes.

Females do not have horns.

ROYAL ANTELOPE

Protective horny plates

GIANT ARMADILLO

CHAMPION DIGGER

Massive claws on its front feet enable the giant armadillo to smash its way inside rock-hard termite mounds. It also digs for other insects, worms, and spiders, and eats snakes.

Each ocelot has different fur markings.

RARE PAINTED LEOPARD

The ocelot, or painted leopard, lives in the rainforests of Central and South America. Hunting at night, the ocelot has large, keen eyes for navigating the dark forest, and its spotted coat gives camouflage as it creeps up on prey. Ocelots are rare because of forest destruction and hunting for their fur.

JUNGLE APES

TROPICAL RAINFORESTS are home to all the
world's apes, including gibbons, chimpanzees,
gorillas, and orangutans. Unlike
monkeys, apes do not have
tails. Gorillas and chimpanzees spend
much of their time on the ground, while
gibbons and orangutans swing through
the trees. Apes usually live in families
and feed by day.

HANGING AROUND
Gibbons are mainly vegetarian and live
in small groups in Asian rainforests.
Confident, skilled climbers, gibbons
can run upright
along large
branches and swing
effortlessly through the trees.

*Lower spine is short and
inflexible, and rib cage is
solid to avoid distorting
the trunk while swinging.*

*Arms are longer
than legs.*

OUR CLOSEST RELATIVES?
This chimp is investigating
a toy block. Chimps are
intelligent, communicating
by sound and gesture.

AMAZING APE FACTS

• The heaviest ape was
a zoo gorilla weighing
683½ lb (310 kg).

• Some apes can live to
be over 50 years old.

• Chimps have learned
over 20 different ways of
using everyday objects –
such as stones, leaves,
and twigs – as tools.

GIBBON SWINGING
THROUGH TREES

*Arms are twice as
long as legs, at a
span of about
6 ft (2 m).*

*Flexible hooklike
hands quickly grasp
branches or prey.*

*Hand-over-
hand swinging
movement is
called brachiation.*

*Making "rowing"
movements with its legs
helps the gibbon propel
itself through the air.*

GENTLE GIANT

This male gorilla is the head of
a family group that wanders
through the forest, eating fruit and
ferns. Females and young climb trees,
but males rarely
do because
they are so
big and
heavy.

*Mature male
gorillas have
silvery gray hair
on their backs
and are called
"silver-backs."*

*Fatty
throat
pouch*

*Long,
powerful
arms*

FIVE YEAR-
OLD MALE

KING OF THE SWINGERS

In the forests of
Borneo and Sumatra, shy
orangutans live a solitary
life, except in breeding
season. Males are much
heavier and larger than
females, and mature males have
wide cheek flaps on their faces.

MALE GORILLA

405

GRASSLANDS

LYING BETWEEN wet forests and dry deserts, grasslands fall into two categories– tropical, such as the African savanna, and temperate, such as the prairies or steppes. Grassland mammals include plant-eating herds, small burrowers, and the predators that feed on both groups.

Prairie dogs live in colonies of thousands in underground tunnels.

PRAIRIE DOG

Horns measure up to 16 in (40 cm)

Strong, grinding teeth to reduce tough grasses and leaves.

Long legs and sharp hooves to run swiftly away from danger

THOMSON'S GAZELLE

BURROWERS
To avoid the heat and cold, and to escape predators and fires, many small mammals burrow underground. Their burrowing, meanwhile, mixes the soil and encourages plant growth.

GRAZERS
The most common large grassland herbivores are grazers – grass-eating mammals like antelope, bison, and horses. Grasses, which sprout again when the tops are bitten off, produce a continuous supply of food. Grazers, such as Thomson's gazelle, live in herds of up to 100 for protection against predators.

HUNTERS

Most large hunters – like lions, cheetahs, leopards, and hyenas– are found on the African savanna. Since they hunt in groups, lions and hyenas can prey on animals much bigger than themselves. Cheetahs hunt alone but can run fast enough to catch swift antelopes.

CHEETAH → THOMSON'S GAZELLE

LION → WILDEBEEST

HYENA → ZEBRA

GRASSLAND CATS

Cats, big and small, are common grassland hunters. Small cats, like caracals and servals, have longer legs than forest cats and rely on speed and surprise to catch their prey. Cats overpower prey with a vicious bite from their powerful jaws, which are armed with sharp, dagger-like teeth.

Fur tufts on ears can be 1¾ in (4.5 cm) long.

Caracal is a Turkish word meaning "black ears."

Sharp teeth for tearing prey apart

A swipe of the paw can kill a bird in mid-air.

CARACAL

PAMPAS AND STEPPES

THE PLAINS called pampas in South America and steppes in Europe and central Asia have hot summers and cold winters. Many small mammals, such as cavies on the pampas and hamsters on the steppes, shelter underground. Herds of wild grazers have mostly been replaced by domesticated cattle and horses.

Coat turns white and thickens in winter

Nostrils can be closed during sand storms

SAIGA ANTELOPE

STEPPE GRAZERS
The saiga antelope's long nose helps to warm the air it inhales during cold winters on the steppes. Huge herds of saigas once roamed the steppes; they are now a protected species.

As anteaters have no teeth, food is mashed up by hard ridges in the mouth and a muscular stomach.

Tongue pushes out 150 times a minute.

MANED WOLF

GIANT PREDATOR
Insects are the main grazers of the pampas, and make a tasty meal for the giant anteater. Anteaters feed mostly on ants and termites, ripping open nests with their big claws and licking the insects with their sticky tongues.

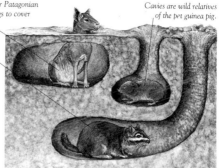

To escape danger, maras or Patagonian hares can use their back legs to cover 6½ ft (2 m) in one leap.

Viscachas dig with their strong front legs and can close their nostrils to stop soil from getting in.

Cavies are wild relatives of the pet guinea pig.

BUSY BURROWERS
Underground burrows provide safe shelter for small mammals of the pampas, such as the mara, cavy, and viscacha. Maras and cavies may live in old viscacha burrows in groups of up to 40.

Maned wolves run fast but usually ambush prey rather than chasing after it.

LONG-LEGGED HUNTER
The maned wolf, which is actually a large fox, has long legs to help it to see over tall grasses. If it is threatened, its mane stands up to make it appear bigger and more frightening. The maned wolf lives alone and hunts at night for cavies and other small mammals and birds.

AMAZING FACTS
• A giant anteater's tongue is about 24 in (60 cm) long.
• Saigas were over-hunted for their horns, which were used in Chinese medicines. Now, they are protected and their numbers have increased.

AFRICAN SAVANNAS

THE HUGE GRASSLANDS of Africa are called savannas. They are home to the last great herds of mammals, such as elephants and antelope, and their predators, including hyenas and large cats. There are two main seasons – wet and dry – and many grazers migrate regularly in search of fresh grass to eat.

Meerkats sit up on their hind legs to watch for danger

Annual rainfall is greater in the north

Dry season

Serengeti National Park, Kenya

Direction of wildebeest journey

Wet season

SUN LOVERS
Meerkats live in family groups, sharing lookout duty and diving for cover if alarmed. Active during the day, meerkats are often found basking in the sun near the entrances to their burrows.

SAVANNA JOURNEY
Wildebeest trek 1,000 miles (1,600 km) across the savanna, following seasonal rains that bring the dry grass back to life. Living in herds gives them some defense against predators.

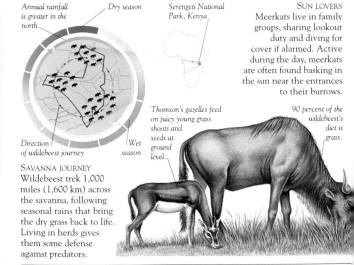

Thomson's gazelles feed on juicy young grass shoots and seeds at ground level.

90 percent of the wildebeest's diet is grass.

Large, rounded ears

Giraffes can reach leaves up to 20 ft (6 m) above the ground

Only four toes on front foot

EFFICIENT PREDATORS

Living in packs of 6 to 30, African hunting dogs are nomadic animals, roaming a wide area in search of prey. By hunting together, the dogs can bring down prey larger than themselves, even wildebeest. The pack shares a kill.

Many savanna animals have patterned skin for camouflage.

SHARING FOOD

Various mammals live together on the savanna, sharing resources. Giraffes feed on the highest leaves; zebras crop the top of the grasses; wildebeest eat the medium-length grasses; and Thomson's gazelles nibble grass close to the ground.

Zebras feed on tough, grass tops and also dig for roots.

AMAZING FACTS

• Hyenas have jaws so strong that they can crunch through bones.

• Young wildebeest can run very soon after they are born.

• African hunting dogs may start to feed on their prey while it is still alive.

GRASSLAND CATS

INTELLIGENT, POWERFUL hunters with sharp senses, grassland cats, both big and small, have strong claws and teeth and a rasping tongue to scrape meat off bones. The spotted coats of leopards, cheetahs, and servals, and the tawny-colored fur of caracals and lions, provide camouflage in the golden grasses. Lions are the only big cats to live in social groups.

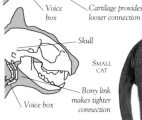

Skull BIG CAT

Voice box

Cartilage provides looser connection

Skull

SMALL CAT

Bony link makes tighter connection

Voice box

Male lion's mane makes him look fiercer and protects his neck during fights

MALE

TO ROAR OR PURR?
In most big cats, such as lions or tigers, the skull and voice box are loosely connected, allowing the cat to roar but not purr. In pumas and wildcats, the link between the skull and voice box is tighter and less flexible. They can purr, but they cannot roar.

Streamlined body *Flexible spine*

At top speed, all four feet are lifted between strides.

Tail helps the cheetah balance when sprinting

Long legs for fast running

Exposed claws grip the ground.

Claws are made of keratin, like human nails.

RELAXED

EXTENDED

FAST CAT
Cheetahs hunt by day, stalking and attacking prey with a short burst of speed. They can reach 60 mph (96 km/h) in just three seconds.

KING OF THE CATS
Lions live in groups called prides, made up of 5 to 15 related adult females and their young and 1 to 6 adult males. Males defend the pride while females hunt and care for the young. Lions are the only cats to hunt together, share prey, and help rear one another's cubs.

CAT CLAWS
All cats, except cheetahs, can draw in their claws. This allows the cat to creep up on prey. A cat has four claws on its back paws and five on its front.

Male and female lions look more different than the two sexes of any other cat.

FEMALE

AMAZING CAT FACTS
• Lions sleep or doze for up to 20 hours every day.
• A lion's roar can be heard up to 3 miles (5 km) away.
• A cheetah can only run at top speed for 60 seconds, or it overheats.
• Adult lions eat as much as 40 lb (18 kg) of meat in one meal.

DESERTS

VERY LITTLE RAIN falls on the world's deserts. Most of them, such as the Sahara, are scorching hot all year round, although they get very cold at night. Some, such as the Gobi, have freezing winters. Many small desert mammals are nocturnal, burrowing by day to protect themselves from the extreme heat. Most desert mammals can survive with very little water. Their fur keeps out heat as well as cold.

Both sexes have thin spiral horns, but the female's are thinner.

The addax gets as much moisture as it can from food.

Addax travel around the African deserts in herds searching for food and water.

Wide-spreading feet stop addax from sinking into the sand.

ADDAX

LARGE MAMMALS
There are few large desert mammals because there is not enough food and water to keep them alive. Only a few kinds of specialized mammals, such as addax, camels, gazelle, antelopes, and kangaroos, manage to survive. They often have to travel long distances in search of water.

DESERT DEFENSE

By coming out at night, small mammals avoid predators as well as the heat of the day. The light color of their fur helps them to blend in with the sand and rocks. Small mammals often leap out of the way of predators.

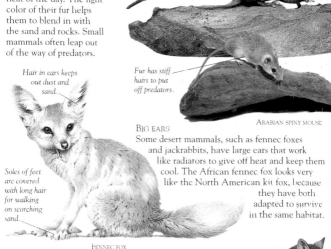

EGYPTIAN SPINY MOUSE

Tail can be shed if grabbed by predator.

Fur has stiff hairs to put off predators.

ARABIAN SPINY MOUSE

Hair in ears keeps out dust and sand.

BIG EARS

Some desert mammals, such as fennec foxes and jackrabbits, have large ears that work like radiators to give off heat and keep them cool. The African fennec fox looks very like the North American kit fox, because they have both adapted to survive in the same habitat.

Soles of feet are covered with long hair for walking on scorching sand.

FENNEC FOX

DESERT BURROWERS

Most burrowing mammals, such as mulgaras, stay underground until the heat of the day has passed. The sand is much cooler slightly below the surface. The mammals' breath creates a moist atmosphere in the burrow, reducing the amount of water evaporating from their bodies. Many small mammals store food in their burrows to last them through lean times.

MULGARA

Mulgaras never drink and excrete concentrated urine to preserve water.

HOT DESERTS

TEMPERATURES IN THE deserts of western North America, Australia, and the African Sahara are scorching during the day. Because there are no clouds to retain the heat, however, they drop to freezing at night. There are few plants to provide shelter from the extreme temperatures. Most mammals avoid the daytime sun. Others have large ears or light coats to lose heat, and some pant to cool down. The dew that forms at night may provide much needed moisture.

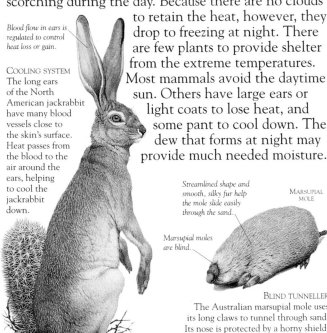

Blood flow in ears is regulated to control heat loss or gain.

COOLING SYSTEM
The long ears of the North American jackrabbit have many blood vessels close to the skin's surface. Heat passes from the blood to the air around the ears, helping to cool the jackrabbit down.

Streamlined shape and smooth, silky fur help the mole slide easily through the sand.

MARSUPIAL MOLE

Marsupial moles are blind.

BLIND TUNNELLER
The Australian marsupial mole uses its long claws to tunnel through sand. Its nose is protected by a horny shield. The burrows are not permanent – the sand is soft and tunnels collapse quickly.

Large ears to listen for prey and keep cool

UNSINKABLE CAT
Thick fur on the soles of the sand cat's feet prevent it from sinking into the soft sand. Sand cats shelter in a burrow or under scrub vegetation during the day and hunt at night. They don't drink, getting all the water they need from their prey.

Yellow brown coat blends into desert background.

SAND CAT

NO SWEAT
Like all rodents, kangaroo rats conserve water by not sweating and by producing only a small amount of urine and dry droppings. Kangaroo rats are nocturnal and travel long distances looking for food. When they find seeds, they carry them in their cheek pouches.

Long tail helps the kangaroo rat balance while hopping and running.

Big ears to listen for danger

Strong back legs for leaping away from predators

KANGAROO RAT

AMAZING FACTS
• Jackrabbits can bound at 35 mph (56 km/h).
• The kidneys of a kangaroo rat are four times more efficient than those of a person.
• Lions once lived in the Sahara but died out due to hunting by man and increasing dryness.

COLD DESERTS

CENTRAL ASIA'S COLD DESERTS, such as the Gobi desert, are harsh habitats for mammals. Besides great swings in temperature between day and night, there are freezing winters of -42°F (-40°C). Some mammals, such as Bactrian camels and dwarf hamsters, rely on their thick coats to keep warm. Small mammals survive desert conditions by spending a lot of time in burrows. Many have long legs to escape from predators.

The onager's coat is thicker in winter

MIGRATOR
Also called the Asiatic wild ass, the onager can run away from enemies at speeds of 40 mph (65 km/h). It migrates to find fresh grass and water.

Some turn white in winter for camouflage in the snow.

Camels can close their nostrils to prevent sand getting in.

Even the soles of the feet are hairy.

HAIRY HAMSTER
As they forage for seeds and nuts, dwarf hamsters push food into their cheek pouches and then carry it underground for storage. Dwarf hamsters have very thick fur to help them survive the extreme climate. They also stay in their burrows much of the time.

DESERT JUMPER

In the darkness of the desert night, jerboas emerge from their burrows to feed on seeds, shoots, and insects. Jerboas are like tiny kangaroos, able to jump away from enemies on their strong back legs. Their long tail helps them to balance when they jump and supports their body when they rest.

Large ears and eyes to sense danger.

Back legs are four times as long as the front legs.

WALKING WATER TANK

The thick fur of a two-humped Bactrian camel holds in body heat during the bitterly cold Asian winters. These camels molt fur in spring when the weather gets warmer. Camels have long, thick eyelashes to protect their eyes from sharp grains of sand.

Humps store fat, which can be broken down to provide energy and water.

Fur is molted in spring.

Webbed feet with thick pads prevent the camel from sinking into the sand.

AMAZING CAMEL FACTS

• A camel can drink up to 13 gallons (60 liters) of water in minutes.

• Camels do not sweat until their temperature reaches 105°F (40.5°C) – a high fever in a human.

• A 1,100-lb (500-kg) camel can store more than 110 lb (50 kg) of fat in its hump(s).

MOUNTAINS AND POLAR

LONG, FRIGID WINTERS, fierce winds, intense sunlight, and cold air with little moisture typify the climate of mountain and polar regions. Mammals in these habitats rely on thick fur coats or layers of fat to keep warm. Some of these mammals' coats change color seasonally, for camouflage. To escape the extreme winter cold, many polar mammals migrate to warmer habitats.

Vicuñas have thick fur and can run at up to 29 mph (47 km/h).

VICUÑA

MOUNTAIN CLIMBERS
Large plant-eating mammals living on mountains have to keep moving to find food and avoid predators. These herbivores include wild mountain sheep and goats, as well as the vicuñas and alpacas of South America. Sure-footed and agile, these hearty mammals have sharp, pointed hooves that grip on steep, slippery slopes.

About 600–700 sensitive whiskers to help find food.

POLAR OCEANS
In polar regions, the sea is often warmer than the air. It is also very rich in food. Some mammals migrate to polar oceans for the summer months, while others live there all year round.

Fatty blubber more than 4 in (10 cm) thick.

ARCTIC FOX IN
SUMMER COAT

TUNDRA CAMOUFLAGE
In the Arctic tundra – the permanently
frozen lands around the edge of the Arctic
– mammals may change color with the
seasons. The Arctic fox, snowshoe hare, and
stoat, for example, turn white in winter for
camouflage against the snow. In the summer,
when the snow melts, their coats change to
brown or gray to blend with the landscape.

*Chest and belly stay
a pale, grayish white.*

*Hollow hairs trap
warm air near
the body.*

*Furry paws act
like snowshoes.*

*Two
layers of
thick fur keep
the bear warm.*

KEEPING WARM
Thick layers of fur
and fat insulate
polar mammals
against the cold, and
blubber acts as a food
store for hard times. In
winter, small mammals,
such as marmots, hibernate
in burrows, while
female polar bears
give birth to their
cubs in cozy dens dug in the snow.

*Nonslip soles
to grip the ice*

POLAR
BEAR

ARCTIC TUNDRA

AROUND THE EDGE of the icy Arctic ocean is a flat, treeless region called the tundra, where the sub-soil is always frozen. Some mammals, such as musk oxen, are hardy enough to live here all year round. Others, including caribou, or reindeer, cannot stand the harsh climate and migrate here only for the summer months.

Long, curved horns for defense against wolves

Two-layered coat keeps out the cold.

MUSK OX

SHAGGY COAT
Musk oxen have long, woolly coats lined with underfur eight times warmer than sheep's wool. Some hairs in the outer coat are over 3 ft (1 m) long. Musk oxen have sharp hooves for digging through snow or ice to find food.

ARCTIC WOLF

BIG FEET
The wide hooves of the caribou, or reindeer, help it to walk on deep snow without sinking in. Caribou breed on the tundra, moving south for winter.

Thick, waterproof fur turns gray-white in winter.

Big feet

CARIBOU

SIBERIAN LEMMING

FAST BREEDERS
When food is plentiful, lemmings nibble shoots and roots and breed fast. In some summers, lemming populations "explode," forcing thousands to wander great distances to find food.

Sensitive ears track sounds from 2 miles (3 km) away.

Long, powerful legs to run great distances after prey

CAMOUFLAGED PREDATOR
Arctic wolves have thick fur, which turns white in winter. This allows them to blend into the background and creep close to prey, such as musk oxen. Pack hunting enables wolves to kill larger prey than if they hunted alone.

AMAZING FACTS
• Wolves can leap up to 15 ft (4 5 m) and can even jump backward!

• Musk oxen have the longest fur of any mammal.

• Adult caribou munch their way through 10 lb (4 5 kg) of food a day.

MOUNTAIN TOPS

MAMMALS ARE SCARCE on mountaintops. To cope with the cold and wind, many have adapted like Arctic mammals. They have thick, shaggy fur coats to keep warm and may move up and down the mountain with the seasons. Some small mammals, such as groundhogs, hibernate in winter after building up layers of fat in the summer. The internal organs of mammals on high mountains also may differ from those in the lowlands. Many have developed larger hearts and lungs to help them get enough oxygen from the thin air at high altitudes.

BATHING MACAQUE
To keep warm in winter, these monkeys from the mountains of northern Japan take hot baths in volcanic springs.

Thicker fur grows in winter.

RARE HUNTER
The snow leopard, or ounce, hunts wild sheep and goats at elevations of up to 18,000 ft (5,500 m) in the Himalayas. It roams its huge territory alone, and is rare as it has been hunted for its thick fur.

SNOW LEOPARD

Broad, furry pads to walk on soft snow and grip ice.

Thick, spotted fur camouflages the snow leopard against snowy rocks.

FURRY CHINCHILLA

High up in the Andes mountains, chinchillas huddle
in rocky holes. Many have been hunted for
their coats, so they are rare
in the wild. Chinchillas
eat plants, holding
food in their paws.

*Bushy tail is 6 in
(15 cm) long*

*Soft,
dense fur
coat*

CHINCHILLA
*Summer coat is short and smooth;
winter coat is long and dense with
soft underfur.*

*Both
sexes have
horns.*

CHAMOIS

SURE-FOOTED CHAMOIS

The chamois has a
very good sense of
balance and can jump
about 13 ft (4 m) up
sheer rock faces in the
mountains of southern
Europe and western
Asia. Chamois browse
on plants, moving
down from the
peaks in winter.

*Hooves have a
hard, thin edge
for gripping rocks.*

*Shock
absorbing legs
and spongy
hoof pads for
extra grip
on steep or
slippery
slopes*

AMAZING FACTS

• The yak is the
highest-living large
mammal, grazing at
20,000 ft (6,000 m)
in the Himalayas.

• Chamois can live for
two weeks without food.

• According to legend,
yetis, or abominable
snowmen, live in the
Himalayas, but no one
has proved they exist.

OCEANS AND SEAS

LIVING NEAR THE SURFACE of the world's oceans and seas are a variety of marine mammals that come to the surface regularly to breathe. Some, such as whales and dolphins, never leave the water; others, such as seals, return to land to mate and have their pups. Sea mammals are streamlined, with modified limbs and tails for swimming and thick fat, or blubber, to keep them warm.

FURRY WARMTH
Unlike other sea mammals, the sea otter has no blubber for insulation. Instead it relies on thick, waterproof fur for warmth. An adult may have as many as 800 million hairs, which help provide buoyancy in the water.

SEAL GROUPS
Seals fall into three main groups. True seals, like the one below, swim with their back flippers and have no visible ear flaps. Eared seals, like the sea lion on the right, swim with front flippers. Walruses are the third group.

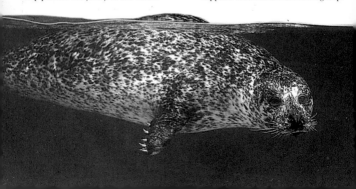

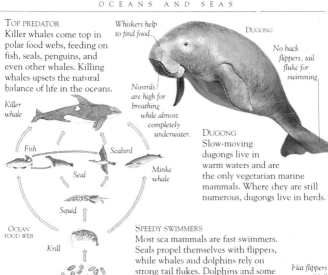

TOP PREDATOR
Killer whales come top in polar food webs, feeding on fish, seals, penguins, and even other whales. Killing whales upsets the natural balance of life in the oceans.

Whiskers help to find food.

DUGONG

No back flippers, tail fluke for swimming

Nostrils are high for breathing while almost completely underwater.

Killer whale

Fish

Seabird

Seal

Minke whale

Squid

OCEAN FOOD WEB

Krill

Plankton

DUGONG
Slow-moving dugongs live in warm waters and are the only vegetarian marine mammals. Where they are still numerous, dugongs live in herds.

SPEEDY SWIMMERS
Most sea mammals are fast swimmers. Seals propel themselves with flippers, while whales and dolphins rely on strong tail flukes. Dolphins and some seals porpoise, or leap, out of the water when swimming.

Flat flippers to "fly" through the water

POLAR OCEANS

HARDY WHALES AND SEALS, such as beluga whales and ringed seals, survive in polar oceans all year round. Many other sea mammals migrate to these cold waters in summer, when food is plentiful. This surge in sea life is fueled by the vast numbers of tiny creatures called plankton, which form the basis of food webs that include fish, whales, squid, seals, and seabirds.

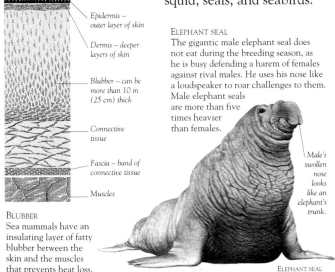

Epidermis – outer layer of skin

Dermis – deeper layers of skin

Blubber – can be more than 10 in (25 cm) thick

Connective tissue

Fascia – band of connective tissue

Muscles

BLUBBER
Sea mammals have an insulating layer of fatty blubber between the skin and the muscles that prevents heat loss.

ELEPHANT SEAL
The gigantic male elephant seal does not eat during the breeding season, as he is busy defending a harem of females against rival males. He uses his nose like a loudspeaker to roar challenges to them. Male elephant seals are more than five times heavier than females.

Male's swollen nose looks like an elephant's trunk.

ELEPHANT SEAL

Fan-shaped tail pushes narwhal through the water.

Blow hole for breathing

Tusk grows in counter-clockwise spiral

NARWHAL

Thick blubber can make up 40 percent of body weight.

NARWHAL

Living in the remote waters of the Arctic, narwhals migrate with the seasons. One of the male narwhal's two teeth grows into a tusk, which can be more than half as long as its body. Male use these tusks to assert dominance, like male deer use their antlers. Females do not usually have tusks.

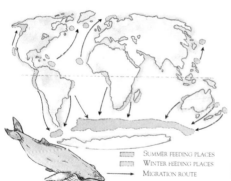

MAP OF WHALE MIGRATION

☐ SUMMER FEEDING PLACES
☐ WINTER FEEDING PLACES
→ MIGRATION ROUTE

WHALE MIGRATION

In summer, many whales travel to the cold polar waters of the Arctic and the Antarctic to feed. In winter, when the sea freezes over, the whales swim back to warmer waters in the tropics to mate and have their young. They eat little in the winter, using up the energy stored as body fat from the summer feast at the poles. Migrant whales include gray, blue, and humpback whales.

AMAZING FACTS

• Gray whales travel more than 12,000 miles (20,000 km) during migration.

• The elephant seal can survive without food for about 100 days.

• Male humpback whales sing the longest and most complex songs in the animal kingdom.

WHALES AND DOLPHINS

GIANT WHALES and smaller dolphins travel the world's oceans, mating and giving birth in the water. They dive deep into the ocean, surfacing frequently to breathe air through a blowhole on the top of their head. Whales and dolphins have large, complex brains, live in groups, and communicate over vast distances using sound, which travels well through water. There are about 88 species of whale, which fall into two main groups: toothed whales and baleen whales.

GRAY WHALE

Scratches from fights with other whales or from collisions with boats

The gray whale is half the size of the gigantic blue whale.

BALEEN WHALE
Blue, fin, gray, and humpback whales are all kinds of baleen whale, which are larger than toothed whales. They feed by straining fish and plankton from the water, using fringed plates of horny baleen, which hang from their great arched jaws like curtains.

BLUE WHALE

An elephant could stand on a blue whale's tongue!

Grooves allow throat to stretch so whale can gulp huge amounts of water.

*Smooth,
streamlined body
shape cuts through
the water,
increasing speed.*

*Powerful muscles
pull tail flukes up
and down*

*Flippers and fins are used
to steer and change direction.*

COMMON DOLPHIN
SWIMMING SEQUENCE

PORPOISING

To breathe while swimming fast,
dolphins sometimes porpoise, or leap
in and out of the water. Some hurl
themselves 23 ft (7 m) into the air.
Spinner dolphins spin around as
many as seven times in a single leap.

Stubby dorsal fin

*Underneath the whale's fat,
or blubber, are powerful
muscles.*

*Powerful tail flukes push
the whale through the water.*

BLUE WHALE

The world's largest animal, the blue whale
can reach 100 ft (32 m) long and weigh 220 tons
(200 tonnes) – as much as 40 rhinoceroses! It can eat up to
4½ tons (4 tonnes) of krill (shrimplike crustaceans) every day.
The blue whale, which was once widely hunted, is now very rare.

*Rows of sharp, cone-shaped
teeth snap up penguins, sea
lions, fish, and squid.*

KILLER WHALE

Orcas, or killer whales, live and hunt in
groups called pods. They have stronger
teeth than dolphins and feed on a great
variety of prey – even attacking other
whales and dolphins. Orcas, sperm
whales, and dolphins are categorized
as toothed whales, which are
smaller than baleen whales.

SKELETON
OF A
KILLER
WHALE

*Powerful
jaws*

RIVERS, LAKES, AND SWAMPS

RIVERS, LAKES, AND SWAMPS provide inviting environments, rich in food and nesting places, that attract a wide range of mammals. These water-loving mammals are strong swimmers, gliding through the water to find food or escape danger. Some, like otters or river dolphins, spend most or all of their time in the water. Others, like raccoons, visit freshwater habitats to feed. These ecosystems are often threatened by drainage or pollution from industry, towns, or agriculture.

FRESHWATER SEAL
Living in and named after Siberia's largest lake, the Baikal seal is the only seal that lives in fresh water. About 70,000 seals live in the lake, feeding on fish and resting on lake shores and islands. Ancestors of Baikal seals may have migrated to the lake from the Arctic along a river during one of the ice ages.

BAIKAL SEAL

UNDERWATER LIFE
Otters are well adapted for swimming underwater. They have waterproof fur, webbed toes, and a long tail that acts as a rudder. Cubs are taught to enter the water but instinctively know how to swim.

Ears and nostrils can be closed under the water.

Otters swim by undulating their body and tail and pushing with their back feet.

Thick, fleshy, muscular tail

Front legs steer.

FISHING FOR FOOD

Fish are an important source of food for water mammals. The fishing cat of southern and southeastern Asian marshes and swamps can flip fish out of the water with its slightly webbed paws. It also dives into the water after fish and catches them in its sharp teeth.

FISHING CAT

Open mouth displays huge teeth in a show of threat.

Eyes, nose, and ears stay above the surface when hippo is underwater.

HIPPOPOTAMUS

RARE MAMMALS

Large mammals are not common in watery habitats. The hippos and antelope of African lakes and swamps are an exception, as are the manatees of western Africa, the Amazon, and the Everglades. More commonly found smaller mammals include mink, muskrats, and beavers.

RIVERS AND LAKES

MANY MAMMALS MAKE their home in safe freshwater lakes, ponds, and rivers. Homes can be hidden away in riverbanks or lakesides, and beavers have even learned to build their homes in the middle of lakes where predators find it hard to reach them. Some mammals use sound or electric fields to find food in muddy water.

PLATYPUS

BOTTOM FEEDER
Feeding mainly along the bottom of lakes and rivers, the platypus probes the mud with its sensitive bill for small aquatic animals such as worms, insects, and crayfish. Platypuses, which have no teeth, crush food between horny, ridged plates inside their bill. They nest in burrows.

Webbed feet with claws for burrowing

Underwater, the platypus can shut its eyes and ears to keep water out.

EXCELLENT SWIMMERS
Muskrats have webbed hind feet and long, flattened tails, which they use as a rudder. They feed mainly on water plants, but also eat fish and frogs. Muskrats dig burrows or construct homes from plants.

Waterproof fur

MUSKRAT

AMAZING FACTS

• The platypus can detect electric fields given off by its prey.

• Strong enough to hold a horse with a rider on its back, the largest beaver dam measured 2,300 ft (700 m) long!

• Using its sharp front teeth, a beaver can fell a small tree in ten minutes.

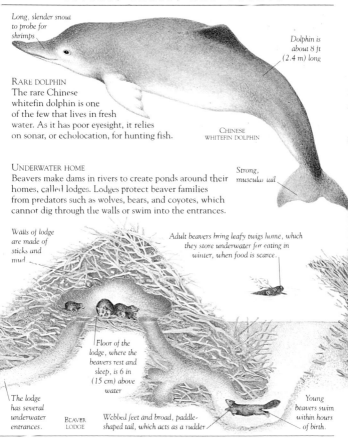

Long, slender snout to probe for shrimps

Dolphin is about 8 ft (2.4 m) long

RARE DOLPHIN
The rare Chinese whitefin dolphin is one of the few that lives in fresh water. As it has poor eyesight, it relies on sonar, or echolocation, for hunting fish.

CHINESE WHITEFIN DOLPHIN

Strong, muscular tail

UNDERWATER HOME
Beavers make dams in rivers to create ponds around their homes, called lodges. Lodges protect beaver families from predators such as wolves, bears, and coyotes, which cannot dig through the walls or swim into the entrances.

Walls of lodge are made of sticks and mud

Adult beavers bring leafy twigs home, which they store underwater for eating in winter, when food is scarce.

Floor of the lodge, where the beavers rest and sleep, is 6 in (15 cm) above water

The lodge has several underwater entrances.

BEAVER LODGE

Webbed feet and broad, paddle-shaped tail, which acts as a rudder

Young beavers swim within hours of birth.

SWAMPS

WATERLOGGED FORESTED AREAS, swamps can be fresh-
or saltwater and are more extensive in tropical than
in temperate areas. At different times of year, the
water level in swamps may rise and fall, affecting
the lives of the mammals who live
there. These mammal inhabitants
may swim through the water, wade
through the mud, or live high up in
the trees. For the few that can
survive the variable water
level and muddy conditions,
food and shelter are plentiful.

*Nose goes red
if monkey is
angry or
excited*

BIG NOSE
The agile proboscis monkey leaps through the
branches of mangrove trees in the swamps of
Borneo. The male, which is much larger than
the female, has a long nose that makes his
honking danger calls strikingly loud.

PROBOSCIS
MONKEY

*Long 2½-ft
(76-cm) tail
for balance*

UNSINKABLE ANTELOPE
The long hooves and flexible ankles
of the sitatunga antelope allow its feet
to splay, preventing it from sinking
into mud. The sitatunga swims well
and often hides underwater.

WINGED HUNTER
The graceful fisherman bat detects its
prey by echolocation, then uses its huge,
powerful wings to swoop down into the
water and catch it.

*Sharp claws
snatch fish
and insects.*

AMAZING FACTS

• The nose of the male
proboscis monkey can
reach 7 in (17.5 cm).

• Fisherman bats are
superb swimmers, using
their wings as oars.

• Manatees munch
through 165 lb (75 kg)
of vegetation a day.

• Manatees live for
50 or 60 years.

*Large, rounded tail
pushes manatee
through the water
at speeds of
15 mph (25 km/h).*

*When breathing,
only the tip of the
manatee's snout
is above the
surface.*

SHY PLANT EATER
Manatees, often
called sea cows, are
shy, rare animals that
feed at night mainly
on sea grasses. Florida
manatees, of the
Everglades, reach a
maximum size of almost
13 ft (3.9 m) and weight
of 3,650 lb (1,660 kg).

MANATEE

DOMESTIC MAMMALS

WHAT IS A CAT?

CATS ARE NATURE'S most efficiently designed hunting carnivores. They have powerful bodies, superb vision, and razor-sharp teeth and claws. Most cats are self-reliant, stalking their prey alone in dusk or darkness. One species has also succeeded in living with people and is now kept as a pet around the world.

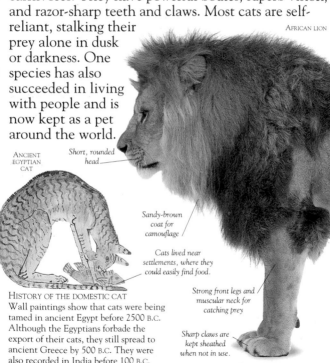

AFRICAN LION

ANCIENT EGYPTIAN CAT

Short, rounded head

Sandy-brown coat for camouflage

Cats lived near settlements, where they could easily find food.

Strong front legs and muscular neck for catching prey

Sharp claws are kept sheathed when not in use.

HISTORY OF THE DOMESTIC CAT
Wall paintings show that cats were being tamed in ancient Egypt before 2500 B.C. Although the Egyptians forbade the export of their cats, they still spread to ancient Greece by 500 B.C. They were also recorded in India before 100 B.C.

MOTHER AND KITTEN

TYPICAL MAMMAL

Like other mammals, cats are warm-blooded and have a skeleton and a four-chambered heart. The female gives birth to live young and produces milk to feed her kittens.

Loose skin for freedom of movement

Flexible backbone increases length of stride as cat runs.

CAT FACTS

• Cats survive on any meat or fish they can catch. When hungry, even the largest cats will eat insects.

• Australia and Antarctica are the only continents with no native cat species.

• Except for tigers, most wild cats attack people only if they are too old to catch their usual animal prey.

Tail is one-third the length of the body.

Back legs are powered by the largest muscles in the cat's body.

Long, dark hair at tip of tail is used for signaling.

THE HUNTER

Virtually everything about a cat, including the domestic cat, is designed for hunting. Cats are lithe, intelligent, and strong, and react with lightning speed. A cat approaches its prey using stealth and camouflage, then overpowers its victim. Lions are the only cats that hunt in groups.

CAT ANATOMY

ALL CATS ARE AGILE and athletic predators. Their bodies are powerful and flexible, specially designed for running, jumping, and climbing. Some types of cat even excel at swimming. Superb hunters, cats first swiftly chase and then overpower prey with their strength. Sharp teeth are used to finish off the catch.

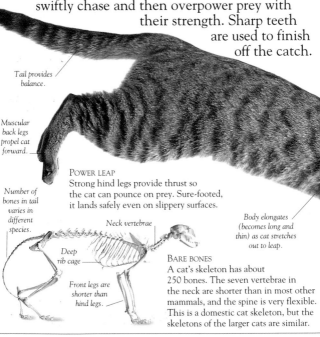

Tail provides balance.

Muscular back legs propel cat forward.

POWER LEAP
Strong hind legs provide thrust so the cat can pounce on prey. Sure-footed, it lands safely even on slippery surfaces.

Number of bones in tail varies in different species.

Neck vertebrae

Deep rib cage

Front legs are shorter than hind legs.

Body elongates (becomes long and thin) as cat stretches out to leap.

BARE BONES
A cat's skeleton has about 250 bones. The seven vertebrae in the neck are shorter than in most other mammals, and the spine is very flexible. This is a domestic cat skeleton, but the skeletons of the larger cats are similar.

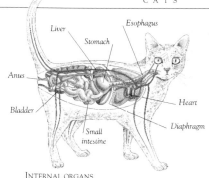

Esophagus

Liver

Stomach

Anus

Bladder

Heart

Small intestine

Diaphragm

ANATOMY FACTS

• A cat breathes four times faster than a human, and its heart beats twice as fast.

• Cats do not chew their food, but swallow it in large chunks.

• The back muscles of a cat are very flexible.

• The record body length of a domestic cat is 41.5 in (105 cm).

INTERNAL ORGANS

The intestines of a cat are short and simple since they need to digest only meat and not plants. Most of the nutrients from the food are absorbed in the small intestine.

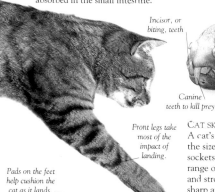

Powerful jaw muscles attach to side of skull.

Incisor, or biting, teeth

Canine teeth to kill prey

Carnassial teeth tear prey apart.

Front legs take most of the impact of landing.

Pads on the feet help cushion the cat as it lands.

CAT SKULL

A cat's skull is large compared to the size of its body. The eye sockets are big to allow for broad range of vision. The jaws are short and strong. All of a cat's teeth are sharp and scissorlike for tearing and cutting, rather than flat, like a human's, for crushing.

Eyes and ears

As predators, cats depend on their highly developed senses of sight and hearing to find prey. The majority of cats hunt at night, so they need to be able to see in near darkness. A cat can see about six times better than a person can at night. However, a cat's color vision is not as developed as ours. Cats also rely on their acute hearing to pinpoint the exact location of prey. Sounds inaudible to humans, or even dogs, can be detected by cats.

SOUND DETECTORS
The serval, a cat from the African savannah, has large, mobile ears. It can pick up the high-pitched calls of rodents hidden in the grass.

THE OUTER EAR
A cat's outer ear acts like a funnel, channeling sounds to the eardrum. Each ear can rotate to locate sounds precisely.

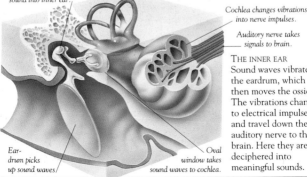

Ossicles (ear bones) send sound into inner ear.

Semicircular canals are filled with fluid.

Cochlea changes vibrations into nerve impulses.

Auditory nerve takes signals to brain.

THE INNER EAR
Sound waves vibrate the eardrum, which then moves the ossicles. The vibrations change to electrical impulses and travel down the auditory nerve to the brain. Here they are deciphered into meaningful sounds.

Eardrum picks up sound waves.

Oval window takes sound waves to cochlea.

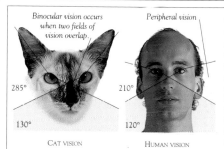

Binocular vision occurs when two fields of vision overlap.

Peripheral vision

285°
130°

CAT VISION

210°
120°

HUMAN VISION

THROUGH A CAT'S EYES
Cats can see at a wider angle around their heads than people can. This allows them to be alert to movements to the side or slightly behind them. Binocular vision allows them to see images as three-dimensional, as well as to judge distance and depth very accurately.

PUPILS IN DARKNESS

PUPILS IN DAYLIGHT

PUPIL DILATION
At night, the cat's pupils enlarge to let in more light. In bright light, some cats' pupils narrow to slits; others contract to small circles.

SEEING IN THE DARK
Cats see well in semidarkness. This is because of a "mirror" of glittering cells (called the *tapetum lucidum*) behind the retina. These cells reflect light back, making objects clearer in the dark.

The mirrorlike structures in cats' eyes shine when light reflects on them at night.

In the dark, the pupils dilate to become almost round.

Smell, taste, and touch

Cats have extremely acute senses. They rely on smell to identify the things around them, and on touch to feel their way around, particularly in the dark. Another sensory device cats possess is the Jacobsen's organ, located in the roof of the mouth. This structure seems to respond to both smell and taste, and helps the cat to detect scents that their nose cannot – for example, when a female is ready to mate.

The senses of smell and taste tell the cat if this toad is edible.

Cats never eat anything without carefully sniffing it first.

SENSE OF SMELL
A cat's nose contains some 19 million smelling nerves, compared to a human's 5 million. Cats are especially sensitive to rancid odors, such as meat that has gone off. They normally seek out fresh meat rather than scavenge dead animals.

ENTICING CATNIP
Many cats, especially tomcats, find the smell of catnip irresistible. This garden herb contains a chemical that relaxes cats, or can make them roll around. About 50 percent of cats do not react to catnip at all.

TOUCH-SENSITIVE HAIRS

Whiskers are specialized, stiff hairs with highly sensitive nerves in their roots. They help a cat like this leopard to familiarize itself with its surroundings. A cat uses its whiskers to gauge if it can fit through a gap.

The cat's saliva leaves its scent.

Cats groom each other to spread their scent, and also to show affection.

CAT COMMUNICATION

Cats use smell to communicate far more than people do. They recognize the familiar scents of their companions. Because their skin is covered in touch-sensitive nerves, cats also communicate by grooming each other.

Characteristic lip-curling known as flehmening

FLEHMENING

The curious way that a cat curls its upper lip is called flehmening. It does this to draw smells into the Jacobsen's organ in its mouth. Male cats flehmen to detect the scent of nearby females. The Jacobsen's organs of the lion and tiger are more sensitive than those of domestic cats.

Paws and claws

A cat uses its paws for everything from gentle grooming to fierce fighting. To aid a cat in one of its most important skills, running, the bones of the feet have evolved so that a cat permanently walks on its toes. In the wild, injuries to the paws can prove fatal, since these can prevent a cat from hunting successfully.

CLAWS FOR CLIMBING
Most cats are masterly climbers, and can make even a vertical ascent with ease. Coming back down is more problematic, since the claws curve the wrong way to grip when descending. Cats awkwardly make their way down a tree backward.

Claws are made of keratin, like human nails.

Dewclaw on front leg is placed like a thumb and helps grip.

Claws dig in to anchor the cat.

Carpal pad on front paw prevents skidding when cat lands.

SPECIALIZED FEET
A cat has furless pads of tough leather on the underside of its paws. These pads enable the animal to stalk silently, and they cushion the impact of landings. Pads also help the cat to "brake" suddenly in mid-run. The cheetah has unique grooved pads to improve its control when running.

SCRATCHING ITS MARK
This jaguar, like other cats, scratches trees to keep its claws clean and sharp. Scratching also marks a cat's territory. A cat leaves behind its scent from glands between its toes, while the scratches themselves show the cat has been in the area.

Claws extended to grasp toy

HUNTING WEAPONS
Watching a cat play will reveal many of its hunting techniques. Cats use their front paws to swipe at, scoop up, rake, or grip their catch. Playing with toys is one way domestic cats practice these moves. Pets tend not to use their claws ferociously against their owners

This 3-week-old kitten is already beginning to develop its hunting skills.

RETRACTABLE CLAWS
When a cat rests, ligaments keep its claws protected under extensions of the toe bones. The claws are only extended when needed. A cheetah, however, has its claws out permanently so it can grip the ground when it runs.

CLAWS RETRACTED

CLAWS EXTENDED

Relaxed cat with claws retracted out of sight

Ligaments slacken to unveil claws when necessary.

CAT MOVEMENT

NORMALLY GRACEFUL and controlled, cats can also react with a sudden burst of energy. Balance, strength, speed, and quick judgment help cats to chase and seize elusive prey. The only physical quality cats lack is endurance. The cat is a particularly talented leaper, able to jump four and a half times its body length and land on a chosen spot with great accuracy.

JUMPING

Cats can leap vertically when necessary. The caracal and lynx are expert jumpers, leaping up into the air to swipe a bird as it takes off. With one paw, they can knock their catch to the ground.

A kitten extends its paws and claws to prepare for landing.

Head outstretched as cheetah accelerates to its full speed.

CHEETAH

Claws help a cat climb and maintain its balance.

Looking before leaping, to judge its distance from the ground

TERRITORIAL MOVEMENTS

One of a cat's main daily movements is to patrol and mark its territory. It will roam around looking out for other cats or potential prey. Cats climb both to survey their area and because a higher position gives them an advantage over competitors.

LEAPING

A cat's most characteristic movement is its leap, demonstrated here by a lioness. The back muscles flex and relax as the cat leaps, with the tail extended for balance. The powerful back legs lift the cat and are the last part of the body to leave the ground.

The lioness stretches her body forward as she takes off.

Tail is turned up for balance.

Slender, light body and long legs enable the cheetah to reach high speeds.

The tail is more than half the length of the body. It swings to counterbalance the body during sharp turns.

RUNNING

Most cats can leap better than they run, but the cheetah is built for speed. Its backbone is extremely flexible, so when the front legs touch the ground, the back end springs forward. In midstride the body stretches full out and all four legs leave the ground. At full sprint the cheetah can reach 60 mph (96 km/h).

When running, the front paws never touch the ground at the same time as the back paws.

Balancing and falling

Some types of cat spend a significant part of their lives in trees, moving confidently along even the narrowest branches. However, if it does fall, the cat has evolved a unique method of protecting itself. Its eyes, brain, and sensitive balance organs in the inner ear ensure that the cat always lands on its feet.

The head rotates first to align with the ground.

1 INSTANT REACTION
The inner ear instantly reacts if the cat is off balance. This warns the brain that it needs to begin to respond to the fall.

2 ROTATING RAPIDLY
The front of the body receives signals from the brain and twists to follow the head. The backbone is so supple that it can rotate 180°.

Front legs pull around to upright position.

GEOFFROY'S CAT

LIVING THE HIGH LIFE
Many of the small wild cats hunt and sleep in trees. The Geoffroy's cat from South America uses its sharp claws, powerful vision, good reflexes, and superb sense of balance to stalk mammals and birds in the treetops.

This cat lives in the mountainous forests of southern South America.

PERFECT BALANCE
This leopard looks precariously balanced, but it will easily secure its kill off the ground and away from scavengers. The leopard is one of the biggest members of the cat family that spends a lot of time in the trees. It is strong enough to drag up a carcass heavier than its own body weight.

FALLING FACTS

• One cat is known to have survived a record fall of 200 ft (61 m).

• From heights of 60 ft (18 m), cats travel at 40 mph (64 km/h) before they hit the ground.

• If the front legs cannot absorb the force of impact, the cat's chin crashes into the ground. This is likely to cause a jaw fracture.

Back end still recovering

Eyes checking where it will be landing.

The back legs will help to absorb the force of impact.

4 LANDING ON ITS FEET
Only seconds after losing its balance, the cat is well positioned to land safely. The head and soft underparts are protected from injury. The cat instinctively relaxes its body before impact, which prevents it from tearing its muscles or jarring its joints.

3 READY FOR IMPACT
As the cat's front legs begin to stretch out to make contact with the ground, the back of the body is still swiveling around. The collarbones at the top of the front legs will act as shock absorbers when the cat lands.

Legs prepared to run when cat touches ground

Front legs take most of the shock of the landing.

HUNTING

VIRTUALLY ALL CATS hunt on their own, so they must attack with surprise and speed. They stealthily approach their unsuspecting prey using any available cover. When they are close enough they suddenly pounce, seizing their quarry in a deadly grip.

HOUSEHOLD HUNTER
The domestic cat is famed for its prowess as a mouser. Some cats also excel at catching lizards, birds, or insects. However, hunting is a learned behavior, so not all pet cats make efficient hunters.

GROUP CHASE
Unlike most cats, lions hunt in groups. This means they can kill animals larger than themselves. The lionesses of the pride do nearly all of the hunting. To improve their chances of a kill, they single out a weak-looking animal, surround it, and then chase it down.

Cat holds its body and tail close to the ground.

FATAL BITE
This leopard pins down its victim to stop it from escaping. Then it bites through the neck of its catch to sever the spinal cord. If a cat cannot eat its kill all at once it will drag the carcass under cover to protect it from scavengers.

FRUSTRATED KILLER
Domestic cats will play with a toy as if it were a prey animal. They creep up on the object, then bite and shake it. Wild cats sometimes play with their quarry before killing it.

Spotted coat pattern keeps the animal camouflaged.

Mature cats play occasionally, but not as often as kittens.

ASIAN LEOPARD CAT

SILENT STALKER
Except for the cheetah, cats can manage only short bursts of speed. They must steal quite close to an animal before they bound forward. Approaching slowly and silently, the stalking cat is alert to every movement. When it is within striking distance it springs on its prey without warning.

The cat runs forward in this position, then stops and crouches down.

FUR TYPES

SLEEK AND FINE, or long and luxurious, a cat's fur is its finest feature. The coat insulates a cat in hot or cold weather, carries its scent, and is sensitive to touch. Fur type is often suited to where a cat lives, although the wide variation of coats in domestic breeds is due to selective breeding by people.

Awn hairs

Down hairs | *Guard hairs*

BRITISH SHORTHAIR
This breed is typical of short-coated cats. It has a short, dense, crisp coat. The thick, plush fur stands out from the body like a rug.

Coat is about 2 in (5 cm) thick.

A CAT'S COAT
There are three kinds of hair in a cat's coat, although not every breed has all three. The longest are the coarse outer guard hairs. In wild and domestic cats, these carry the pattern. Slightly shorter awn hairs lie beneath. Short, soft down provides insulation.

Persians have thick down and up to 4-in-long (10 cm) guard hairs.

PERSIAN
Persian cats have the longest and densest fur of any cat breed. The hairs are silky and fine, giving the cat a very fluffy appearance – even the paws are tufted. In warm summer months the cat molts, which makes its coat look shorter.

Fur is especially curly on back and tail.

CORNISH REX

The unusual fur of the Rex breeds is wavy and crimped. All of the hairs in a Cornish Rex's coat are short and curly. The coat is made up solely of down and awn hairs, both of which are very soft to the touch. The fur is fine, so Rexes can be susceptible to the cold.

AMERICAN WIREHAIR

This cat's fur is distinctively wiry and springy. Every hair, including those in the ears and on the tail, is crimped, or even coiled. The Wirehair's fur is of medium length and very frizzy. It feels like lamb's wool to the touch.

Wiry coat makes pattern look raised.

WILD CAT FUR

Wild cats have coats of two layers: warm down hair underneath and a resilient outer coat. In cold climates, cats have thicker fur. The Pallas's cat from Asia has the longest coat of any wild cat. It was once mistakenly believed to be the ancestor of domestic cats with long hair.

Longer fur on underside for warmth when lying on cold ground

PALLAS'S CAT

"HAIRLESS" SPHYNX

Although the Sphynx looks bald, it has traces of fur on its tail and a light covering of down on its body. It also has very short eyebrows and whiskers. This breed's lack of hair means that it is vulnerable to sunburn.

Coat is like suede.

Colors and patterns

Cats come in a huge variety of colors and patterns. Many have distinctive markings that originally evolved to help cats in the wild stay hidden from their prey. Domestic cats often come in more conspicuous colors because they have little need for camouflage. Breeders have achieved some very striking color and pattern combinations.

SEAL TORTIE
POINT SIAMESE

CORNISH REX
TORTOISESHELL

HIMALAYAN POINTS
Siamese cats have a characteristic pattern of darker areas on the tail, legs, ears, and face. These markings are described as points. Young kittens develop their points as they mature.

Black and red randomly but evenly distributed

TORTOISESHELL
For genetic reasons, tortoiseshell patterns occur almost entirely in female cats. Tortoiseshell fur is a combination of black and red.

COLOR RANGE
Some cats have unpatterned coats of one pure, solid color. There are many varieties, some simply paler versions of the basic colors. Here the typical darker colors are shown above their lighter variants, with white shown on its own.

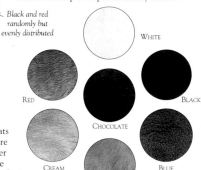

WHITE

RED

BLACK

CHOCOLATE

CREAM

BLUE

LILAC

TABBY MARKINGS

This cat's spotted coat exemplifies the dark markings typical of tabbies. In different tabby cats, the patterning might be stripes, spots, or patches. These patterns are left over from the natural camouflage markings of wild cats. Tabby patterning is very common in feral cats (domestic cats that live in the wild).

SILVER SPOTTED BRITISH SHORTHAIR

Black spots are striking against a silver background.

WILD CAT PATTERNS

The stripes or spots of a wild cat's coat are vital because they help the animal blend into its surroundings. Patterns camouflage a cat by breaking up the outline of its body shape. The markings of wild cats vary so considerably that the shape of the patterns is one way to distinguish the species. Individual cats of the same species also have slightly varying patterns.

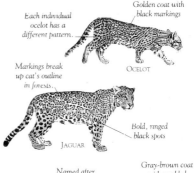

Golden coat with black markings

Each individual ocelot has a different pattern.

OCELOT

Markings break up cat's outline in forests.

Bold, ringed black spots

JAGUAR

Unique striped markings

TIGER

Named after its cloudlike pattern

Gray-brown coat with marbled markings

CLOUDED LEOPARD

WHAT IS A DOG?

THE DOMESTIC DOG, scientific name *Canis familiaris* (from the Latin *canis*, meaning "dog"), is one of 34 living species of canids – meat-eating animals that evolved for the pursuit of prey across open grassland. The dog family ranges from the tiny Fennec Fox to the large Gray Wolf.

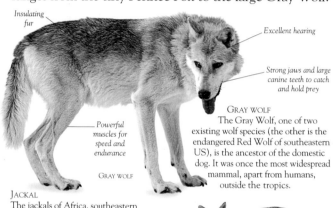

Insulating fur

Excellent hearing

Strong jaws and large canine teeth to catch and hold prey

Powerful muscles for speed and endurance

GRAY WOLF

GRAY WOLF
The Gray Wolf, one of two existing wolf species (the other is the endangered Red Wolf of southeastern US), is the ancestor of the domestic dog. It was once the most widespread mammal, apart from humans, outside the tropics.

JACKAL
The jackals of Africa, southeastern Europe, and Asia, have an undeserved bad name. Jackals are good parents to their young and do not scavenge as much as is supposed. Their diet ranges from fruit to small gazelle.

RED FOX

RED FOX
The Red Fox, like all foxes, is a small canid with a slender skull, large ears, and a long, bushy tail. Its coat comes in three colors – a flame red, a blackish silver, and the intermediate, "Cross" fox.

JACKAL

Dogs are social animals that adapt to their surroundings easily

PACK INSTINCT
Unlike more specialized carnivores, such as cats, which tend to hunt alone, most canids hunt in packs. Pack members also have a strong instinct to guard pack territory. Such instincts helped domestication, as canids readily adopted a human family as their "pack."

EVOLUTION
About 50 million years ago, in the Eocene epoch, *Miacis*, a small, weasel-like mammal with a well-developed brain, was the forefather of all canids, as well as more distantly related carnivores.

By the Miocene epoch, more than 40 ancestors of modern canids had emerged. Tomarctus had the beginnings of modern canine tooth anatomy.

TOMARCTUS

Hesperocyon was a long-bodied, short-limbed canid living in the later Eocene epoch. Fossils have been found in North America.

Miacis had the distinctive teeth of a canid, and also spreading paws, indicating adaptation to life in the trees.

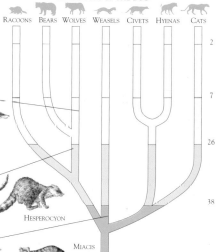

ANCESTORS OF THE DOG

| RACOONS | BEARS | WOLVES | WEASELS | CIVETS | HYENAS | CATS |

2

7

26

38

HESPEROCYON

MIACIS

54

MILLIONS OF YEARS AGO

DOMESTICATION

DOGS WERE FIRST DOMESTICATED from wolves more than 10,000 years ago. Human–dog contact may have evolved as wolves scavenged around human settlements and when wolf cubs were raised as pets. The dog's potential as a reliable guard and excellent hunting companion was soon realized.

Early Asian dogs migrated and interbred with North American wolves

EARLY HUNTING SCENE
Ancient cave paintings depict dogs assisting the hunt, as followers of human "pack" leaders.

The Carolina Dog may be descended from half-wild dogs brought across the Bering Straits by Asian peoples 8,000 years ago

MEXICAN HAIRLESS

The Chihuahua is possibly the oldest breed on the American continent. It may have been introduced to Mexico by traders from China

MEXICAN HAIRLESS
This primitive dog, descended from the Indian wolf, has much in common with the Chinese Crested Dog of mainland Asia, and may be related.

Wolves did not migrate to South America; dogs were brought here by early traders

PHARAOH HOUND
This oldest-recorded breed graces the tombs of ancient Egyptian pharaohs. It was probably a descendant of the Phoenician hound – the Phoenicians traded dogs throughout the Mediterranean.

PHARAOH HOUND

DOG OWNERSHIP FACTS

• Worldwide, over 200 million dogs are kept as pets.

• North America has the largest number of pet dogs (60 million); next is France (10.8 million), followed by Russia (10 million). Japan and Britain each have around 7 million dogs.

Sheepdogs originated in Europe more than 1,000 years ago

Mastiff-type dogs were domesticated in the Stone Age and later used in battle by the Greeks

The Greyhound is portrayed on 8,000-year-old Mesopotamian pottery

Wolflike dogs similar to spitzes, such as the Elkhound and the Siberian Husky, originated in Arctic regions

DINGO
The Dingo was brought to Australia 4,000 years ago. It is now a feral dog (a domesticated dog that has reverted to the wild).

DINGO

BASENJI
The Basenji's roots lie lost in the mists of antiquity. This nonbarking African breed has remained more or less pure for thousands of years. It is depicted on Egyptian tombs.

BASENJI

DOG ANATOMY

THE BASIC DESIGN of the dog is that of a highly developed carnivorous mammal of the hunt. Over the centuries, humans have modified dog anatomy to exploit particular talents, and for aesthetic appeal.

Insulating coat

Loin

Brush, or tail

Croup

Flank

Stifle

Lower thigh

Knee

Hock

Pastern

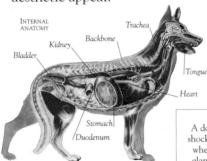

INTERNAL ANATOMY

Trachea

Backbone

Kidney

Bladder

Tongue

Heart

Stomach

Duodenum

INTERNAL ORGANS

The organs of the dog are essentially the same as those of humans, and function in the same way. Although its attitude toward food is that of a hunter-scavenger, the dog is not a pure carnivore, tending toward an omnivorous diet. Its digestive system can cope with anything from fruit and nuts to shellfish and raw meat.

PAWS

A dog's paws carry pads that act as shock absorbers, provide a good grip when running, and contain sweat glands. The claws, unlike those of most cats, cannot be retracted.

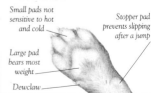

Small pads not sensitive to hot and cold

Stopper pad prevents slipping after a jump

Large pad bears most weight

Dewclaw

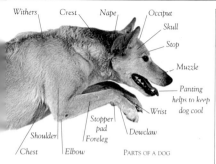

Withers Crest Nape Occiput
Skull
Stop
Muzzle
Panting helps to keep dog cool
Wrist
Stopper pad
Shoulder Foreleg Dewclaw
Chest Elbow PARTS OF A DOG

CLASSIC DESIGN

The classic canine design is seen in most wild or feral dogs and many domesticated mongrels: a lithe body, long legs, a long tail for balance and communication, efficient prick ears, and excellent vision – all ideal features for a resourceful hunting animal with plenty of stamina.

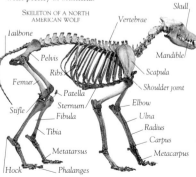

SKELETON OF A NORTH AMERICAN WOLF

Skull
Vertebrae
Tailbone
Pelvis
Mandible
Ribs
Scapula
Femur
Shoulder joint
Patella
Sternum
Elbow
Stifle
Fibula
Ulna
Tibia
Radius
Metatarsus
Carpus
Hock Phalanges Metacarpus

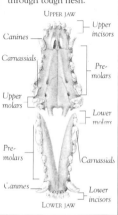

TEETH

An adult dog has 42 teeth, including four stabbing, canine teeth and four molar teeth called carnassials that are designed to shear through tough flesh.

UPPER JAW

Canines
Upper incisors
Carnassials
Premolars
Upper molars
Lower molars
Premolars
Carnassials
Canines
Lower incisors

LOWER JAW

THE SKELETON

The basic dog framework provides strength, flexibility, and speed. However, selective breeding has resulted in some breeds possessing weak areas. Extra-long spines can lead to "slipped disks"; compressed skulls to breathing troubles; and short legs to knee problems.

More on anatomy

All predatory animals depend on their sight, hearing, and sense of smell to catch prey. A dog's sense organs are some of the most sophisticated in the animal kingdom. Dogs' reproductive systems follow the basic mammalian pattern, but with some distinct features in the male.

Cerebral cortex
Frontal sinus
Nasal membranes
Vomeronasal organ
Tongue
Soft palate
Windpipe

CROSS SECTION OF THE HEAD

SMELL AND TASTE

Dogs are marvelous smellers, in fact about one million times better than humans. Their long noses contain "smelling membranes" about 40 times larger than ours. Taste is not as important, as dogs "gobble" rather than "savor" food.

SIGHT

Dogs' eyes are more sensitive to light and movement than ours and they can often "miss" creatures that stand very still. Yet shepherds claim their working dogs will react to hand signals at a distance of 0.6 miles (1 km). Dogs are not totally color-blind, but see mainly in black, white, and shades of gray. The anatomy of a dog's eye is very similar to ours.

Lacrimal gland
Pupil
Cornea
Iris covers anterior chamber
Lower eyelid
Third eyelid
Lens
Sclera
Uvea
Optic nerve
Retina

CROSS SECTION OF THE EYE

DOG'S EYE VIEW 250°–290°
HUMAN'S EYE VIEW 210°

VISION

A dog has a wider field of vision than a human because its eyes are set toward the sides of its head. Its carnivorous, hunter ancestors needed lateral vision.

HEARING

Dogs have excellent hearing. Equipped with large external ears served by 17 muscles, they can prick and swivel these sound receivers to focus on the source of noise. They can register high-pitched sounds of 35,000 Hz (vibrations per second), compared to humans' 20,000 Hz. This greater hearing range assists in tracking down quarry.

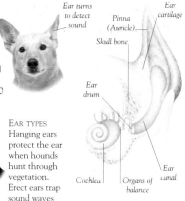

Ear turns to detect sound

Pinna (Auricle)

Ear cartilage

Skull bone

Ear drum

Cochlea

Organs of balance

Ear canal

INSIDE THE EAR

EAR TYPES

Hanging ears protect the ear when hounds hunt through vegetation. Erect ears trap sound waves most effectively.

HANGING EARS   POINTED EARS

REPRODUCTIVE ORGANS

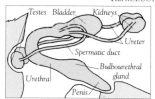

Testes *Bladder* *Kidneys*

Ureter

Spermatic duct

Bulbourethral gland

Urethra

Penis

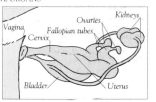

Vagina *Ovaries* *Kidneys*

Fallopian tubes

Cervix

Bladder *Uterus*

MALE
The dog's penis contains a bone, through which the urethra passes, and a bulbourethral gland that swells up, thereby "tying" the dog and bitch together during sexual intercourse.

FEMALE
The female has a typical mammalian arrangement: vagina, cervix, uterus, fallopian tubes, and ovaries. When a bitch is neutered, the ovaries, fallopian tubes, and uterus are surgically removed.

LIFE CYCLE OF DOGS

ON AVERAGE, a dog's life span is about 12 years, though small breeds generally live longer than larger ones. In terms of aging, the first year of a dog's life equals 15 human years, the second equals nine years, and thereafter each dog year counts for four human years.

GETTING ACQUAINTED

Exploratory sniffing before mating begins

THE "HEAT" PERIOD

The female is called the bitch. She becomes sexually mature at 8–12 months old. Twice a year, she goes into "heat," usually for 18–21 days. This is when ovulation occurs.

MATING

Female remains willing but passive

MATING

The male is sexually active all year and is attracted to the scent of a female in "heat." When a female is ready to mate, she draws her tail to one side. The transmission of sperm is completed within a minute but the couple remain "locked" together for half an hour.

DEVELOPMENT OF A PUPPY

7 DAYS
At this age the puppy only sleeps or nurses. Its eyes and ear canals are closed, but it responds to its mother's touch.

14 DAYS
The eyes are opening but they cannot focus properly for another 7 days. Between 13 and 17 days the puppy begins to hear.

3 WEEKS
At 3 weeks the puppy can focus its eyes and move around. Its nails should be trimmed to prevent it from scratching the mother.

1. The yolk sac provides nourishment to the embryo for the first few days

2. By the third week of pregnancy, the embryo has a developing head, eyes, and limbs

3. By midpregnancy, all the internal organs are developed

Yolk sac

Embryo

Most puppies will emerge head first in diving position

PREGNANCY

Pregnancy in the bitch lasts an average of 63 days. The swelling of her tummy is noticeable from the fifth week onward. The breasts and nipples become bigger, and milk can often be produced 5–6 days before labor begins.

4. At six weeks, the skeleton has developed

BIRTH

When the puppies are almost ready to be born, the mother may stop eating and find a nest site. She gives birth to the first puppy soon afterward, and may rest for minutes or hours after each puppy is born. Each puppy's placenta usually comes out within 15 minutes.

Mother sits contentedly while puppies nurse

Puppies huddle together for food and security

BONDING WITH MOTHER

30 DAYS
The puppy begins to play. Teething starts at 3–5 weeks. It should receive its first worming dosage.

6 WEEKS
Milk teeth are present, but the puppy is still nursing, and it should not be separated from its mother.

8 WEEKS
Mother and pup can be separated now, and the puppy should receive vaccinations against major diseases.

DOG BEHAVIOR

DOGS EXHIBIT A BROAD RANGE of behavior patterns
that spring from their origins as social, hunting
animals. Ear and tail movements are
obviously expressive, but all
patterns are vital rituals
that express a dog's
relationship with
its environment.

SCENT MARKING

A dog marks out territory via deposits
of urine or feces, or by
scratching the ground
with its hind legs.

SCENT GLANDS

Distinctive scents are produced by
sebaceous glands in the dog's anal sacs
(anal glands) that are passed on to feces,
and by sweat glands in the hind paws.
These scents lay down sniffable
information that only dogs can interpret.

*Dog shows
interest in a scent*

HOWLING

Howling is an
ancient form of dog
communication.
Wild dogs and wolves
howl to let other pack
members know where
they are and, in some
cases, to inform strangers
that they are in possession
of territory. It can also be a
sign of distress or loneliness.

DIGGING

Dogs inherit their love
of digging from their
ancestors, who
stored food in order
to survive when
hunting was poor.
It leads well-fed
dogs to bury
bones and
dig them
up later.

AGGRESSION

Aggression can indicate possessiveness of prized objects, territory, or animals. It can be directed at outsiders who are not members of the home pack. Fear and pain also cause aggression.

DOMINANCE

Dogs asserting their dominance make eye contact, with tail raised and ears erect, and often place their neck on the other dog's shoulder. Size, though helpful, does not necessarily affect dominance.

Tail carried high indicates boldness

SUBMISSION

Submissive individuals in the canine hierarchy reveal their position by their crouched postures, and by rolling onto their backs, looking away, and appearing meek and defenseless.

PLAY BOW

The play bow, often exhibited by puppies, is a clear request to human or fellow dog to meet on friendly terms. Indicating total lack of aggressive intent, it is usually an invitation to play.

Body is lowered to ground

Human pack leader offers food

Dog pack leader shows authority by rising above other dogs

HIERARCHY

Packs of wild canines have leaders to exercise authority and coordinate activity. This is usually, but not always, a male. Gatherings of domestic dogs behave in the same way.

INTRODUCTION TO BREEDS

AMONG DOMESTICATED ANIMALS only the dog has been selectively bred to produce such a wide variety of types. Worldwide, there are over 500 different breeds. National kennel clubs differ in the way they group breeds so, for the purposes of this book, general categories have been used.

GUNDOGS

Gundogs were developed to pick up the air scents of game and also be good sporting companions. They are highly responsive and amenable workers. Field trials are held regularly to test working skills.

IRISH RED AND WHITE SETTER

BORDER COLLIES HERDING SHEEP

CHOW CHOW

SPECIAL DOGS

This is a miscellaneous collection of breeds. Many, such as the Chow Chow, are highly distinctive, and some have specialized in particular types of work. Most make good companions; many popular pets fall into this category.

HERDING DOGS AND GUARD DOGS

These dogs were bred to protect and herd livestock, work as guards, pull and carry loads, or assist police and armed forces. Most of these dogs are happiest when they have access to open spaces and a job to do.

HOUNDS

These athletes with sensitive noses and sharp eyes were the first dogs used by humans. They helped their (much slower) masters by hunting down animals, such as deer, for food.

FOXHOUNDS

BREED FACTS

• Archaeological finds show that that there were four types of Bronze Age dog: wolflike dogs, sheepdogs, hounds, and small house dogs.

• Breeds least likely to bite: Labrador, Golden Retriever, Shetland Sheepdog, Old English Sheepdog, Spinone.

TERRIERS

Developed from hounds to tackle small, burrowing animals, terriers are generally small, short-legged, stocky animals with alert and spirited temperaments. No group of dogs is more expert at burrowing than terriers.

NORFOLK TERRIERS

TOY DOGS

These breeds' main function is to be loyal, decorative, and friendly companions. Many are useful for raising the alarm and nipping intruders' ankles. Small and dainty, they play a vital role in people's lives.

PEKINGESE

MONGRELS

Most dogs in the world are mongrels or "crossbreed" dogs that have interbred at random. Apart from their individual endearing qualities, they are often better-tempered, less disease-prone, and more adaptable than purebreds.

WHAT IS A HORSE?

SOME 60 MILLION YEARS AGO the first horses ran on the plains of North America. The modern horse has single-hooved feet and a greater length of leg than its earlier ancestors. Like all mammals, horses suckle their young, and as herbivores, their natural food is grass. They are social creatures, and prefer to live in groups.

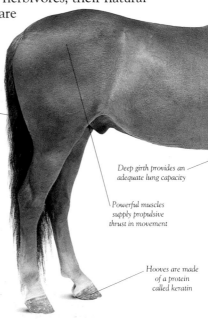

Long tail helps to keep flies off the body

Deep girth provides an adequate lung capacity

Powerful muscles supply propulsive thrust in movement

Hooves are made of a protein called keratin

HORSE FACTS

• Horses are measured from the ground up to the withers, which is the highest point of the shoulders.

• In 1910, North America had about 20 million domestic horses.

• There are over 150 officially recognized horse and pony breeds.

• Most modern horse breeds have been deliberately created to do a specific task.

Long hair on the back of the neck is called a mane

Horses have an excellent sense of hearing

Withers

Long head and neck allow horse to graze while standing

It takes over two years for a horse foal to take on adult proportions

Long legs developed to run from danger

HORSES AND HUMANS
As this cave painting shows, early humans hunted horses for their meat and skin. By keeping horses in herds, these essential items became more readily available. Eventually, horses were used for riding and pulling carts, and later they were bred to perform all kinds of work.

BORN TO RUN
Both wild and domestic horses give birth to fully developed offspring. This is because in the wild the young foal must keep up with its mother and the herd, as well as escaping from predators.

MAIN HORSE TYPES

MOST MODERN HORSES are thought to be descended from four types that inhabited Europe and Asia over 6,000 years ago. Their features can still be seen in some breeds today. Domestication led to the variety of modern breeds and their spread across the world.

Broad forehead with straight profile

Lean with narrow body

PONY TYPE 1
This hardy pony looked similar to today's Exmoor breed of Great Britain. It lived in northwestern Europe.

HORSE TYPE 1
Originating from central Asia, this horse lived in dry, arid conditions and resembled the modern Akhal-Teke.

Small head

PONY TYPE 2
Similar to Przewalski's horse, the Type 2 was powerfully built with a heavy head. The breed roamed over northern Eurasia.

HORSE TYPE 2
Living in the hot deserts of western Asia, this slim horse was possibly the ancestor of the Arab and Caspian.

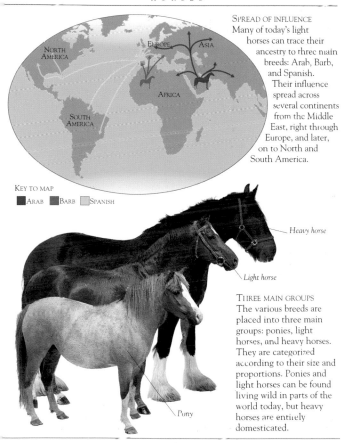

SPREAD OF INFLUENCE
Many of today's light
horses can trace their
ancestry to three main
breeds: Arab, Barb,
and Spanish.
Their influence
spread across
several continents
from the Middle
East, right through
Europe, and later,
on to North and
South America.

KEY TO MAP
■ ARAB ■ BARB ▢ SPANISH

Heavy horse

Light horse

THREE MAIN GROUPS
The various breeds are
placed into three main
groups: ponies, light
horses, and heavy horses.
They are categorized
according to their size and
proportions. Ponies and
light horses can be found
living wild in parts of the
world today, but heavy
horses are entirely
domesticated.

Pony

BODY AND CONFORMATION

A HORSE'S BODY IS perfectly designed for its way of life. The neck is long so it can stoop to graze, and long, muscular legs allow it to run away from danger. The proportions of a horse's body, or conformation, may vary according to the group or breed.

Points

The external features of a horse are called the points. Each point has a different name and together they make up the horse's conformation.

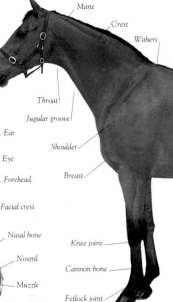

Mane

Crest

Withers

Throat

Jugular groove

Shoulder

Breast

Knee joint

Cannon bone

Fetlock joint

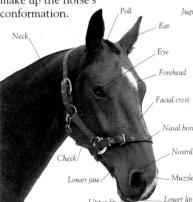

Neck

Poll

Ear

Eye

Forehead

Facial crest

Nasal bone

Nostril

Cheek

Lower jaw

Muzzle

Upper lip

Lower lip

PROPORTION

In a perfectly proportioned horse, certain measurements of the body should all be equal. Those shown in blue should correspond to each other, as should the lines drawn in both red and gray.

Head should be same size as side of blue squares

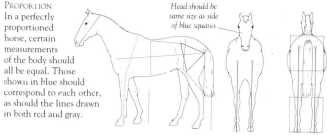

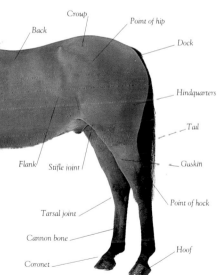

Croup

Back

Point of hip

Dock

Hindquarters

Tail

Guskin

Flank

Stifle joint

Point of hock

Tarsal joint

Cannon bone

Hoof

Coronet

FRONT AND REAR LIMBS

When viewed from the front, a line from the shoulder should pass through the center of the knees, fetlock, and foot. A straight line should also pass through the rear legs.

ANATOMICAL FACTS

• The body and head of a horse are streamlined and this helps to reduce wind resistance.

• A long neck and well-sloped shoulders may indicate that the horse is fast and good for riding.

• Large eyes usually show not only that the horse has good vision, but also a calm nature and intelligence.

Skeleton and muscles

The framework of the horse consists of a skeleton, made up of a
number of connected bones that are moved by muscles. Along the
spinal, or vertebral, column, which runs from the head to the tail,
is the spinal cord – the connection between the horse's brain and
body. When a horse wants to move, it
sends a message from its brain down
the cord via nerves to signal the
appropriate muscle.

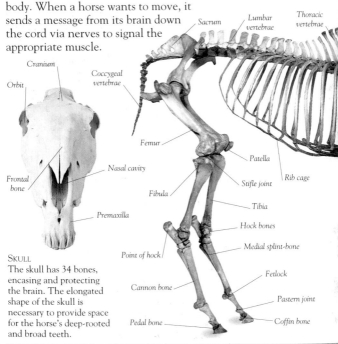

Sacrum

Lumbar vertebrae

Thoracic vertebrae

Cranium

Coccygeal vertebrae

Orbit

Femur

Patella

Stifle joint

Rib cage

Frontal bone

Nasal cavity

Fibula

Tibia

Premaxilla

Hock bones

Medial splint-bone

Point of hock

SKULL

The skull has 34 bones,
encasing and protecting
the brain. The elongated
shape of the skull is
necessary to provide space
for the horse's deep-rooted
and broad teeth.

Cannon bone

Fetlock

Pastern joint

Pedal bone

Coffin bone

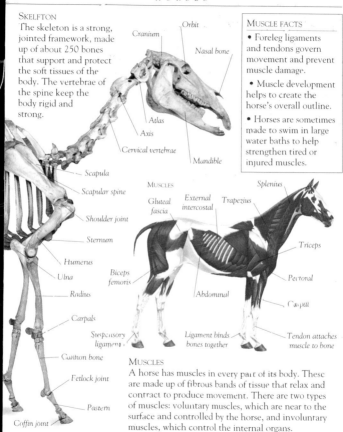

SKELETON

The skeleton is a strong, jointed framework, made up of about 250 bones that support and protect the soft tissues of the body. The vertebrae of the spine keep the body rigid and strong.

Cranium
Orbit
Nasal bone
Atlas
Axis
Cervical vertebrae
Mandible

Scapula
Scapular spine
Shoulder joint
Sternum
Humerus
Ulna
Radius
Carpals
Suspensory ligament
Cannon bone
Fetlock joint
Pastern
Coffin joint

MUSCLE FACTS

• Foreleg ligaments and tendons govern movement and prevent muscle damage.

• Muscle development helps to create the horse's overall outline.

• Horses are sometimes made to swim in large water baths to help strengthen tired or injured muscles.

MUSCLES

Splenius
Gluteal fascia
External intercostal
Trapezius
Triceps
Biceps femoris
Abdominal
Pectoral
Caput
Suspensory ligament
Ligament binds bones together
Tendon attaches muscle to bone

MUSCLES

A horse has muscles in every part of its body. These are made up of fibrous bands of tissue that relax and contract to produce movement. There are two types of muscles: voluntary muscles, which are near to the surface and controlled by the horse, and involuntary muscles, which control the internal organs.

Patterns and markings

Individual horses can be identified by body markings, which can be either natural or acquired. Natural markings are often areas of white hair on the head, legs, and hooves. Acquired markings are the result of branding or injury. Branding has been carried out for more than 2,000 years and can help to identify the horse if it is stolen.

FACE MARKINGS
While some breeds are defined by their coat patterns, face markings help to identify individual horses. The most common face markings are named below.

BLAZE

WHITE MUZZLE

SNIP

LIP MARKS

WHITE FACE

STRIPE

STAR AND STRIPE

STAR

ERMINE   SOCK   STOCKING   ZEBRA

LEG MARKINGS

These markings are often white. They are called ermine if they are just above the hoof, a sock if they extend below the knee, and a stocking when extending above the knee. Zebra markings are dark rings.

HOOF MARKINGS

The blue hoof is made of hard blue horn and is most often associated with ponies. Hooves of black and white vertical stripes are seen on the Appaloosa and other spotted horse breeds.

BLUE HOOF   STRIPED HOOF

DORSAL STRIPE

This mark extends from the tail to the withers. It is found on primitive horses such as the Tarpan, and is associated with dun-colored coats.

IDENTITY MARKINGS

Artificial markings help identify ownership and sometimes breed. Brand marks are applied by a hot iron rod which stops the hair from growing back. Freeze marks are frozen on in a similar way.

BRAND MARK   FREEZE MARK

FOOD AND DIET

LIKE ANY ANIMAL, horses get their energy from food. They are herbivores, which means they do not eat meat. In the wild, horses can survive on grass and herbs as long as their grazing area is large enough. In the winter, when it is cold and there is less food, wild horses get out of condition, while in the summer they put on weight.

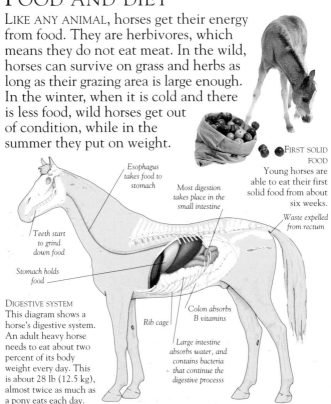

FIRST SOLID FOOD
Young horses are able to eat their first solid food from about six weeks.

Esophagus takes food to stomach

Most digestion takes place in the small intestine

Waste expelled from rectum

Teeth start to grind down food

Stomach holds food

Rib cage

Colon absorbs B vitamins

Large intestine absorbs water, and contains bacteria that continue the digestive processs

DIGESTIVE SYSTEM
This diagram shows a horse's digestive system. An adult heavy horse needs to eat about two percent of its body weight every day. This is about 28 lb (12.5 kg), almost twice as much as a pony eats each day.

TEETH AND JAWS

Grazing wears down the foal's milk teeth and by the time the horse is five, these are replaced by a set of 36 adult teeth. The incisors cut the food into small pieces, and the molars grind it down, ready for digestion.

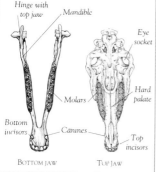

Hinge with top jaw

Mandible

Eye socket

Hard palate

Molars

Bottom incisors

Canines

Top incisors

BOTTOM JAW

TOP JAW

BALANCED DIET

Horses need a balanced diet, with enough vitamins and minerals to help them stay healthy and in condition. Horses should be fed little and often, and allowed constant access to fresh water.

Fruit and root vegetables must be chopped up lengthwise so the horse does not choke

Feed bowl holds carrots, corn, linseed, nuts, chaff, and a slice of apple

Hay is grass that has been cut and dried

Bucket of clean, fresh water

FOOD DANGERS

• Plants like deadly nightshade, bracken, and ragwort may poison a horse if it eats them in any quantity. Pastures where horses are left to graze must be cleared of these plants.

• Horses should not graze in an area within 14 days of any spraying.

BEHAVIOR

TODAY'S DOMESTIC HORSES show the same patterns of behavior as their wild ancestors. The herd instinct still dominates, and horses prefer to be kept in groups rather than on their own. Much of their behavior is linked to the way they communicate with other horses.

Horses sleep for only short periods at a time

SLEEPING
Horses are able to sleep standing up. In the wild, this increases their chances of escaping from predators.

EARS
The position of a horse's ears is an important indicator of its mood. If the ears point forward, this shows curiosity. When the horse is uncertain, it keeps one ear forward and the other backward.

SHIRE HORSE

FLEHMENING
When a mare is close to a stallion, the stallion may fold back his lips and draw air into his mouth, over its Jacobson's organ, to detect the mare's scent to sense if she is ready to mate. This action is called flehmening.

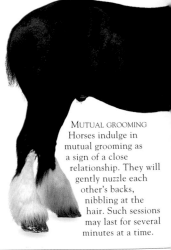

MUTUAL GROOMING
Horses indulge in mutual grooming as a sign of a close relationship. They will gently nuzzle each other's backs, nibbling at the hair. Such sessions may last for several minutes at a time.

ROLLING OVER
By rolling, a horse can exercise the muscles in its back, and also clean its coat. Horses often roll when turned out to graze in a field.

REARING
A stallion rears up to intimidate a rival, often lashing out with his front feet at the same time.

Horse uses its front legs to balance

Horses often rear in play

Stallions rear naturally in the wild

Horses nuzzle each other to establish their relationship

SHETLAND PONY

BEHAVIORAL FACTS

• Horses will call out to warn others of approaching danger.

• The tail is used as a fly swish rather than for communication.

• Repeated pawing at the ground with the hooves is often a sign of nervousness.

• A horse's ears are very mobile and can rotate independently 180° forward and back.

USES OF THE HORSE

IN SPITE OF THE SPREAD of mechanization, the horse still has a place in society. Today, horses can be found hard at work in cities, forests, and farmland. While traditional horse sports like racing and steeple-chasing remain popular, they are now being joined by activities such as trail riding.

Working horses

Horses work in forests because they cause less damage than tractors. Farmers in developing countries also find horses easy to keep, as they can live off the land. Though no longer used in war, horses are retained in many countries for ceremonial duties and the police horse has so far proved to be irreplaceable.

London police horses undergo about 40 weeks of training

MULE TRAINS
Even in the late 20th century, it has been hard to find anything to replace the mule to transport goods over uneven ground. Mules are still used in many parts of the world.

ROYAL
ARTILLERY
HORSE AND
RIDER

CEREMONIAL DUTIES
Many countries still
use horses for
ceremonial duties.
This dates from wars
where horses were
used as cavalry and to
haul artillery.

POLICE HORSES
Mounted police can be seen in many
cities today. Horses offer the rider a
good view and mobility, and can move
through crowds more easily than either
motorcycles or cars.

WORKING HORSE FACTS
• More horses are bred
in the United States
for leisure riding than
for herding cattle.

• India employs more
mounted police than
any other country in
the world.

• Heavy horses are
used in Canadian
forests to pull up trees
and take them away,
and to cultivate the
soil afterward.

*Working cow ponies
in the US tend to
average 15 hh*

*Average working
life of a police
horse is about
14 years*

QUARTER
HORSE

BRITISH POLICE
HORSES AND
RIDERS IN
CEREMONIAL
DRESS

HERDING CATTLE
Horses are still used to herd cattle and
sheep in the Americas, the former USSR,
Australia, and New Zealand.

Horses for sport and leisure

Since the end of World War II, there has been a tremendous increase in the use of the horse for pleasure. Sports such as horse racing remain as popular as ever, and interest in such competition as show jumping and dressage has been heightened by television. Riding vacations are now a popular and relaxing pastime for many people.

POLO
Probably originating in Persia, polo has been played for 2,500 years. Modern polo is played by two teams of four using long mallets to hit the ball into the opposition's goal.

DRESSAGE
The American Morgan Horse, once favored by the US cavalry, is shown in ridden and harnessed classes. It is also used for Western and pleasure riding, and jumping.

Rider sits on the horse's center of balance

A hard hat protects the rider's head in case of a fall

Pony will cover 3–6 miles (4.8–6.4 km) in an hour

The use of plain snaffle bridles for recreational riding is almost universal

RACEHORSES

Horse racing has become a huge international industry. This statue in the Kentucky Horse Park in the US, is of the famous racehorse *Man O' War*, or *Big Red*, who was beaten only once in 21 races. When he died in 1947, more than 1,000 people attended his funeral.

HORSE SPORTS FACTS

• The longest-running horse race is the Palio in Siena, Italy, begun in the 1200s and still run today. The winning horse attends a special banquet afterward.

• The word polo comes from the Tibetan *pulu*, meaning ball.

• The first steeplechase was held in 1830 at St. Albans, England.

Riders learn to use aids such as the reins

Each rider keeps a pony-length away from the next

A novice rider is given a quiet, reliable horse

Riding school ponies are frequently cross-bred animals

RIDING VACATIONS

Those who want to ride occasionally or just for pleasure, can take a riding vacation. These rides can last from a single day to a whole week. The distance covered in each day varies between 10–25 miles (16–40 km). Trips are always supervised and provide an opportunity to reach beautiful and inaccessible areas of a country.

Index

Acknowledgments

Contributors to this title include:
Editors: Elise Bradbury, Laura Buller, Alan Burrows, Bernadette Crowley, Alastair Dougall, John Mapps, Susan McKeever, Miranda Smith, Leo Vita-Finzi, Selina Wood, Sarah Watson.

Designers: Alexandra Brown, Sarah Crouch, Janet Allis, Tanya Tween.

PAGEOne: Melanie McDowell, Chris Stewart, Suzanne Tuhrim, Sophie Williams.

Dorling Kindersley would like to thank: Hilary Bird and Mark Lambert for indexing, Robert Graham for research and editorial support, Caroline Potts for picture library services, Natural History Museum, University Museum of Zoology, Cambridge, Thurston Watson for model making.

Photographs by:
Julie Anderson, Dennis Avon, Akhil Bakhshi, Simon Battensby, Geoff Brightling, Jane Burton, Peter Chadwick, Gordon Clayton, Geoff Dann, Philip Dowell, Mike Dunning, Neil Fletcher, Steve Gorton, Frank Greenaway, Steve Gorton, Marc Henrie, Kit Houghton, Colin Keates, Dave King, Bob Langrish, Cyril Laubscher, Ranald Mackechnie, Andrew McRobb, Ray Moller, Tracy Morgan, Stephen Oliver, Oxford Scientific Films, Nick Parfit, Tim Ridley, Bill Sands, Karl Shone, Steve Shott, Harry Taylor, Kim Taylor, Michael Ward, Jerry Young

Illustrations by:
Graham Allen, Janet Allis, Stephen Biesty, Joanna Cameron, Rowan Clifford, Karen Cochrane, John Davis, Ted Dewan, Gill Ellsbury, Samantha Elmhurst, Angelica Elsebach, Giuliano Fornari, Chris Forsey, Will Giles, Craig Gosling (Indiana University Medical Illustration Department), Tony Graham, Nick Hall, Nick Hewetson, John Hutchinson, Mark Iley, Stanley Cephas Johnson, Aziz Khan, Richard Lewington, Kenneth Lilly, Ruth Lindsay, Mick Loates, Janos Marffy, Malcolm McGregor, Sean Milne, Richard Orr, Maurice Pledger, Sandra Pond, Bryan Poole, Sally Alane Reason, Colin Salmon, Tommy Swahn, John Temperton, Simon Thomas, Kevin Toy, David Webb, Amanda Williams, Ann Winterbotham, John Woodcock, Debra Woodward, Colin Woolf, Dan Wright.

Picture credits:
t=top b=bottom c=center l=left
r=right

The publisher would like to thank the
following for their kind permission to
reproduce their photographs:
Dennis Avon 286b, 323bl;346bl;
Professor Edmund D. Brodie Jr. 165cr;
Lester Cheeseman 251c; Dr. Barry
Clarke 23tr; John Holmes 175cl; Colin
Keates 27cl; Dave King 25cr; Bob
Langrish 487tl; Leszczynski 157cl
Ardea/M Krishnan 257bl; Eric Ingren
238tl
BBC Natural History Unit/Galleria
Degli Uffizi, Florence 168tl
Bridgeman Art Library/210tl, 233br
Centaur Studios/175bl
Bruce Coleman/231bc; Jen and Des
Bartlett 279tl; Erwin & Peggy Bauer
258-259, 216tl; Fred Bruemmer 203bl;
John Cancalosi 236tl, 342bl; Eric
Crichton 80cl; Gerald Cubitt 81br;
Geoff Doré 81bc; M.P.L Fogden 154
155; P.A. Hinchcliffe 60rr; Dr. M. T.
Kahl 344tr; Jan van de Kam 338br;
Stephen J. Krasemann 379tl; Gordon
Langsbury 354-355b, 355r; Cyril
Laubscher 290br; Werner Layer 366-367;
Luiz Claudio Mango 307tr; George
Mcarthy 287b;351tl; Michael McCoy
237tl; Rinie van Meurs 338 tr; Charlie
Off 330bl; Dr. Eckart Pott 30-31, 133tc;
Dr Sandro Prato 139tr; Hans Reinhard
99tl, 352cl, 361b, 365bc, 438-439;

Hector Rivarola 349bl; Kevin Rushby
63tl; Dr Frieder Sauer 79br; Pacific
Stock 142-143; Kim Taylor 51tr, 88cr,
94cr, 133tl, 272-273b, 302cr; 276c,
305b; 313cl; Norman Tomalin 106c
Corbis/Tony Arruza 50c
Mary Evans Picture Library/69ac, 151tr
FLPA/L Chance 237bl
Robert Harding/300cl; 301cr; 302cr;
353bl; 475tr
Chris Mattison Nature Photographics
185b
**Musée Nationale d'Histoire
Naturelle**/158tr 159tc
Naturhistoriska Riksmuseet/158c
Natural History Museum/Frank
Greenaway 98cr; 99br, 16cr, 170cl,
170bl, 170br, 171tl, 172t, 172b, 173t,
173c, 173br, 177c, 179tl, 212bl, 212cl,
215cl, 216bl, 217t, 218b, 219t, 221tl,
223cr, 223br, 224tl, 225b, 226t, 226bl,
227br, 228b, 229c, 230-231, 230cr, 230b,
231c, 231r, 233t, 237tl, 241cr, 243bl,
248r, 252bl, 256b, 437br
Nature Photographers/289tr; E.Lemon
300br, H. Miles 358bl; Paul Sterry
337br; 341r; 337br
Natural Science Photos/C Banks 221cr,
256tr, 256cl; M. Boulard 131bc; P.
Bowman 92cl; M. Chinery 135cl; C
Dani & I Jeske 209br, 221bl; Carol
Farneti 106bl; Adrian Hoskins 95cr;
G Kinns 246cl; JG Lilley 204c, 204b;
Chris Mattison 227t, 246br; Jim Merli
176cr, 180bc, 188cl, 193tr, 255tl, 253t,
257tr; Pete Oxford 203tl, 205bl;

Queensland Museum 253c; Richard Revels 92tr, 132cr, 252tr; C & T Stuart 249bl. P.H. & S.L. Ward 61cr, 137c; David Yendall 101tr

N.H.P.A/Stephen Dalton 437tl; Melvin Grey 271cl; Peter Johnson 362 bl; R & D Keller 373tl; Peter Parks 153br, 282tr; Philippa Scott 301tl; John Shaw 301br; 348r

Frank Lane Picture Agency/ E&D Hosking 281t; 303tr; 355tl; 362-363; 365cr;/ T&P Gardner; F.Polking 304br; Silvestris 328tr;/Roger Tidma 353t;/ Roger Wimshurst 307tr;/ W.Wisniewski 359br

Mark O'Shea 199cr, 239t, 241bl

Oxford Scientific Films/Doug Allen 364l; Larus Argentatus 274-275, 301bl; Kathie Atkinson 57tr; G.I. Bernard 101cl; Raymond Blythe 130bl; Densey Clyne 127tr; C.M. Collins 68bl; J.A.L. Cooke 79c, 134tl; David B. Fleetham 387tr; Michael Fogden 125tl; Peter Gathercole 67tr; Howard Hall 153t; 387cr; Stan Osolinski 166-167; Papilio 296br; Alan Root/Okapia 371cr

Mantis Wildlife Films/32cl; Peter O'Toole 68cr; James Robinson 76cr, 99br; Harold Taylor 83c; Steve Turner 81cr, 125tr; P & W Ward 124cr

Museum der Bildenden Kuenste, Leipzig/24cl

Planet Earth/K & K Ammann 387br; Andre Barttschi 321 bc; John R. Bracegirdle 386cl; Richard Coomber 436bl; Carol Farneti-Foster 449tr, 459tr,

386br; Daniel Heuclin 245bl; Gerard Lacz 217cr; John Lythgou 308b, 347tr; Mark Mattock 336cl; E Hanumantha Rao 244cl; Brian Kenney 232t, 236bl, 238bl, 255bl; Jonathan Scott 387bl, 387tl; Anup and Manoj Shah 451tr; Yuri Shibbnev 311tl; Martin Wendler 239c

Premaphotos/K.G. Preston-Mafham 59tr, 67br, 71br, 73cl, 74br, 80br, 106br, 110bl, 123t, 123cr. Dr Bill Sands 70cr

Science Photo Library/Dr Jeremy Burgess 47tl; Mark Deeble & Victoria Stone 213cr; John Downer 214br; Michael Fogden 215tr, 249br; J.C. Revy 114cr; Tui de Roy 186cr; David M. Schleser/Nature's Images 74br; Alastair Shay 247cr

Tony Stone Images/Mike Surowiak 101bc; 196cl; Maurice Tibbles 189c

Werner Forman Archive/14cl

Wild Images/Romulus Whitaker 193br; 214tr; Howard Hall 153 cl

Jerry Young/12c, bl, br

Zefa/J. Schupe 7tr; 447tr, 455t.

Every effort has been made to trace the copyright holders and we apologize in advance for any unintentional omissions. We should be pleased to insert the appropriate acknowledgment in any subsequent edition of this publication.

All other images © Dorling Kindersley For further information see:
www.dkimages.com